Jerusalem, Take One!

Jerusalem, Take One!

•

Memoirs of a Jewish Filmmaker

•

Alan
Rosenthal

Southern Illinois University Press
Carbondale and Edwardsville

03 02 01 00   4 3 2 1

Library of Congress Cataloging-in-Publication Data
Rosenthal, Alan, 1936–
    Jerusalem, take one! : memoirs of a Jewish filmmaker / Alan Rosenthal.
       p. cm.
      1. Rosenthal, Alan, 1936– . 2. Television producers and directors—Israel Biog-
raphy. 3. Television broadcasting of news—Israel. I. Title.
PN1992.4.R58A3 2000
791.43'0233'092—dc21
[B]   99-43223
                                                CIP
ISBN 0-8093-2311-7 (cloth : alk. paper)
ISBN 0-8093-2312-5 (pbk. : alk. paper)

The paper used in this publication meets the minimum requirements of American
National Standard for Information Sciences—Permanence of Paper for Printed Library
Materials, ANSI Z39.48-1992. ∞

For Miki,
Gil and Tzofnat,
Tal and Yifat,
and for my brothers and sisters,
especially Raymond,
who shared the journey

Contents

Preface ix

1. New Boy at Israel TV 1
2. Only Madmen Go There 26
3. Next Year in Jerusalem 46
4. Eichmann on TV 65
5. Six Days in June 88
6. Selling Zion 115
7. The Wars: Yom Kippur and After 137
8. Of Heroes and Treasures 169
9. The Brink of Peace 201
10. *Civilization and the Jews* 235
11. Moses, Come Home! 260

Selected Filmography 277
Index 279

Illustrations following pages 18 and 114

Preface

I see you a Stranger.
I see you a Stranger.
    Tell me, where have you come from.
Tell me, where are you going . . .
Stranger.

—African tribal tale

My friend Andrew Tracey used to recite these lines to me at college, in between telling me exotic tales of growing up in Kenya, learning Swahili, going on safari, and hunting for diamonds. My own background was more prosaic, more banal. It could be told in fewer words. English. Jewish. London. Middle class. Oxford. Law. It would all have led to a very conventional journey had not Israel inserted itself into my life in a most devious way and had I not become a documentary filmmaker.

In the sixties I was living in London, working as a solicitor, and making the occasional short film. I'd flirted with the idea of Israel for years and then in 1968 was invited to Jerusalem to help set up the new television station. I thought that would just mean a year off. Now, a few decades later, to my amazement I find I'm still here, have made about fifty films about the place, am still bemused by it, still intrigued by it, and am still wondering whether I love it or hate it.

It's an Israeli journey I never expected to take. This book explains a little bit about that journey. The stranger is telling where he came from and what happened on the way. It's a wandering that starts with the filming of the Eichmann trial, the recording of kibbutzim under fire, and Bedouin life and goes on to cover all the wars, the Intifada, and the peace process. It's been a bit of a haphazard drunken progression, so that stops on the way have included hunting for the Temple treasures in southern France, looking for underwater archaeology in the Red Sea, and trying to fathom the secrets of Jerusalem.

So, for many years, my life has revolved around putting Israel on record. As a documentary filmmaker I was, of course, privileged. I was invited, so to speak, into secret rooms, shown secret passages, and allowed to see and observe goings-on hidden from many others. I was allowed to poke, probe, insert, ask, and generally make a nuisance of myself, all in the name of the supposed good of the public. It is this privileged recording of Israel that I want to tell about in this book.

The view, of course, is that of the outsider. If you haven't been here fifty years, been to the kindergarten with Dudu at the age of three, been on the Negev hike with Yossi at the age of twelve, and been in the scouts and in the army, you are, ipso facto, an outsider. It all reminds me of the American who comes to Oxford and examines the immaculate emerald lawns of one of the colleges. "What wonderful grass," says the American. "How do you grow it?" "Easy," says the college gardener. "You plant grass seeds and water the ground. When the grass comes up, you cut it and roll it. You do that for six hundred years, and you'll have a lawn." As with England, so with Israel.

At first I thought this would be a very serious memoir, but it didn't work out that way. As I wrote I found that it was the bizarre and comic sides of Israel that kept surfacing rather than a profound scholarly analysis. After thinking this over, I realized that wasn't a bad thing. To write properly about Israel, you have to have a deep sense of the absurd as well as a feeling for historic destiny. I'll give you just one example.

A few years ago, following the success of the film *Jurassic Park*, an enterprising Israel milk firm decided to decorate its plastic yogurt containers with pictures of dinosaurs. The rabbis were enraged. Dinosaurs were said to have existed millions of years ago. Yet strict Jewish tradition maintains the world was only created six thousand years ago. The rabbis therefore ruled that the milk company was deliberately insulting tradition, and the yogurts had to be condemned as unkosher.

When I came to Jerusalem in 1961, people used to say, "Where shall we meet? Oh, at the traffic light." At that time there was only one traffic light in the city, at the junction of Jaffa Street and King George. For that matter there seemed to be only one car in the city, my brother's. It was a tiny red Morris Minor, and since he was unique in having a car, the girls treated him like a prince. Today there seems to be at least a thousand traffic lights, half a million cars, and to get to work early you have to leave home the night before.

Clearly, change and flux is the name of the game, with a lot of it recorded on film. And it's salutary to look at the old stuff. Not just for the nostalgia kick. Without seeing what Israel was like in the past, you can have no idea how far you've come.

When I made my films I never realized they would be witnesses to these changes, but in retrospect I see that a number of them caught a particular moment of time. And that's why I want to write about them. The Eichmann trial, for example, was not just about Eichmann but marked the first real confrontation of young Israelis with the Holocaust. Again, the Yom Kippur War and Project Renewal can be seen as marking the high point of an Israeli-diaspora relationship that seems to have gone down the drain. And all this was captured on film.

So the films mark a journey. They mark my own personal wanderings and changes (which are not very important) and a little bit of the Jewish and Israeli journey in the twentieth century. And these latter wanderings, meanderings, and maybe even possibly progressions matter very much.

The French director Jean Luc Godard once said, "Films should have a beginning, a middle and an end, though not necessarily in that order." Being English, and not Gallic, I have actually decided to start at the beginning, which for me means looking first at the films I did about the past—the Jewish past, the European past—and telling a bit about my roots in England. The middle part of the book deals with Israel in the seventies and eighties, and the book ends with a note about the making of my most recent films, *On the Brink of Peace* and *Into the Future*.

The question that underlies these last films, and the question for myself, my friends, my family, and most Israelis and Arabs, is where do we go from here? Will there be real peace in this region? And will there be peace among the Jews themselves? Or are we heading for chaos and tragedy? This is the key question, which only the next part of the journey will answer.

Besides expressing gratitude to my family, who read the early chapters and helped me with their comments, I particularly want to thank my friends Donald Staples and Henry Breitrose for their immense help in shaping the final manuscript. Thanks are also due to Bobby Cramer, who encouraged me from the beginning, and to Jim Simmons, the best and most supportive of editors.

Finally I'd like to acknowledge my debt to 13/WNET and Abba Eban, who allowed me to reprint part of my scripts and who, between them, kept me going for years.

Jerusalem, Take One!

1 - New Boy at Israel TV

Outside the graveyard, the soundman was looking at me as if I were a cross between Dracula and Frankenstein. "I don't care what you're filming . . . I can't go in."

"Why not?" I asked, puzzled.

"Because I'm a Cohen, a member of the priestly caste. And under Jewish law a Cohen can't go into a cemetery." The "priest" was dressed in stained Levi's and an old denim shirt and carried the tape recorder and two gun mikes. Some priest, I thought. Doesn't look a bit like the Archbishop of New York. But because of his hesitations, we shot the scene from outside the offending area.

That wasn't the first such incident. There had been one like it a few days earlier. I'd shot an innocuous ten-minute film profile of Yaakov Pins, a Jerusalem artist, and was going over the rushes, the raw material of the film, with the editor. He was an ex-Chicago hippie, one of the best cutters around, but had recently embraced a very strict Jewish orthodoxy. This meant he had to work with the Bible open next to the editing table.

His alternative praying and splicing I could take. It didn't really disturb me to have him make a cut and then turn to the Bible for a few verses of declamatory prayer. In fact I was quite in the mood for him to tell me about the sins of the flesh because since I had been in Israel I hadn't had time to indulge in any. This was all fine till suddenly, in the midst of viewing, he stopped and threw up his hands in horror. "Graven images! You've shot graven images. And you've brought them into my house. Fegh upon you. I'm not touching any footage that has idols in it." I looked again. In my shot the artist was admiring the head of a Buddha he had acquired in Indonesia. This was the idol that had offended my editor. We argued, but the scene came out.

Of course, he didn't always win. The Friday before, we had been editing a sequence that included a scene in a Tel Aviv café. Suddenly Yoel downed tools. The thought had occurred to him that maybe the food they were eating in the film wasn't kosher. And if it wasn't kosher, the film would pollute his editing table. "Yoel," I assured him. "the Sephardi chief rabbi eats there twice a week, and they have four *glatt kosher* certificates (highest fitness approval given to traditionally prepared food) on the back wall. So please continue the cutting because the place is blessed from heaven."

These three incidents were typical of the rather bizarre surrealistic atmosphere surrounding my first few months filming in Jerusalem. It was May 1968, and I'd been invited to Jerusalem for a year to help set up Israeli television. For ages there had been talk; now suddenly there was to be action.

Israel was very late coming onto the television scene, deciding to set up a government-controlled station only after the Six-Day War. (Israel TV takes the BBC independent corporation idea as its model but in practice is subject to much more political pressure.) This was after years of dallying with the idea and after years of anti-TV sentiment among the conservative and religious elements of the country. Some argued that TV would lead to an abandonment of religious values. Others feared that television would lead to personalization and would debase the regard for politicians and the parties. And the pro-TV lobby wasn't helped by the fierce opposition of David Ben Gurion—the once seemingly permanent prime minister—who fervently believed that TV would destroy Israeli cultural values.

Prior to the '67 war there were a mere thirty thousand TV sets in Israel, mostly in the hands of Arabs or Arabic-speaking Jews, and tuned to the broadcasts of the Egypt, Jordan, and Lebanon. When the war broke out, the screens were flooded with violent propaganda from these surrounding countries. Israel could only watch in silence. But the lesson was quickly absorbed. The power and propaganda value of television had been demonstrated in the most dramatic way, and now the government wanted TV as fast as possible. On the one hand, it could counter the Arab broadcasts, and on the other hand, who knew whether it might also play a part in reconciling Arab and Jew.

So after decades of hesitation, things began to move. A Hebrew University communications professor, Elihu Katz, was engaged as the TV's first director. American CBS experts arrived in Brooks Brothers suits carrying wondrous organizational charts conjured out of the realms of fantasy. Over two hundred would-be filmmakers were corralled (mainly from the radio and the press). And finally, to cap the whole thing, eighteen foreign advisers, including myself, were invited to spend a year teaching Israelis the splendid art of film and television and to assist in getting the operation off the ground.

Prior to the invitation, I had lived a double life, working both as a lawyer and a filmmaker in England and the States, establishing during this time a fairly good reputation in documentary. I'd also filmed a few times in Israel: I'd covered the Eichmann trial in 1961 and had shot a piece on kibbutzim in 1964. Having taught film in San Francisco also helped. On paper I looked great. How I appeared in the flesh was another matter. In London I was sagging under the weight of a never-ending court battle over a feature film. My eyes were hollow. My mouth was parched. My knees were bent. I definitely wanted out of law for a while, so the invitation was seen as manna from heaven.

Israel had always faintly beckoned me, but never quite strong enough till this moment. But now they were really laying it on. Good pay. A return ticket after a year. A choice to be in on things from the start. Who could resist? Not me. So I closed the legal files and signed on the bottom line. Only later did I realize that the dreams and the promises used by the TV were exactly the same techniques that the press gangs used in the seventeenth century when their ships were unmanned and they didn't want to reveal the true state of affairs. But go know!

When I told my family (two parents, four sisters, two brothers), they just shrugged. More gallivanting. More day-dreaming. California. New York. Finally, after all these years, we thought you had settled down, a steady job, a steady income. But no! Where will it all end? My answer was in a year's time. They sighed and looked at each other. They knew me better than I knew myself. "Just one year?

Well, from your mouth to God's ear. But we doubt it." As usual, they were right.

To come from the United States with its hundreds of stations to Israel with its one fledgling station was to enter a weird and wonderful world—a world where very little of what one knew before counted or even made sense. (In fact, a small educational station had been set up in Tel Aviv by the Rothschild Foundation in the early 1960s. In 1968 it was still broadcasting but only to a limited audience of a few thousand.) But it was a stimulating and vibrant world, where talent was high and technique was low, where almost anything could be tried (at least once), and where nobody paid the slightest attention to anyone else, least of all the advisers.

The Israelis, of course, would have you believe they knew everything. Eisenstein might know just a little bit more than them about editing, but not much. And if only Hitchcock would listen to them, he could learn a thing or two. This didn't worry me because I knew my TV experience was limited, and when I worked with the Israelis it was very much a case of the blind leading the lame. But there were others there at the station who were veritable gods but were dismissed as kindergarten children.

Stuart Hood, for example, ex-head of BBC news, was brought in to teach news techniques. Tony Hatch, a veteran CBS correspondent, was brought in to organize current affairs. Both of them told me they could have been talking to the wall, for all the attention the Israelis paid to their advice. Both were lost in a world where chaos and improvisation quickly chased out sanity and order. But then chutzpa, chaos, and improvisation had won the Six-Day War, so who were they to argue with the Israeli system?

Altogether it was a crazy world. Take the TV station itself. It was housed in an abandoned diamond factory on the edge of an industrial quarter and had all the gray appeal of Attica prison. One mini-elevator serviced the whole building, while a tiny café gave the workers something that only with imagination could be called food. Yet there was a cheerfulness in the building. Television had arrived. A new world was being born. There were opportunities there to be seized, and anything was possible if you had the drive and the cheek. Thus it was a world where the students studied directing on Monday and promptly set up their own school for production techniques on Tuesday. Outside the station it was just as mad, so that within a week of the first TV broadcasts every Israel newspaper boasted its own expert, world famous, and *experienced* media critic.

The training of TV crews started in April 1968, and by September the station was already broadcasting a few programs. In the beginning there was, of necessity, a deliciously haphazard quality to everything. Schedules were nonexistent. When a program arrived from the States, OK, that was an excuse for a broadcast. Someone had finished a film, again fine, we might as well broadcast today. It was almost like the early days of cinema: so long as your program moved, and maybe even spoke, let's broadcast it. Its sheer existence in a country hungry for TV was what counted, not its quality.

For a documentary filmmaker, this was wonderful. So I rushed around the country filming religious festivals, sports festivities, and Bedouin life and rejoiced in the fact they were broadcast about an hour after being completed. However, anarchy didn't last very long. In less than a year, the station was in full swing and broadcasting between two and three hours a day to 80 percent of the country. The idea at first had been to emphasize Arabic programming over Hebrew programming. This seemed to make sense since it had been the worry about external Arabic broadcasts that had prompted the formation of Israel TV. In practice things worked out very differently, with Hebrew programming becoming the clearly dominant partner.

Broadcasting began at 7:00 P.M. with news in Arabic, followed by Arabic light entertainment. Later came overseas programs such as *The Defenders* or *You Are There* followed by a Hebrew news program and some general Israeli program such as a short documentary or a quiz show. Although there were the occasional specials, such as the postwar parade, the anniversary concert of the Israeli Philharmonic under Bernstein, and Christmas masses from the Church of the Nativity in Bethlehem, it was the news programs that captivated the Israelis.

Till the advent of TV, news had meant the viewing of the Carmel or Geva newsreels that accompanied feature films in the theaters. News is probably too optimistic a description since these items were really mostly light fashion or sports or promotional Zionist magazine programs. Now the Israelis were being treated to *real* news, featuring the politics and personalities of today, rather than the passe events and pseudo news of yesterday. This was a real revolution. And as in England and the United States, the news created stars. Thus while Arabic news had a pretty woman news reader called "Gloria," Hebrew news had as its front man Chaim Yavin, a handsome, amiable, and extremely talented ex-radio man who went on to dominate Israeli news for thirty years. Gradually his face came to decorate not just TV, but magazines covers and boxes of children's games. And woe to you if you had a public function without Yavin as announcer. It was just not done.

The Hebrew news show had started with an ambitious forty-five-minute time slot and was made up of short documentaries, panelists, and art pieces, as well as regular news. Even though it was broadcast, at first, only three times a week, it was a hard show to sustain. Necessity forced it to be cut to thirty minutes and then again to fifteen minutes. Here the problems were equipment, bureaucracy, space, and staff.

Put simply, the station was underequipped, subject to too many rules, and going through the usual teething problems. The administrative staff were too few and had little television training. Forms for everything had to be filled out in triplicate or quadruplicate and lodged days in advance, from hiring a taxi to booking lodgings for crew. And even when that was done, personal whims and insider grabbing knocked the system to hell. Thus if you thought you would be smart and use a station car for your filming, as likely as not you would find it had been borrowed by a junior lighting engineer to take his family to the beach for the weekend. If you thought yourself lucky that the production manager had actually ordered you a hotel for your day's research in Tel Aviv, you would learn, like my friend André Kaminsky, not to be surprised when this turned out to be a cheap brothel in Hayarkon Street.

The fight for insufficient equipment and space soon produced bitter feuds that lasted for years. Nowhere was this more evident than in the news departments where both Arabic news and Hebrew news fought merciless battles to get into the one tiny studio or to get access to the best cameramen and editors. Occasionally the feuds turned into literal sabotage of the other's programs and facilities. Cooperation and help became forgotten concepts in the rush to become the dominant TV department.

For most of 1968 and 1969, I worked full time on the TV staff. My job consisted in the main of training film crews, trying to build a documentary department, advising on policy, and acting as producer-director on six or seven films. I then left Israel for a couple of years, and in 1971 came back to try my hand as a freelance filmmaker. As anyone can easily guess, the story then became very different and the work conditions much more difficult and confining.

The way a freelancer worked was fairly simple. Although Israel TV preferred to make all its films with tenured staff, by 1971 it had begun to contract films out to private companies. Those companies in turn then contracted out the writing and directing to freelancers, and it was at this last stage that I entered the game.

Because I was a founding father, so to speak, the work was fairly easy to come by, but the most appalling restrictions applied. For the staff of Israel TV, neither time nor materials mattered very much. One could take between three and six months making a half-hour film, and not too many questions would be asked. Nine months on a film was not unusual, and one friend of mine boasted that quality demanded that he not do more than one film a year. The point is, no matter how long the film took, the TV paid a fairly good salary to the staffer once a month.

Working as a freelancer, you saw the other side of the coin. Israel was broke, we were told, and the TV could only afford a pittance for our films. Thus—regrettably—time, money, and materials all had to be restricted.

At that time, the total budget for a freelance film was somewhere between four thousand and six thousand dollars. For such a film you were allowed four days for research, three days for filming, and, with luck and a lot of pressure, nine or ten days for editing. As often as not the research was done by the writer-director without any backup, and the production help was minimal. You never went out with a production assistant, and a production manager was uncommon.

In telling how he made the film *Cast a Giant Shadow* in Israel, director Mel Shavelson says that he met with his first-time actors at 9:00 A.M., and by noon they had already formed a union and were demanding higher pay. Hearing the story, I envied the actors. In the TV, unions didn't yet exist, and the private production companies took full advantage of that fact. Thus an average shooting day would run some thirteen or fourteen hours. Why didn't we complain? Because it was a classic buyer's market with everyone dying to get into the industry no matter how lousy the conditions. You didn't want to direct? Fine. There was always another director waiting outside the door.

A typical example of the situation is a film I did in the early seventies, *Battle Officer*, about two lieutenants in the Israel army stationed near the Suez Canal. For research I was allowed one day to drive from Jerusalem to the canal, tour the length of the canal, do the interviews, and then drive home the same evening. All together that involved six hundred miles of driving, between myself and my assistant, mostly through desert, sandstorms, and flash floods.

The shooting merely repeated the story, though this time I was with a crew and didn't drive. We left Tel Aviv at noon on a Tuesday and drove across the northern Sinai desert to get to the canal in the evening, where we started filming immediately. On Wednesday we arose at 5:00 A.M.; we shot through Wednesday and Thursday until midnight; and we traveled back through the desert early Friday morning. No one said anything—it was simply standard procedure.

The film itself actually stayed in my mind for many years. The war of attrition with Egypt was still on, and all along the canal I could pick out the bunkers, and the isolated wire surrounded outposts of the Israeli fortifications. In the bunkers the men were cheerful, but there were constant warnings to be careful traveling between the outposts as Egyptian commandos occasionally made forays across the canal. This gave rise to one of the more memorable scenes in the film, where the Israeli soldiers are seen in silhouette as dusk falls, patiently combing for mines.

The officers whose stories I was telling were actually tank commanders, and before doing the research I had wonderful visions of myself directing a blockbuster of a documentary, falling only just short of *Patton* and *Battle of the Bulge* in visual pyrotechnics. I saw myself lining up seven tanks over here, fifteen tanks over there and having them race across the horizon, with cannons pounding and machine guns firing. When I talked to the commanding officer, he quickly brought me down to earth. I could use one tank for the main filming, and no—repeat—no use of live ammunition.

The men, short-term officers, tank commanders barely out of their teens, interested me more than the weapons. How did they feel with the enemy only a few hundred yards away? Why had they volunteered for the armored corps? And what did they want to do with their lives when they'd finished their four years of service? One of them, Danny, twenty-two, would have looked good in a Hollywood film. He seemed the earnest guy next door, the solid guy all the girls want as a best friend. Yet his background was astonishing. He came from a deeply religious family who had cut him off for volunteering for the army.

"The only thing they wanted for me was to go to a *yeshiva* [rabbinical college] and become a rabbi." Like most of their Hassidic sect, Danny's parents totally opposed the idea of a secular Jewish state, and going into the army was a total betrayal of all their beliefs. "When I told them I was going into the army, they treated me as a total outcast. Yet I had to go. Unlike them I feel part of this country and don't want to be confined to the ghetto and the old ways. I'm proud of what I'm doing, and I wish they were. It hurts. Now I rarely see them and spend most of my leaves with my girlfriend."

The opposition of Danny's parents didn't surprise me. In Israel few religious young men join the army, following a ruling of Ben Gurion that religious boys are excused from the army if they join a *yeshiva*. Till today this ruling is one of the most divisive issues between Israel's religious and secular communities.

Yuval, the other officer also came from a religious background, but had studied in one of the rare *yeshivas* that actually encouraged its students to join the army. Like Danny he was extremely proud of what he was doing and was glad to be able to prove that you could be sincerely and devoutly religious and yet still fight for your country. His plans after the army were to go to Bar Ilan University and study physics.

Danny and Yuval both came to my mind four years later when the Yom Kippur War broke out. I had last seen them getting ready to lead their men across the Sinai dunes in a training exercise. Had they been involved in the Canal battles, or had they been used on another front? This I was never to learn. But there was a postscript. One day I got a call to show *Battle Officer* to two grieving parents. Their son had been killed at Suez, and they remembered he had appeared in my film. They had no other pictures of him on film. Could they take a look? So we sat in the editing room where they cried softly and then raised a glass to their son's memory.

Battle Officer was made for the TV's Documentary Department, but nonfiction films could just as well be made for the Religious Department or as cultural specials. For the most part the films were in Hebrew, but occasionally they had to be in Arabic for the Arabic department. At that stage my Hebrew was fairly fluent since I had attended a government language course, but I had practically no Arabic. This didn't matter too much as I could interview in Hebrew or English or through an interpreter and then write the full commentary in English and have it translated into Arabic. There was only one catch: Arabic comes out about three times as long as English. So when I wrote, "I like you," which takes a second and a half in narration, I had to keep in mind that in Arabic the phrase would emerge as "Your eyes are as luscious as dappled swans floating over the moonlight sea" and allow ten seconds for the commentary.

For a while Arab programming was pushed very strongly at the television. The belief was that following the dramatic reunification of Jerusalem and the takeover of a big Arab population on the West Bank, TV might help promote a message of peace. As Elihu Katz, the head of TV put it, television by itself wouldn't cause the Arabs to like Israelis, but it might help broaden the picture of Israel beyond the highly political image that was current in 1968. Maybe the television might show that there were mutual concerns between the two peoples—agriculture, medicine, family—whereby Arab and Jew might find a common interest. So along with many others, I started making documentaries for Arab audiences on town expansion, culture, musicians, industries, artists, and so on. Whether they did any good, I don't know, but they were definitely fun to make.

In working on Arab subjects you always had to allow extra time for cultural necessities. You couldn't just come into an Arab home and say, "Right! Tell me what you think of the city council's plans for a new sewage system." Instead you had to drink endless cups of tea, then coffee, then tea again, while inquiring about the eldest son in Cairo, the son studying to be a doctor in Boston, and the daughter in London. Finally, after about two hours you could begin the interview. Having been brought up in England on a lot of tea and small talk about the weather, this was fine with me.

Like their Jewish counterparts, the Arabs soon became extremely sophisticated in the realities of filmmaking and the costs of giving film services. For example, in my first years in Israel the Bedouin in Sinai would do anything for you for nothing. "Ride my camel past those palm trees. Sure. No problem!" A year later, filming on the same stretch, you would be sure to have your pockets stuffed with five- and ten-dollar notes for handouts.

This business realism struck me in particular one morning when I went to film a Bedouin encampment in the Judean desert, close to Jerusalem. We were doing one of those films where the camels and the donkeys ride across the horizon, and a Charlton Heston voice thunders out, "Unchanged since the dawn of time, these hills bear silent witness to the agonies Abraham must have suffered three and a half thousand years ago," or some such similar twaddle. The film was actually about Syrian archaeology and the Ebla tablets, and I was just doing some pick-up footage for the American director.

The first filming had been fine. I'd got the Bedouin headman to lend us four camels and some donkeys and get three of his men and two girls to lead the animals over the hills. Apart from trying to persuade the Bedouin not to smoke and failing to convince them that jackets and wrist watches weren't around three thousand years ago, it couldn't have been simpler.

Unfortunately something went wrong in the labs, and a week later I sat once more in the headman's tent, going through the tea and coffee routine, explaining why we needed to do the scene again. That was OK, except for one small detail. The headman wanted three times the amount that he had received the week before. Even in those heady days of massive Israel inflation, that seemed to me a trifle extravagant. But the chief had his reasons. "I supplied you with a tribe, dancing girls, extras, the lot. I had to pull my men off grazing to help you. I put up tents. I pulled down tents. We all gave up smoking for two hours. We gave you our best camels. And what did we get? A miserable three hundred dollars."

The real reason for the inflationary spiral was explained to me later by the chief's sidekick. The representative of Menachem Golan's feature film company had visited during the week and had promised them the moon for a few days of shooting. So if they got the moon from Golan, they wanted at least the stars from me. Trapped, and needing the footage, I had to give in.

The filming went well. As we were finishing, the Bedouin chief never left my side but looked anxiously at my shirt pockets containing all my ready cash. Dressed in a long white *galbiya*, flat sandals, and his head wrapped in a red Arab Legion *kaffiya* (Bedouin headdress), he could have passed for a bosom pal of T. E. Lawrence. He could have featured equally well in one of those romantic paintings entitled *A Noble Prince of Eastern Blood*. My daydreaming nostalgia was knocked aside, however, when I saw his watch. It was one of those priceless Guccis that tell you the time seven thousand feet under the ocean and lets you know simultaneously the corresponding hour and temperature in Japan and Korea. This was clearly one sophisticated chief, so I decided to press on with questions of modernity and current Bedouin life.

As I handed him the money (American dollars, not that cheap, worthless Israeli paper currency), I asked him, "Going to spread it around a bit, Chief? Give it to the wives and the children?" He looked shocked at my ignorance and presumption. There was no way that was going to happen. In the tribe, the money stayed with the big boss. That's the way it had always been. That was the way it would be in the future, at least if he had any say in it.

"So what do you do with it? Put the money under the pillow? Buy a few more goats?"

"Are you crazy? What are banks for? I can get at least 12 percent interest in Bank Leumi, or maybe I'll send the money to my stockbroker in the States. I hear General Electric is very good these days." As I left the Bedouin encampment for the second time, I reflected that I had a lot to learn about life and the real ways of the world.

With perseverance and sheer bloody-mindedness, I eventually learned to cope with the practical aspects of the work—even to laugh at them. Coping with the culture and the pressures around Israeli TV, however, was infinitely more tricky and complex.

For example, I was, for the first time, making films about Israel for Israelis and not for a foreign audience. That doesn't sound too hard, but it was a situation I felt quite uneasy about. Put simply, the question I had to ask myself was, did I know enough to make meaningful films about the culture and society without appearing a complete idiot in front of the natives? I just wasn't sure!

Experience would suggest that this area is a minefield, which has taken the toll of many foreign filmmakers. Antonioni's film on China was blasted by the Chinese. Louis Malle's *Phantom India* series was scorned by the Indians. Both filmmakers were ostensibly condemned not because they criticized the culture (though this is certainly part of the reason for the attacks on Malle) but because they failed to understand the subject—the society—and the mores and beliefs with which they were dealing.

Israel, too, has had its share of itinerant foreign filmmakers, and it has usually viewed them with suspicion. There have been too many digests of Israel based on a week's "expertise" or a three-day briefing, too many CBS, ABC, BBC, and *Frontline* films that skim the surface, to provide instant analyses and superficial solutions to the most complex of situations. The irony is that many of these efforts, scorned by the Israelis as sheer ignorant misreadings of a situation or the culture, have been praised to the skies abroad. Thus Susan Sontag's *Promised Lands* (1973), a really dreadful film in the opinion of myself and many of my Israeli friends, was hailed by *Commentary* magazine as possibly the best short ever done on Israel (Oct. 1976, p. 78).

When I came to Israel in 1968, I was seen as a foreigner—my having previously spent six months in the country counted for nothing, nor did the fact that I knew Hebrew. "You're a bloody Englishman and you don't know our ways. You're a new boy. You're wet behind the ears. You're not one of the *chevrah* [group; mostly used to describe a very close-knit circle of old friends]. You haven't been in a youth movement. You haven't been in the army. You haven't climbed Masada at dawn. You haven't got a clue." My students at the TV said this to me. They were pleasant but cocky, arrogant Israelis. They *knew*, because of their birthright—I didn't. And, to my chagrin, they were largely correct. The only thing I could do was look, learn, observe, read, talk, and hope that time would bring insight.

My first problem of filmic acculturation was to understand the audience—to grasp very completely that I was making films for the locals and not for Americans, Australians, or Englishmen. Further, I had to grasp that the difference between making Zionist films and making Israeli films was like the difference between day and night. The first was meant to sell Israel and encourage *aliya* (emigration to Israel), while the second was meant to explore a country in flux, reveal it to itself, and (in my view) encourage and support social change.

This acculturation may sound simple, but it had an immense number of ramifications. I had to understand emotionally, and not just in my head, the sheer diversity of the audience. We were making films for a population of over 4 million, the majority being Jews, but a large minority being Moslem Arabs. Whereas the Arabs were fairly homogeneous, the Jewish population was divided in every way imaginable. There were the sophisticated Berliners who had arrived in the thirties; the Yemenites from Saana who came in 1949; the Jews from Kurdistan, Afghanistan, and Bokhara; the North Africans from Morocco and the semi-Bedouin Jews from the Atlas mountains who came in the fifties; and the Russians from Georgia, Moscow, and Leningrad who came flocking in the seventies.

Israel's fantastic diversity of peoples and visitors was to be seen everywhere. One stumbled on Christian tour groups going over Crusader castle; Greek pilgrims watching with humbled awe as red robed priests washed their brethren's feet at an Easter ceremony held in the courtyard of the Church of the Holy Sepulchre; Moslems celebrating Ramadan; and blue-shirted Jewish youngsters from the youth groups visiting the sites of the Dead Sea Scrolls. Geographically, historically, and religiously, Israel presented a painting of a thousand different colors. And to add to the fantasy, one always saw in the background a Hollywood or Italian television team shooting the story of Moses in the Sinai desert, or reconstructing the fall of Masada. At last I understood the expression *mind-boggling*. For the first year my mind well and truly boggled.

This worked very negatively on my filming. Everything was exotic; everything was a wonder. This included the velvet-gowned rabbi who looked as if he'd walked straight out of a medieval Polish village. It included the Bedouins and their supercilious camels, straight from the central casting of *Ben Hur*. And it certainly included the sexy, flamboyant Greek Orthodox priests with their majestic gray beards and hair tied behind in a bun.

But for the Israelis all this was commonplace, not worth a second glance. I was seeing a *New York Times* travel section on Israel, but what had to appear on the screen was a different Israeli reality—more subtle, more somber, more probing—a vision relevant to life as it was lived in Tel Aviv, in the Negev, and in the kibbutzim rather than to life in the great beyond.

My social acculturation took time. I had thought about the problems before I came and was therefore on my guard. What I hadn't considered too seriously, though, were the areas of censorship and security—how careful you had to be and how the possible impact of your films could never be dropped from your mind for a moment.

In the seventies, Israel was surrounded by countries with whom it was in a state of war. Since the peace treaty with Egypt and the situation post-Oslo, things have changed slightly, but not much. There is still a wariness of one's neighbors. However, because of proximity, nearly all Israeli broadcasts can be seen in parts of Lebanon, Syria, and Jordan. The impact of one's broadcasts on the enemy then, or the potential enemy, while not central to one's filmmaking, is always in the background. The impact of one's films on Israel's own Arab population also warranted serious thought (more on that shortly).

Official censorship was the easiest to handle. It came up mainly in the context of films dealing with the border situation, terrorism, and the army. In nearly all these cases permission had to be sought for filming, and the films had to be cleared before broadcast. Though I didn't deal too much with the first subjects, I made two films on the army, *Battle Officer* and *Letter from the Front*, and so went through most stages of censorship.

The first move was to apply to the army bureaucracy for approval to do the film. The outline idea was submitted, and in 80 percent of the cases it was approved. But occasionally the army would get difficult. No one could be spared to help you! The subject was under wraps! The film would underline army morale! But these were exceptions. In general, and up to the Intifada (the Palestinian uprising on the West Bank)—and that's a later story—the army was slow, but helpful. Restrictions usually extended to saying you could only film in X, not Y, and only do a picture about officer A, not officer B.

Once official permission had been given, your director's credentials had to be approved by the army spokesman's office. During the actual filming itself, an officer from the spokesman's department accompanied you everywhere. His task was to tell you what you could and couldn't film. The battles consisted of the officer saying no, it couldn't be done, and myself trying to recall where I had seen a published picture of that particular tank, that new artillery piece, that new carrier. If I could quote chapter and verse, I could go on filming. Buildings up to eye level could be filmed, but nothing revealing place or situation. Everything was quoted as taking place *esham bamidbar* (somewhere in the desert). General dialogue was OK; specific battle comment and operating procedures definitely out. No names could be mentioned, no units cited.

Later the rushes—the raw unedited film spools—were seen in toto by another supervising officer, and the final censorship took place when the completed print was almost ready. *Battle Officer* had featured some fortifications near the canal, tanks on maneuvers, and searches for mines and terrorists. It had good, exciting material that I was loathe to lose, and I was quite fearful the film would be emasculated. In the end, the censors left in all the visuals except for one night operation and merely cut out three passages of dialogue dealing with a weapons' system, cuts that I recognized as being totally justified.

During the Yom Kippur War, while working on *Letter from the Front*, I saw another aspect of the censorship game. What was unique about the war was the immediacy and involvement of the coverage. This was not a war being filmed a thousand miles away, to be shown to the viewers who were for the most part uninvolved: it was a war being filmed a mere fifty or one hundred miles away from the TV set. It was also a war that was being shown not weeks and months after the battle but scarcely half a day later. In a country as small and as intimate as Israel, few of the faces on the screen were anonymous: all were immediately known and recognizable as sons, husbands, friends, and acquaintances.

All this implied both practical and emotional censorship rules that provoked different reactions among foreigners and Israelis. In the early days of the war, journalists couldn't really get to the front, and when they did, their copy was severely restricted. This irked many of the foreign journalists used to relatively free battle coverage from Vietnam. The Israeli attitude, with which I agreed, was that what was merely a news story for some people involved matters of life and death for others, and that security and human feelings came before world information or war as entertainment.

Yet Israel censorship couldn't stop people from watching Jordanian and Lebanese TV news broadcasts. And this is when the pain was felt. In Israel during the Yom Kippur War, we knew from the start that the war was going badly. Nevertheless the pictures always showed the Israeli tanks going forward. On the Jordanian broadcasts, however, a different story was being told. Here we could see Egyptian troops perched on top of the Israeli bunkers at Suez, waving their rifles proudly and ripping the Israeli flag to pieces. And on Lebanese TV we could see Israeli prisoners of war, sitting on the ground, their hands bound together and their eyes blindfolded. For everyone in Israel this was the blackest, darkest moment.

During the war I had joined a camera team from the Jewish Agency and gone with them as an additional director. *Letter from the Front* was a ragbag of film, grabbed on the run everywhere from the Sinai front to the Golan Heights. Seven camerapersons participated, as did three directors and a couple of editors. I shot two sequences in Safed military hospital, one at Fayid (the old British Egyptian airfield), one around the tank battles in the north, and another sequence of soldiers at a kibbutz.

The material was heartrending—just too much to bear--and I've written about it later in this book. Being very depressed by events, I was happy to leave the film to the two other directors (which word is really a misnomer when applied to battle footage) to finish. I hadn't got a clue what they would do with the material or what shape they would give it. I merely knew they were up against a bind, as the film had to be out within two weeks.

A few days later I got a call from the producer. The film was finished, which is to say totally edited, with picture locked into position and music and effects recorded—but somehow it wasn't working. Could I write a link commentary for it, but . . . er . . . no visuals could be changed, and the commentary had to be ready by tomorrow.

I looked at the film on the editing table. It was half an hour long and went all over the place. One moment we were with the fighting, the next moment with a family, the next moment back at war again. It was a mess, but it had some marvelous sequences, mostly showing the sadness and exhaustion of the men when the battles had ceased. And it was a challenge. Because of its confusion an A-to-Z script was out (thank God), but I felt some interesting things could be done if the script was internalized and personalized and told how people *felt* rather than how wars were fought.

Everything then became simple. I looked at the film a few times, took sequence timings, and went home. In my bedroom I drew out copies of my recent letters to family in England, took out my diary, poured a glass of brandy, and started to work. The script was the easiest I've ever written—to use a cliché, it wrote itself and was finished in about an hour and a half. In retrospect I think it's the most personal film I've ever done and certainly the one that has brought the most satisfaction. Part of it went as follows:

Visual	Narration
Soldiers lying alongside cars and in tents, absolutely tired.	You keep running, and when you stop there is this overwhelming tiredness, not just of your body, but of your whole being. Where are your friends? Where are those you love? And you feel a terrible heaviness covering everything.
Soldiers playing football, barefoot. Mountains behind them.	Okay! So now we have a cease fire, big deal! Mind you, I'm not knocking it. It's good, but I don't quite believe in it, and the silence is strange.
Soldiers talk, write letters, sleep on the grass, etc.	Now I find time completely standing still for me. There's no yesterday and no tomorrow . . . no normalcy, no reference points. There's only the immediacy of this moment.
	We are still mobilized, and plans, future, home life—all these things are vague and unreal.
	A lot of my mood has to do with the fact that we tend to share all our emotions here, both the joy and the pain . . . and of the latter there is quite a lot.

War films and military films were only a small part of my life in those early television years. My films had much more to do with religion, history, urban politics, and the social scene. Here the informal censorship of the system was much more subtle than that of the military censors.

Alan Rosenthal, 1992. Photo by Tal Rosenthal. (Author's collection)

Alan's brother Monty at age nineteen—a few days before joining the RAF. (Author's collection)

Alan at Oxford, 1969. "When I hear these wild Israeli songs," his Oxford tutor remarked, "I now understand, for the first time, why Pharaoh let the Children of Israel go." (Author's collection)

The Rosenthal family gathers before Alan and Ray's departure for Israel in 1961. *Left to right, standing:* Sylvia, Raymond, Phylis, Monty, Iris, and Alan. *Seated:* Lewis (Alan's father), Adele, and Sarah (Alan's mother). (Author's collection)

Alan and Ray on the night before they left for Israel. The plan was that Ray would provide the car, Alan the music. (Author's collection)

Adolf Eichmann in his glass booth in Jerusalem. Not a word of remorse was heard from him during the whole trial. (Central Zionist Archives)

Eichmann as a young lieutenant colonel. (Courtesy Israel Government Press Office)

Gideon Hausner, chief prosecutor at the Eichmann trial. (Central Zionist Archives)

One of the walls that divided Jerusalem between 1948 and 1967, demolished after the Six-Day War. (Israel Government Press Office)

Israeli soldiers at the Suez Canal in 1967. (Israel Government Press Office)

Alan filming at the Suez
Canal during the Yom
Kippur War, 1973.
(Author's collection)

The image of the "new Israeli woman" popularized in Zionist documentaries. (Israel Government Press Office)

The *Exodus 1947*—the most famous of the "illegal" boats that brought over 70,000 Jews to Palestine's shores 1945–48. (Central Zionist Archives)

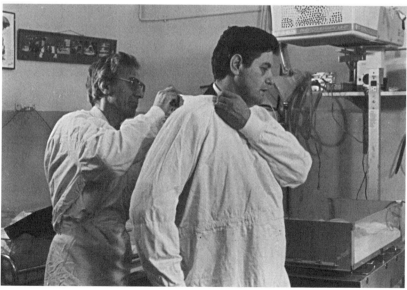

Alan attending the head of Hadassah hospital while making a film on heart surgery, 1988. (Courtesy Richard Nowitz)

Interviewing Yitzhak Rabin for *Hadassah at 75*, 1990. (Copyright © Joel Fishman 1999)

Interviewing Prime Minister Shimon Peres for *Hadassah at 75*. (Copyright © Joel Fishman 1999)

Filming *Hadassah at 75*. (Courtesy Richard Nowitz)

Covering the making of the British/Italian series *Moses the Lawgiver* for Israeli television, 1974. (Author's collection)

Shooting *Bedouin Life*, somewhere in the Sinai Desert, ca. 1990. (Author's collection)

Leon Charney playing the Mexican bandit alongside Anna Karina (*left*) and Geraldine Chaplin. (Courtesy Leon Charney)

Left to right: Bob Lipschutz, Leon Charney, Ezer Weizman, and President Jimmy Carter. Charney alleged that he was the secret peacemaker behind the Israeli-Egyptian accord. (Courtesy Leon Charney)

Sauniere's strange church at Rennes le Chateau, one of the possible sites where stolen treasures from the Second Temple in Jerusalem may have been buried. (Author's collection)

Carcassonne, in southern France, another possible location of the Temple treasures. (Author's collection)

The Temple menorah on Titus's Arch in Rome, filmed for *The Hunt for the Treasures of God*. (Author's collection)

Now every TV system has its own unwritten rules. These can vary from dealing with the Irish situation with kid gloves and being polite to the queen, to keeping quiet about Vietnam, not knocking the FBI, and leaving the president's family in peace. And of course these rules change from year to year. So what I'm discussing is not new but just an indication of where Israel's sensibilities lie as opposed to those of England or America.

Because the TV came into existence only in 1968, the ground rules were at first quite fluid. At least that was my sense of the situation at the time. When I came back to Jerusalem in 1971, the ground rules, though never openly stated, had crystallized very clearly. These guidelines were, first, no criticism of religion. For years the religious parties have tended to hold the balance of power in the government. Their votes have given the ruling party its majority, whether Labor or Likud. Thus, no one is willing to ruffle the feathers of the religious, particularly not in a TV documentary. Luckily, there is a little more freedom in open discussion programs. The second guideline was no documentaries analyzing the roughhouse of politics, political parties, or problematic situations, social or otherwise—in short, no rocking the boat.

From the start the religious affairs department produced a lot of documentaries and was a good bread supply to freelance directors. In the main these films were fairly simple pieces, such as the profile of a young rabbi, the scientist as believer, or a righteous convert. Outside of Judaism there was always something to be done on Ramadan, or Christmas in Bethlehem.

The films on Judaism, however, suffered from three peculiar problems. First, some of the small ultraorthodox groups objected vehemently to being filmed, any time, any place—the old graven-image taboo. Thus they would take refuge from photographers by covering their faces with their traditional *streimels* (black felt hats). This, of course, was their right, as is anyone's to privacy. However, they would often interrupt filming in accepted public places, which could be a bit much. Once, while filming around Shimon Bar Yochai's tomb in Meron at Lag Beomer, I was told to stop, otherwise the objector would write to the Hassidic rabbi of Bessarabia to excommunicate me. Lunch was ready, so I stopped, otherwise who knows what would have happened to my immortal soul.

The second drawback to filming religious subjects was that because of the strictly interpreted ban in Jewish law regarding

Sabbath work, it was forbidden for the orthodox to film or be filmed on the Sabbath and on certain Jewish holidays. Now this makes things a bit tricky when so much of one's filming consists of trying to shoot a Saturday morning bar mitzvah, a New Year celebration, or a Passover seder. The answer—not totally satisfactory—was to stage most of these events and then superimpose a title reassuring the righteous that these events were not shot on the Sabbath or whatever.

All the above was in its own way quite funny and a challenge to the inventiveness of both director and cameraperson. Subject censorship was much more serious. In no way as a documentarist could you get by with a film that might offend orthodox religious susceptibilities or that commented critically on the religious state of affairs. The news and current affairs department, however, because it dealt with immediate events in the public eye, was a much freer department in this respect. Even then, its broadcasts on controversial issues were only made after a struggle.

The result of all this was you knew you couldn't do a film debating the power of the religious courts: the subject was simply out of bounds. You knew this and wouldn't even waste time writing a proposal on the subject. The same was true if you wanted to do a piece looking at some of the slightly shady goings on involved in conversion.

My own run-in in this area came in a film I wanted to do on marriage. In Israel there is no civil marriage, only religious. Thus not only can a Jew not marry a Christian or a Moslem, but the marriage—even for unbelievers—has to be religiously performed. Naturally this state of affairs has been a battleground for years, with traditionalists opposing civil reformers. Like others, I thought this would be a good subject for a film if I could find the right approach. The best answer seemed to be to come at the general subject through the particular incident, and I chose three stories that would illustrate the dilemmas.

My first profile was to be a Jewish girl from a kibbutz who wanted to marry an Arab. Then I found a Cohen (a "priest," like my sound man) who wanted to marry a divorced woman, a relationship forbidden by Jewish law. Finally I wanted to film a director friend who wanted to marry a non-Jewish American girl. He found this was impossible in Israel and was planning to marry in Cyprus.

I thought the film had tremendous potential for investigating the subject. I also thought I was the right person to do it because, although in favor of reform and not particularly religious, I was fairly sympathetic to religious traditions. So, buoyed with high hopes. I took a ten-page proposal to the head of programming at the TV.

We drank a few beers. He slapped me on the back. "Great subject, Alan. Fantastic idea. But of course we can't do it. Maybe in two years' time. Just now it's . . . er . . . a bit sensitive." So the idea got dropped. Instead, the TV did a film on three ethnic wedding celebrations, Bokharan, Yemenite, and Moroccan—what I would call a "lovely, moving wallpaper picture."

My film *Battle Officer* also brought up awkward moments for the TV. Here my central character, the tank officer Yoel, had made two "offending" statements. The first was that few soldiers in his unit wanted to attend morning prayers. The second, also highly personal and mentioned earlier, was that his deeply religious parents objected to his serving in the army.

The executive producer argued that these passages should be cut. The impression he wanted to create was that the army was gung-ho for religion and that the religious community was right behind the army. I argued that the passages were personal and must stay. In the end we compromised. The personal expressions stayed in but were "balanced" by commentary supporting the executive producer's views.

Aside from the religious limitations, many of us were troubled by the unseen political limitations. At the root of the problem was a mistaken belief on the part of the government and politicians concerning the power of television to influence opinion, something professional communicators were and are much more cautious about.

So the unstated message filtered down through the ranks. Not so much "Don't do that subject," but rather, "If you do it, it is going to create a lot of problems for us, so why don't you try something else. Something safer, less noisy." All this was complicated by the fact that you were an independent director. Thus if your controversial films were made and created a ruckus, your chances of getting another film from the system were diminished. As I've said, I don't think it's much different elsewhere, but it's frustrating when you think your films might gradually be able to create a climate of change.

Nevertheless, and happily, people fought this situation. Early in 1968 a friend of mine, Ram Levy, a very talented, impassioned director whom I knew from London, did a film on two families. One was Jewish, one was Arab, and the link binding them was that they had both lost sons in the 1967 war. It was a very sensitive and human story showing that grief and tragedy knew no barriers, and yet it caused a minor storm. The film was finished in 1968 and then reviewed by committee after committee. I'd see them meeting in the editing room next door, pontificating on whether this mild, gentle film would spark riots in the Gallil or would cause Arabs in the Old City to rise in revolt. Eventually it was shown in 1970—a mere two years late.

Sitting in the television basement café with friends in the early seventies we would go through films we had suggested that had been turned down without consideration. They ranged from the obvious "naughties"—Jewish converts to Christianity and the Zionist dirty linen of the twenties and thirties—to more shaded areas, such as drugs, homosexuality, poverty in Israel, and the character and possible corruption of the political parties. This last area attracted me, especially after seeing a BBC film on the British Labor Party, *Yesterday's Men*. But cold water was poured on the idea in the preliminary discussions. According to the pundits, such a film would either propagandize for the party or probe too many grubby secrets. Neither result was acceptable.

I must add at this juncture—in order to be fair—that all this was in the early seventies and that the late seventies and eighties saw an improvement in the situation. All the controversial sex subjects were discussed, poverty was admitted, and the buried pages of history were uncovered. Nor did Judgment Day follow. In fact, one of the highlights of the seventies was a drama, shot documentary style, that showed some of the Israeli actions of the 1948 war in a distinctly unfavorable light. The film, *Chirbat Chiza*, became a cause célèbre, and though there were protests galore, the film was scheduled and screened.

Sometimes the constraints of the Israeli political atmosphere made for a double-edged sword. On one cutting edge lay all the forbidden subjects. The other edge, equally dangerous, represented the special-interest subjects. Here care was needed to avoid being "used" if you were to maintain some kind of integrity as a filmmaker.

In this area the biggest traps were usually encountered in attempts to show aspects of the Israeli-Arab conflict on the screen. Sometimes the problem would be historical, such as dealing with the old Hebron massacres by the Arabs or the Deir Yassin killings by the Jews, or it or it might arise out of contemporary life and problems in the administered territories.

My own turn to be involved arose out of a suggestion from the Arabic department of the TV. Could I write and direct a short film about a village called "Abu Ghosh"? Nothing serious—just a short profile piece depicting its history, its current life, and featuring a few of the village personalities.

The village lies about eight miles from Jerusalem and straddles the old road to the capital. It was founded by the Abu Ghosh brothers a few hundred years ago, and its strategic situation made it a favorite bandit "tax" point for robbing pilgrims and travelers. Today the village shelters hundreds of the descendants of the original brothers. One of them won over a million shekels in the local Israeli lottery, and the fine restaurant built on the winnings welcomes scores of Israelis every weekend. Abu Ghosh also talks of a Crusader tradition, claims a few biblical remains, and boasts a few rather lovely churches. All in all, a dead easy film to do.

The catch lay in the motivation behind the film proposal. Abu Ghosh had been taken as a positive example of an Arab village that didn't flee in 1948 and whose inhabitants had lived ever since in prosperity and peace with their Jewish neighbors. In short, what we had to show was a positive, picturesque story of harmony and friendship to counter the propaganda about Arab refugees. So the underlying interest of the TV was fairly clear. But if the story was true, I was in all in favor of telling it.

My research turned up a rather more complex situation. In the 1948 war, the Arabs had in fact been asked to leave the village so that the Haganah forces (Jewish defense forces before the foundation of Israel) could better defend the entrance to Jerusalem. The Arabs were reluctant to go but eventually complied with the wishes of the Jewish officers after being reassured that they could return in a few weeks. After the war, however, their return was denied them. In the end it took the forceful intervention of Yitzhak Navon—later president of Israel, then a young Haganah officer—against the authorities to ensure the villagers' return and fulfillment of the original promise. Even then the Arabs claimed that much of their land had been forcibly requisitioned, with only a small recompense paid.

This was not quite the story the TV had hoped for. Yet any film on Abu Ghosh would be nonsense unless this history was brought out. I discussed this with the head of Arabic programs, who had proposed the film, and he was rather taken aback. To his credit he decided the story must be told and supported me the whole way through. Given the internal pressures of the TV, this was quite courageous. The only thing he insisted on was that I interview Navon (not in my original script) to get a fuller understanding of the context of the promises and counterpromises.

While making the film I also became prey to a few Arabs who wanted to use it for an anti-Israeli diatribe. Did I know that conditions in the village stank? That social help was being deliberately withheld? That village lands had once stretched from Jerusalem to Tel Aviv and had been taken and ruined?

The charges couldn't be ignored, and I spent about a week tracking down welfare grants to the village, statistics on aid it received, compensation it had been paid, and so on. I also interviewed about ten people from the village to try to cross-check stories as to what had happened between 1948 and 1976. In the end I found most of the charges were unsubstantiated and didn't even refer to them in my program.

Abu Ghosh was one of the last pictures I did for the TV till the early nineties. After *Abu Ghosh* came two films on archaeology in Sinai and a profile of a Bedouin musician, but none of the films had problems. That was in 1978. Afterward I started working almost exclusively for American and foreign networks via my own production company. That has meant better financial rewards but also some emotional loss, as my films are not going to the audience that counts—the Israelis themselves.

On reflection I see that between 1968 and 1978 I made over twenty films for the TV. They ranged from pieces on soldiers, academics, and workers through films on the Holocaust, politics, and Israeli history to social investigations, child welfare, and profiles of musicians. I learned scuba diving for a film on underwater archaeology, did a three-hour climb up Mount Sinai to capture the desert at dawn, traipsed through every religious site in the country, shot factories beyond recall, and amused myself making a film about Burt Lancaster playing Moses.

In all this I count myself very privileged. I saw the country from the ground up (and underwater) and learned to understand firsthand its ways, its nuances, and its peoples. At the same time I would like to think my work made a small impression on a country in a state of flux, a country in the process of defining itself and its character and institutions. Maybe. One never knows.

Looking back, my early days at the TV seem to belong to another world and another time. For years we had no drama on the TV. Now the soap opera has arrived with a vengeance, and you can spend your evenings watching the yuppies of north Tel Aviv in *Ramat Aviv Gimmel*, difficulties of the poor in *Florentine*, or the adventures of the Israeli police in *A Detective in Jerusalem*. Today Israel has two main channels and over twenty cable channels. The minister of communications promises "open skies" and a future one hundred fifty channels. God forbid! I'm not against competition, but I doubt whether any one has thought through seriously what this would really mean in terms of quality of programming. I fear that with the same amount of money now pushing ten or twenty stations instead of one or two, serious programming will go to the dogs, with game shows and quizzes dominating the ratings.

It is easy to be nostalgic, but I see one serious but inevitable loss that has come with time and the proliferation of stations—and that is the loss of social glue. Poor as it was, Israel TV in the beginning bound the country together and in a sense provided a kind of nation-building cement. Those days are gone. They can be mourned, but they can't be brought back.

As can be seen, I still have a very warm feeling for Israel television, though I feel it's beginning to collapse, as its ratings fall and it loses its audience. In spite of everything I recently had a renewed appetite to work for the TV, and gave it a few proposals. One of them dealt with the difference between the Israeli dream and reality. The head of the department liked it but had a few negative comments. "Where are the rabbis? What's happened to the Arabs and the monasteries and the castles? No camels. No deserts. Why can't you begin to think like a tourist?" Hearing that, I knew my time as a "new boy" was over. Graduation day had come at last.

2 - Only Madmen Go There

Sometime in the midseventies, feeling very fed up with Israel, I decided to take a quick trip to London, see family, watch cricket, take in a few shows. In short relax, something that was and still is incredibly difficult to do in Israel. Inevitably my sisters pushed me to visit Aunty Lilly. "She'll be annoyed if you don't, and why should we be the only ones to suffer from her boiled chicken? Besides, she wants to discuss the will with you."

My Aunt Lilly was then a widow in her midseventies. She hadn't seen me for three years, but her greeting fitted the occasion. The door opened. The familiar round, warm face. "Alan, dolly, should I take my teeth with me to America?" My Aunt's conversations were always like that. No preliminaries. Boom. Right into the heart of the matter. The teeth I could cope with, because our conversations always hovered on the brink of the surrealistic. Other times we would talk about aphrodisiacs for the over-eighties and whether Marilyn Monroe and Elizabeth Taylor (two good Jewish girls) knew how to *daven* (pray) in the synagogue.

Lilly was a pretty woman, who against her father's wishes had married for love. My grandfather Alec, born in Warsaw in 1870, had come to England as a young man and opened a fairly thriving wholesale grocery business. And everything had to serve the business. When Lilly was nineteen, my grandfather wanted to marry her off to his best customer, someone who resembled Lazer the butcher in *Fiddler on the Roof*. Lilly demurred. He was too old and smelt too much of pickled herrings. My grandfather saw a nice monthly profit going down the drain. But his protestations were to no avail. Love won out, and Lilly eventually married my Uncle Morry, a baker who sang sweetly both to her and his customers.

Every few years Lilly went to America to see her eldest sister, Annie, also a widow. The preparations took on the kind of complexity that groups must have faced in the nineteenth century when about to cross the Sahara Desert. Should teeth be taken? Should spare dollars be put in the right shoe, the left shoe, or be hidden in the corset? If a millionaire fellow traveler wanted to take you home, could you leave your sister waiting at the airport? And what underwear should you take for this would-be seducer?

Annie, the older sister, was as bizarre as Lilly. She had moved to America when her daughter had married a GI and found her true element there. She was a flamboyant storyteller transplanted to a scene where no one could check on the veracity of her tales. So along with being the lover of Mountbatten (forgetting that he was reputed to be gay), she also held herself to be the intimate of Eisenhower and a close friend of Churchill. She drew the line at the queen. "No," she would say reluctantly, "I have never been to the Palace," leaving you to wonder how the Palace equerry could have been so stupid as to have left her off the list of the annual Buckingham Palace garden party. To balance that she let you know that the chief rabbi never took a decision without her, from whether plastic was kosher to whether five times intercourse on the Sabbath merited a special blessing. When Annie came to America, she worked at Macy's as a shop assistant, but that had to be embroidered. "I'm not really the assistant. Mr. Macy placed me here to keep a secret watch on the department and report personally to him."

Whereas Annie was almost a mythic figure to me, Lilly was very real. She had a lot of my mother's warmth, and lacking children of her own, she was always pleased to see the nieces and nephews. I also enjoyed her stories of the family, regretting as always, not just that my mother had died so young, but also that she had died just when I became interested in roots, origins, and connections.

In retirement Lilly had become an avid writer to the newspapers and would make frequent calls in to British radio. Her favorite topic was the defense of Israel. Had William Waldgrave or Douglas Hurd to make just one throwaway remark praising the Palestinians and disparaging the Israelis and my aunt was in there fighting. "Doesn't Undersecretary Waldgrave realize that the Mufti of Jerusalem had a seven-course dinner with Hitler? Doesn't Douglas Hurd realize that Arafat has five mistresses and billions stashed away in the Swiss banks?" But she saved her real anger for the BBC overseas service. "Dear Editors of the World Today. Can you please explain why you always refer to the PLO bunch of thugs as 'freedom fighters' while the IRA are always called 'terrorists'? Yours sincerely. Lilly Aleck."

I loved my aunt at these moments as she showed me her book of cuttings and went into the tiny kitchen to urge me to take another piece of boiled chicken. But finally we would finish with politics, and she would give me the latest state of her will. "I've cut out Sheila because she couldn't be bothered to phone me when I had the flu. And nothing goes to Doris because she didn't speak to me at the wedding. However, I might give Morry's gold pen to Linda because she bought me a box of chocolates last week." And so it went on, with the possessions being divided and subdivided with more care than the Rothschild millions.

On Lilly's bedside table was a picture of her brother Moishe, who died at the age of forty-four; her third sister, Hetty; and the fourth sister, Sarah, who was my mother. In the photo Hetty looks very nervous. She had the timid frightened look of someone afraid of her own shadow. I was told she had been the beautiful one of the family till she married Willie the gambler. People would look at this fragile ghost of a woman at family gatherings and say, "Willie ruined her. That's what he did. Ruined her."

In contemplation, I have to believe that my mother's sisters, while being quite lovable, were all a bit potty, with eccentricities that increased with age. So how did my mother emerge from such a crazy family and stay sane? I see four answers. First, she was also crazy herself, but being a loving son I never saw it. Second, she had a strong character. Third, my father kept her sane. And fourth, having nine children keeps you inexorably tied to the here and now, to the immediate and the practical, and to necessity and reality.

My parents' match was not inevitable, and both had other irons in the fire before they met each other, especially my father. As a handsome lad who was a master tailor, he was seen as a man with good prospects. But he was also known to like the girls and to be a little unreliable. When he started courting my mother, her parents were a little uncertain whether to tell her to rejoice or be on her guard. After all, Lewis Rosenthal had already been engaged to a couple of girls, and his silver-headed walking cane indicated too much of a poseur.

Yet somehow they married, and Boris photographed them tying the knot. Boris was the great East End Jewish photographer. He'd started his career in Russia and on coming to England had built up a monopoly on photographing Jewish weddings. To get married without a Boris photograph was like getting married without breaking the glass. The marriage was just not kosher. So there they are in the photograph. She is eighteen. Pretty. High boots and a short wedding dress. He is twenty-eight and looks exactly like my younger son, Tal. The black hair is thick, the tie neat. As always he looks the aristocrat, the man in charge. Handsome as hell. My mother would hug him and say, "Well, a nice looking guy like you really fell in the cart marrying a girl like me, didn't you?"

The fact that they produced nine children over forty-two years of marriage always amazed me. I came number eight and was always acutely conscious that if they had stopped when any normal self-respecting couple would have stopped, I wouldn't be around.

Raising a very large family was helped by my father always knowing how to make money, not enormous amounts but enough to get by comfortably. He'd done a bit of teaching in his time and later left that for wholesale dress manufacturing. With my brother Monty's help after the war, he then went into import-export and mail order. The latter ventures brought in more money than the dress business so that different members of the family were brought up in different economic circumstances. This was illustrated by our geographic movements.

The early birds, so to speak, were brought up along the lower numbers of Holloway Road, in north London, close to the darker parts of Camden town and Euston. The middle ranks were raised a couple of miles up the road, while I was born in the classier 700 section. Here you could already breathe the heady air of Highgate and perhaps even pretend you that you touched the fringes of Hampstead. As for my youngest sister, Adele, number nine in the family, we counted her as the nouveau riche. She wasn't really one of us, as she was totally brought up in the bourgeois wastelands of Finchley and had no memories of the old country like the rest of us.

Of course the major problem in a large family was trying to make out who was in it. This wasn't helped by half of us being evacuated and half of us staying in London at the start of the war. At the height of the blitz my father bought a house in Wellingborough and shoved the younger part of the family out there with my mother. While he and my eldest sister, Phylis, stayed in London, all sorts of long lost family members turned up in the country. They claimed to be variously grandmother, great aunt, or twice removed cousin, and so on, but most of them looked like moth-eaten members of a down and out repertory company. Nevertheless, having claimed blood ties, they then invaded our one and only defense against the German bombing, our prized Morrison shelter.

This was a rectangular table made of steel, supported on steel legs, under which were bed springs for a mattress. During the raids, the idea was to sleep under the table, protected from the bombing by a few inches of steel. Great idea! The only problem was that the bed was made for three but normally had to accommodate eight to twelve people. This was accomplished in sardine fashion, five or six with heads north to south, and the rest of the world heads south to north. On a good night I'd vaguely recognize the face next to me as a brother or a sister or my cousin Irvin. On other nights I would wonder who was this woman with the moustache breathing down my neck or whether this man with the pipe wasn't really a German spy. The answer was usually, "This is your Great-Aunt Sarah, or your Uncle Ralph, now shut up and go to sleep."

The problem of the early years was to distinguish who was really family and who were the freebooters who'd just come along for the ride. Eventually I decided those who stayed around most often were probably my brothers and sisters. But it was difficult. There was a thirteen year old called "Sylvia" whom my brother Ray confided to me had been found on the sea shore and wasn't really one of us. As her method of putting me to sleep was to put a pillow over my face, I was ready to believe the worst, but her resemblance to my mother made the story hard to believe. I was also suspicious about a pretty sixteen year old called "Iris," who claimed to have been evacuated with her school to Cambridge. Since she brought us chocolates I was at least willing to give her honorary status as a sibling.

The problem resolved itself when I was six. For my birthday I was given a family chart. It then all became clear. The nine children were reduced to seven, as it appeared two had died before I was born. Of the remaining seven, four were girls, and three were boys with an age range of eighteen years. Simple. And the eldest in the family was Monty. He was fourteen years my senior, and he was the prince. Next came Phylis, the wonderful and understanding elder sister everyone dreams about. Together they probably did more to teach me about life than my parents did. But there was a difficulty. Being so much younger than they were, I didn't really exist for them.

When Monty eventually recognized me as his youngest brother, which must have been when I was seven and he was twenty, I began to think he was quite a nice guy. Later, when I was about twelve, he started piling on the myth. "You see, Al," he would say, "you had it easy. You were born to luxury, to feather beds, to silk curtains, to a car, to a bicycle that worked. In contrast I had it very hard, very hard! In order to help Dad I had to pack parcels to midnight. In fact my hands are still sore." This just didn't accord with reality. In practice he had a bedroom to himself, whereas the rest of us were piled three up or four deep. He never washed up or did housework and to this day cannot make a cup of tea or boil an egg. As for the hard work for my father, I discovered that his first real job after leaving school at fourteen was to test mattresses eight hours a day by lying on them.

During the war Monty went to India with the RAF. Apart from repairing busted bombers and, more bizarrely, roller skating in a maharajah's palace, he discovered India needed umbrellas. My father promptly sent these out to Bombay, receiving combs and curry in return. So was born the family import-export business, which besides keeping my brother off the streets, also kept two of my sisters away from the poverty line.

For a while import-export boomed. Then, in addition, my father and Monty took up the mail order business. I thought the object was to make money, but the prime purpose seemed to be to answer begging letters from Nigeria or Kuala Lumpur which went,

Dear Mr. Mail Order,

I saw your superb advert for a Tommy Steel guitar in the *Daily Mail*. I have five children, my wife has left me, and I have not worked in fifteen years. Christmas is coming, and my youngsters are so sad. Will you not brighten the festival by sending me four of your guitars free for which I am sure Jesus will bless you and make your days plentiful on this good earth. I could also do with a car cover, which I can make into clothes for my grandmummy.

Yours sincerely, and very thanking you,

Surripji Singh

The idea of mail order was to anticipate the nation's whims and get to the customers, particularly those in isolated districts of Britain, faster and cheaper than any local store. So over the years my father and Monty, with the help of my sisters Phylis and Iris, advertised and sold everything from trampolines, crystal radios, guitars, and prams, to team hats for motor bike supporters, car covers, and garden furniture. It was a good business, but it had its dangers, mainly in the form of post and transport strikes. As these always happened at Christmas, and a good part of the business dealt with toys, the tension was often overwhelming. Would the toys arrive at their destination before Christmas, or would the strike and delays bring chaos and disaster? This was the yearly "Perils of Pauline" question.

Often it was touch and go. If a strike was on, then all the family would be called in to avert disaster. My sisters would handle the phones. In calm soothing voices they would tell irate customers that their goods would be there in time, that in fact they were being specially shipped from London to Paris to Sweden to the Orkneys, from where frogmen would swim to Glasgow to make a special delivery, finishing the last leg of the journey on roller skates if necessary. So far so good. The real problem was when the customers came to the showrooms demanding their orders. This was the equivalent of the moat having been crossed, the castle walls stormed, and the realization that the enemy was just across the threshold. Only one person could handle this. My mother.

In retrospect I have to say she had the negotiating qualities of Kissinger at his best, crossed with the advocacy skills of Louis Nizer and William Kunster. One Christmas, seared in my memory, two burly Yorkshire coal miners burst in demanding their Tommy Steel guitars, otherwise "this fucking fancy factory will be fucking finished." My mother knew the lorry was due, but whether it would arrive in five minutes or an hour was anyone's guess. Her strategy was to give them tea, talk to them about their wives, admire their children, and listen to their problems. By the time the guitars arrived, two hours late, they were all sitting around singing music hall songs, perfectly prepared to spend the holiday with my mother or failing that have her come up and visit with them over the New Year.

In order to facilitate her children on their path through life, my mother kept a trousseau closet. In it were placed bed sheets, table cloths, napkins, towels, dishcloths, everything and anything that would help her children set up home once they got married. Although there were variations in patterns and in the year of purchase, everyone had more or less the same amount, as this was part of my mother's basic philosophy. She wanted all her children to be equal. She had seen families with one rich son and one poor son, one spoiled daughter and one neglected daughter, and she wanted to avoid that at all costs.

Though her ideals for her daughters were crystal clear—marry early and have lots of kids—her ideals for her sons were much more vague. She wanted them to be comfortable, though not necessarily rich. Being in business was best, though taking up a profession might just be acceptable. It wouldn't be a bad idea if they got married, but there was no rush, and if the girl was wealthy it wouldn't hurt.

Monty fitted her dreams to perfection. He was a first-class entrepreneur and carried my father's business to undreamed of heights. My brother Ray was more difficult. He had left school at sixteen (common for those days), rebelled against joining any family enterprise, and instead took up accountancy. My father thought this was crazy as the business offered more golden opportunities. In consequence there were frequently family rows on the matter. Ray stuck to his guns, however, and emerged quite brilliant in his field, till he surprised everyone by doing a doctorate in Indian history and also going to Israel.

As the eighth out of nine siblings, I tended to get forgotten. Not exactly overlooked but treated with benign neglect. "Don't worry. We'll get around to you when we've dealt with the rest of the family, got them married off, sent on their way, or set them up in business. Meanwhile get on with school, don't get into too much trouble, go to Hebrew school, and keep away from non-Jewish girls."

This regime of few rules and basic laissez faire was ideal for me. It meant little pressure from above and plenty of time to explore and find my own way. It also meant that my sisters and elder brothers had a much greater influence on me than my parents, and it was also they who set the rules in the house rather than my parents. But there was a radical difference between us. The first half dozen in the family had all grown up in north London and followed my father in his trip from hard times to better times. They had lived over the shop or over the factory, had left school very early, and had been used to helping Dad if and whenever needed. In contrast my younger sister, Adele, and I grew up in northwest London, when the family had, so to speak, "made it." We were the coddled, spoiled, middle-class members from Finchley as opposed to the working-class members from Highgate and Islington.

Well, I wasn't going to worry about that. As the Americans say, that's the way the cookie crumbles. And if you were going to be Jewish and middle class there were worse places to be than Finchley and worse roads to live in than Chessington Avenue. Of course, if you had money, the real place to live in was Bishops Avenue, commonly referred to as "Millionaires Row." Here people would drive up and down the tree-lined boulevard and point out where Shirley Temple had once lived and where Lady So and So had committed suicide. Since then the road has been taken over by Arab sheiks, surgeons, rock stars, and old age homes. Still, if you couldn't live in Bishops Avenue, Chessington Avenue didn't run it a bad second or third.

When my family came to live there in the early forties, they were merely following an earlier Jewish invasion trend from north London, Hackney and Commercial Road. Boris, the successful wedding photographer, had changed his name to Bennett and lived at the top of the road. Almost opposite them, in what seemed from the outside to be a very modest brick house, lived Jack and Tessie Cohen of Tesco fame. Farther down the road was the Young family, with two kids, Stuart and David, later to make their marks in the BBC and in Margaret Thatcher's cabinet.

Also hanging around the vicinity and close friends of mine were two scruffy kids, Jeffrey and Gerald Stillets. Their father ran a successful skirt business, and it was at their house I ate my first post-war grapes and bananas. Till then, all we knew of bananas were the wax effigies decorating the local fruit shops. Jeffrey's housekeeper had once tried to enlighten us about this strange, unknown fruit by making us all banana sandwiches. This was done by grinding up a turnip, mixing some banana essence into the pulverized mass, and spreading it all on bread. Afterward it took us years to appreciate the worth of real bananas.

With other nine-year-old friends, Bert and Bernie, I broke into the bombed houses off Chessington Avenue, where with stones and bits of wood we completed the destruction started by the Jerries. In between times I watched my cousin marry an American and Elizabeth marry Philip. I watched the Australians Don Bradman and Keith Miller play cricket at Lords and bemoaned the fact that my father hadn't purchased a television set and was content to spend the evenings playing chess with Raymond and myself.

My father's pleasures were few: a good book, a good film, the Yiddish theater, and now and then watching a good variety turn at the Golders Green Hippodrome, and failing anything else, a chat with friends at the *shul* (synagogue). He had been a founder member of Highgate synagogue, and it was natural, on moving to Finchley, for him to join the local *shul* in Kinloss Gardens, which was just around the corner.

His Saturday morning synagogue going wasn't done out of piety but rather expressed his identification with the community. Like so many of his generation he belonged to the orthodox congregation because that was the thing to do. His own views, however, were far from orthodox. Like many of his friends he had worked out a place where he was comfortable but not *meshugah* (crazy) about his Judaism. Changing crockery for passover . . . absolutely! Keeping kosher . . . absolutely! *Shul* going, well why not if it didn't interfere with business. Occasionally the other *shul*-goers would try to entice him to come for a Talmud lesson, or a Gemarrah *shiur* (a lesson that debates commentaries on the Mishnah), but he would shake his head. His Judaism was from the heart and the senses, from an identification with a past and a tradition and had little to do with learning and dissecting the ancient laws.

Nevertheless, he insisted that Ray and I learn a little bit more about Judaism than just how to read our bar mitzvah portions. This meant religious classes not just on Sunday but three evenings a week. The classes were awful. Everything was taught by rote, without explanation or meaning, in a stuffy, damp outbuilding. The teachers were dull and ancient and we students bored and indifferent. For fun we introduced mice into the class, stuck pins into each other, jumped out of windows in the middle of lessons, and set fire to the chairs, anything to relieve the tedium as we studied the Amidah (daily prayer; done while standing) for the thirty-seventh time in order to exhibit our prowess at the chief rabbi's annual visit.

My relations with our own local rabbi were never good, and the problem was not helped by the fact that we lived too close to the synagogue for comfort. Thus every time I went to play cricket for the school on a Saturday, I would run into the rabbi. He would spot my cricket gear, sniff, and look away in disgust. And it didn't matter what time I went out, whether it was 7:00, 9:00, or 11:00 A.M.. He would always be there, chatting with the regulars about an offending article in the *Jewish Chronicle* or chatting with the rabbetzen (rabbi's wife) about the dearth of women wearing modest *sheitels* (wigs).

Was it chance he always caught me? Was he put there outside our house by divine providence to make me change my ways? Did he look up the cricketing schedules of all the boys in the *shul* and visit all the houses on the day they had sport? None of these explanations would have surprised me.

Retribution always came from the *bima* (pulpit), in one of the rabbi's sermons. Could our parents please pay attention? If so, our Jewish souls could yet be saved. Books on the Torah and the Mishnah should decorate our homes, not cricket bats and football boots. Rashi and Maimonides should be studied, not the latest England batting averages of Compton and Edrich.

We sports transgressors and Sabbath breakers were about number five on the rabbi's sins list. This was somewhat comparable to the best-sellers' list or the top of the charts. There were the subjects that occasionally appeared, soared spectacularly to number one, and then vanished a few weeks later. Other sins appeared lower down on the list but were old favorites so to speak and stayed longer on the hit parade.

Thus transgression number one for January might be the sons of the congregation who were evidently marrying *shiksas* (non-Jewish girls) by the dozen. A week later we would find that *avera* (the sin) had been overtaken by a hot newcomer, married congregants who flirted with their Swedish au pair girls. A month later both might have vanished from the charts, with the finger of shame now being pointed at families who flaunted their wealth by hiring the steamship *Queen Elizabeth* for a transatlantic bar mitzvah party.

Eating *treife* (nonkosher food) was a steady number three. That was the sin that, as they say, had legs. It was a time-worn favorite, good for a mention when the rest of the week's news was low. But though well and truly loved because of familiarity, it had to be introduced with variations. The rabbi couldn't just say, "According to the latest Gallup poll in the *Jewish Chronicle*, eating *treife* is on the increase." Even he knew the subject had to be dressed up and flaunted with a little more artifice. So the rabbi would shake his head, pause, stroke his wispy beard, and deliver his oration with the sadness of King Lear admonishing his rebellious daughters.

"It has come to my attention that a new Chinese take-away has opened near Temple Fortune. A place that serves shrimps [gasps from the congregation], that serves crabs [more gasps], that serves sweet-and-sour pork [tears and beating of breasts]. But that is not all. This abomination of a shop has a picture of one of our brethren in the window with the caption 'Two-Gun Cohen ate here.' Mr. Cohen of Haslemere Gardens has asked me to tell you that Two-Gun Cohen is no relative of his, nor has he ever been to Shanghai [gasps of relief from the congregation]."

Once he hit his stride, the rabbi could keep the *treife* attack going for twenty minutes without pause. Aside from the failure of new brides to go to the *mikve* (ritual bath), it was clearly his favorite subject, hotly seconded by kosher butchers whose *kashrut* (certificates certifying adherence to Jewish dietary laws) were in question. He did all this weeping and wailing and gnashing of teeth out of the best of motives, but I couldn't help wondering whether in the end he didn't achieve exactly the opposite effect from that intended. Till he mentioned it, no one had heard of Cohen's Cozee Chinese. Now, with all the "awing" and "oohing" at the mention of the shrimps and the crabs, I'm sure the place was packed the following Monday, to the astonishment and delight of the proprietor.

Looking back it seems to me our rabbi was a total amateur as compared to some of the Israeli rabbis I met in my later life. They were *the real* experts in creative sin, able to invent a transgression at the drop of a *streimel* (a fur-decorated hat worn by the extreme orthodox). Thus one hotel I stayed at in Jerusalem had its *kashrut* lifted for employing belly dancers. Another lost its kosher license because it allowed a New Year's Eve party—a heathen celebration—on its premises. All this required tremendous original thinking, which luckily was then absent from our London Beth Din.

Though I tried to keep out of the way of the rabbi, the *chazan* (cantor), was something else. Born in Israel, he seemed as modern as the rabbi was ancient. If the rabbi's sermons drove away the worshippers, the *chazan*'s joyous Adon Olam brought them back in droves. His singing was one of the things that made me keep coming on the odd Saturday, and it was due to his prodding that I eventually joined the synagogue choir.

Apart from three teenagers like myself, the choir was composed of seven men of all shapes and sizes. Joe, five foot two and dressed like a refugee from Royal Ascot, was a middle-aged bookkeeper and had a voice like an angel. Basil, his tenor partner, was six foot two and bald, looked as if he came straight from a doss house, but was in fact a beginning lawyer. Martin and George shared the same digs and sang bass. Harry was a baritone and a piano tuner and could have passed for Stan Laurel. Roger, all of forty-five, was the oldest and was the one who told the worst jokes during the reading of the law. Frank, who sat next to me and like me sang tenor, was a nineteen-year-old articled clerk studying accountancy.

Altogether it was a disparate group held together by two common factors. First, everyone had a very good voice, loved singing, and truly earned the one pound that was paid for a Saturday morning session. The second factor was that all the adults apart from Frank, though confessing a surface Judaism, were either atheists, agnostics, or believers in some strange religion.

Harry's religion was women. He was the expert on Soho, on Scandinavian girlie magazines, and on books that could only be sent under brown paper covers. Normally he would huddle at the back of the choir with Basil, unfold the center pages, and admire the immense dimensions of the Swedish misses while trying not to miss too many choruses of Adon Olam.

Joe's religion was betting on horses. As Saturday was the racing day par excellence, he was always under pressure. As he was the best singer in the choir, we all turned to him for a lead. This was often a futile gesture. As likely as not Joe would have his head buried in *The Turf Goers Guide to Racing Form* and would miss the lead into the song. I sat behind Joe, and after a while got to prodding him when to be ready. In consideration for these kindnesses he would recommend Betsy's Baby to me for the 3:30, or Zanzibar for the 2:15 at Epsom.

Most of the discussions about horses or Swedish anatomy were conducted during the quiet time of the rabbi's sermon or during the Reading of the Law. The rabbi's sermon always lasted at least twenty minutes, or twenty-five if he had a good subject such as Israel's worship of the golden calf or the transgressions of King Ahab. So that was a good stretch. Again, the Reading of the Law would also take a good forty minutes, so all in all, we had plenty of time for discussion, debate, and general discourse on the welfare of the nation.

Martin and George stayed aloof from our wide-ranging surveys on horse racing and feminine form and my discussions on au pair girls with Frank. They considered themselves above all that, men of a higher moral quality, which they exhibited by their passion for the hereafter. They had met at a spiritualist gathering at the Albert Hall and to their amazement discovered they shared the same favorite medium, Indian Brother-Who-Walks-on-One-Foot.

Most Saturdays they came armed with copies of American séance magazines and discussed among themselves the merits of the latest gurus and the newest techniques for reaching across time and space. Both believed fervently in reincarnation, prophecy, hand reading, and foretelling the future. Joe chided them severely. How come, with all this back-up, they had never won the football pools? Like true believers they treated his mocking with disdain. With a vision of so many glorious worlds to come, who cared about football pools.

Roger also disdained the pools, but then Roger was a died-in-the-wool Communist. When I told him that, as a kid, I had peed very near the spot where Karl Marx was buried in Highgate cemetery, he stopped speaking to me for two weeks and interred himself in the *Daily Worker*.

The socialist experience was a direct result of his having been brought up in the East End and confronting Moseley's Blackshirt Fascists in the thirties. Since then he'd prospered and ran a small menswear shop. But the old habits died hard, and the flourishing of the *Worker* was probably his way of convincing himself he still hadn't become a member of the dreaded bourgeoisie.

Sometimes I thought that Alf, our choir master, must have been born with the patience of a saint. The scene in front of him, hidden behind a thin partition and bars from the congregants' gaze, usually looked like a busy morning in the British Museum reading room. Yet he would take it all in his stride. As he heard the rabbi rolling up the sermon, he would say, "OK gentlemen, time to put away Marilyn Monroe. Would you mind leaving the horses for five minutes, Joe? And Martin, forget about the next world and concentrate on this. We're going to do Sulzer's Keddusha, and make sure you get those high notes."

We would then stand. The sex manuals, the racing papers, the *Spiritual Times* and the *Daily Worker* would all be left on the seats, and instead we would take up Levinson's *Manual of Jewish Liturgical Song*. Then, with beatific looks on our faces, we would burst forth with *"kodosh, kodosh, kodosh, hashem tzevos, melo chol hooretz kevodoh"* ("Holy, holy, holy, is the Lord of Hosts. The whole earth is full of his glory"), hoping that on the other side of the barrier it sounded as if the heavens had opened and the angels were indeed singing the Lord's praise.

Occasionally in his sermon the rabbi would mention Israel but always seemed a bit ambivalent about it. It was as if he hadn't made up his mind whether the idea of Zionism was good for the Jews or bad. He'd never visited Israel, but he'd heard of wild goings on in the kibbutzim, and of the running of buses on the Sabbath in Haifa. All these things tended to dampen whatever little enthusiasm he'd ever had.

Unlike the rabbi, the cantor, our own local *sabra* (native-born Israeli Jew), fed us Zionism with a passion. Through his urgings we were subject to the odd Sunday morning showing of Jewish National Fund (JNF) films on an old 16 mm projector. Of course it didn't mean much, these guys—who didn't look very Jewish—driving tractors, and water gushing out of pipes. So what! What did it mean to us? However, the skies looked blue, and the girls in the films had ample breasts, so all together it was a pleasant diversion from studying the Mishnah or the Gemarrah.

Twice a year the local Zionist society recruited the senior kids in the Hebrew Classes to go out and raise money for the JNF. Each of us was allotted a few streets, given a blue box, and instructions. "Don't you dare pinch any money for yourselves. We know what Jonny Maurice did last year, and we don't want that to happen again."

Not knowing that stealing from JNF boxes was a worldwide tradition, that would later embrace people such as Woody Allen and Mordecai Richler, and being cautiously English, we usually kept our grubby fingers out of the till.

If you got a good road it was no sweat. The people gave easily and occasionally threw in a piece of cake. A bad street was something else. Not all the Jewish houses had *mezzuzas* (tiny holders fixed to doorposts that contain holy verses) and asking a bewildered Scotsman whom you'd just roused from sleep to contribute to some foreign charity wasn't the pleasantest experience in the world. Many times you rang the doorbell, people peered through the curtains but never came to the door. Or they came to the door and argued. "A tree in Israel? Seven bob [about a dollar]? That's bloody highway robbery. I can get a tree here for three bob. Anyway, I've already bought so many I must own a forest. And my husband's a member and he gave at the office."

My own parents were not Zionists, though they contributed to the JNF drive like everyone else. Neither did we have relatives in Israel, so the subject rarely came up at home. Yet in those immediate years following the surrender of Germany and the end of the Second World War you had to be blind, even as a kid, not to sense that the subject of the Jews and Palestine was being discussed and argued about everywhere.

Two incidents stick in my mind. It is 1947. I am ten years old and attending drama classes at a local school. Going home I travel on the same bus with Susan, a rather pretty girl from my class; she is all freckles, blue eyes, and blonde hair. I like her very much, and usually we talk. Today she is crying, and innocently I ask why. Her brother is in Palestine doing his national service with the British occupation forces. A week ago his jeep ran over a mine placed by Jewish saboteurs. As a result of the explosion, two soldiers died, and her brother lost a leg and an eye. Through her tears, ten-year-old Susan tells me the Jews did it, and she hates Jews.

A few days later I am in the Ionic, a picture palace as we used to call it, close to Golders Green station. The main film is about the Mounties and stars Gary Cooper, but before the Mounties we get the news. A man appears with protruding lips and thick glasses. He is short and stout, dressed in a dark suit, and obviously a politician. As he starts speaking the audience in the cinema starts hissing and booing. Some people even start yelling and banging on their seats. In all of my ten years I have never seen anything like this, and I wonder what this man has done. My brother Ray whispers, "That's Ernest Bevin," but the name means nothing to me.

Bevin disappears from the screen to be replaced by pictures of a battered passenger ship. Parts of its sides seem to be torn apart. Old men and women are waving frantically from the decks. A Jewish flag flutters weakly and is taken down. Now women and children are leaving the boat, while masses of armed British soldiers look on with gray faces. Two stretchers pass carrying mute bodies, followed by a limping man, his head swathed in bandages. The soldiers are silent, but everyone around me in the cinema is crying.

The scene changes. Now the men and women are mounting the narrow gangway stairs to board another ship. Again they are between guards. Again they are on deck, but something is wrong. The decks are fenced in by twenty-foot-high railings against which the people are clawing and pushing in desperation. Two faces, an old man and a child, are seen in close-up looking straight into the camera. The last shot is of their hands, agonizingly clutching the bars of their new cage.

I was too young to know I was watching the tragedy of the *Exodus*, too young to follow the story of the return of its passengers to Hamburg after their desperate attempt to break the British naval blockade of Palestine, too young to know why the audience had booed British Foreign Secretary Ernest Bevin. And even if you had told me that besides his responsibility for the *Exodus* fiasco he had also declared blithely, "The Jews of Europe must not push to the front of the queue," I still would not have been much wiser. Understanding would come later.

As I got older, the issue of Zionism figured more and more among my friends. It was a splendid vision that at first I tended to admire from a distance. Whenever my friends whispered to me, "There's a place for everyone in Israel," I would whisper back, "Yes, my place!" Romanticism, as far as I could see, had a place in Wordsworth and Coleridge, but I was suspicious of it in general life. Besides, it also seemed to me that many of my friends' aspirations for *aliya* (emigration to Israel) and life in Israel arose from simple dreams of escape. Louis hated his mother, so at the age of seventeen he hopped off to a kibbutz in the South. Good-bye, Mum. Hello, tomato crops. For a while it doubtless seemed a good swap.

While Louis was irrigating the Negev desert, I was trying to get to grips with what to do with my own life. I'd passed some major school exams at the age of sixteen, but it was the next step that was confusing. As I drew fairly well, I sounded my father off about architecture. "Are you mad?" he said. "Architects are next to artists in starving in garrets." As I didn't like starving and thought garrets were overrated, whatever Puccini had to say about them, that one was out. My father's business had its attractions, but I thought that could always wait. Even at that early age I knew there was more to life than mail order. Ray was doing well as an accountant, but I knew that accountancy was a spreading Jewish disease I definitely wanted to stay clear of. Law, however, seemed to me to have possibilities.

My parents weren't sure. They knew no lawyers. *The Defenders* had yet to appear on television. The writers of *L.A. Law* were still in their diapers. There were few role models I could show them. The one boy up the road who'd become a barrister was still dependent on his father for support. So though my parents weren't opposed to law, they weren't unduly thrilled by it. But at least it wasn't as bad as architecture. So we compromised, as I argued, "Let me stay on at school and take the advanced level certificate. Let's see if I can even get into university. Let's put the whole subject on hold and discuss it again in two years." Some compromise.

Once my fate from sixteen to eighteen had been agreed upon, life settled into a very pleasant groove: A bit of studying; a lot of cricket; choir Saturday mornings; a girl friend Saturday evenings; here a family wedding; there a family bar mitzvah; occasionally a Marx Brothers film at the Hampstead Everyman cinema; sometimes even a play in the West End.

Clearly, everything was being set in motion for a nice, complacent, satisfying, undemanding London Jewish life. All the pieces were gradually falling into place. My parents had even accepted the fact that my studying law might not be quite the tragedy they had thought at first. And Israel—well that wasn't an issue. Was it? Definitely not, because we certainly never talked about it at home, except once.

My father on this occasion had elected to go on holiday to Israel. It was a change from Bournemouth, as he put it. On his return, once the kisses and presents had been disposed of, he asked my brother Ray and me to come and have a drink with him, in private. Pouring the whiskey, he looked at us solemnly. "You're good kids, right? Right! I want the best for you, right? Right! Well it's not the place for you, so forget it. Put it out of your minds. Don't think about it. Forget it."

Ray and I were a bit bewildered by all this. What on earth was Dad referring to? The new theater in Golders Green? Surely not. Had Mum told him about the gambling clubs in Tottenham Court Road? Couldn't be. Had Ray gone to a brothel in the East End and kept it from me? Impossible. Then we realized Dad was talking about Israel.

"You won't believe this boys, but they don't put milk in their tea. They don't have fish-and-chip shops, and as for their pubs, forget it. Their orange juice is like acid, and their favorite dish is raw eggplant, which tastes like boiled car grease. If you don't like eggplant, they give you hummus, which I think is made from cement powder. As for their cognac, they should try marketing it as paint stripper."

Ray and I looked at each other. We weren't accomplished gourmets, nor were we wine cognoscenti, but hummus cement and cognac paint stripper was a bit severe even for our modest tastes. Ray stirred his whiskey and ventured a question. "Well, what about all that draining the swamps and making the deserts bloom? What about all those films we've seen? What about all those boys and girls, plucking oranges with song by day and dancing those crazy Cossack dances at night? You're not going to tell us, Dad, that's all . . . all make-believe?"

My father motioned us to sit. My mother joined us with cakes from the local patiserrie. I tasted them gingerly. They were without cement. I looked at the tea. It had milk in it. Thank God for Britain.

"Well boys, it's not all illusion. I did meet a man in Haifa who told me thirty years ago he had heard someone singing in the orange groves. But I think that was because his divorce had come through. And the swamps probably do need draining, though I'm told they're filling them up again to keep the newcomers in work. But that's only half of it.

"You know what our Houses of Parliament look like? Majestic. Imperial. With Richard the Lion Heart outside on his horse. Well their parliament is over a butcher's shop in King George street, with donkeys and camels outside. What an insult to King George. And when I asked them whether the prime minister Ben Gurion was in residence, they told me—pardon me boys—he was shoveling shit on a Negev kibbutz. OK, Churchill lays bricks, but shoveling manure? I ask you, what sort of a hobby is that?

"They have shacks and tents outside all the towns, old cement buildings in all the cities, and their foreign office is a row of tin huts that the British army abandoned before Waterloo. They have one toilet to every fifteen people, and they have yet to discover bathtubs. And you know what's worst of all? You can't get a decent salt beef sandwich there for love of money. Some Jewish state! Now you see why it's not for you."

Ray and I looked at each other and then at the pastrami sandwiches my mother had thoughtfully provided during Dad's discourse. Neither of us had ever seriously thought we would go to
Israel. It was clear from what my father said only madmen went
there. Israel was clearly not for us. Well, thank goodness that
was settled.

Boy, were we wrong.

3 - Next Year in Jerusalem

The truth is neither Ray nor I was being totally open with Dad. Israel *had* begun to interest us but in a removed and safely distanced way. And that's how it stayed till I was fifteen and Ray was nineteen, and all reason went out of the window. But even at those tender ages, both of us had our heads screwed on and knew the basic facts of life. And the facts of life boiled down to one incontestable truth. Simply stated, it was this: There are four or five good reasons for going to Israel, but Zionism isn't one of them.

A friend of mine, Hernandez, a gaunt, tall South American with whom I worked at Israel TV, produced the best reason I ever heard. His grandfather had left him three hundred thousand dollars on condition that he live in Israel for at least four years. When I last saw Hernandez, he was in the middle of his third year. No longer was he the gay spark I knew when he first came to work in Jerusalem. His beard had grayed and occasionally he twitched. But now and then he would grasp my hand and say, "Alan, only fourteen months to go, just fourteen lousy months and it'll be mine." Then his eyes would light up, a look of rapture would suffuse his face, and he would be lost in contemplating what he would do eventually with his grandfather's millions.

Of course, as time went by, he lived in increasing fear and anxiety. "Just suppose," Hernandez would say, "I get to the last month and have a traffic accident. Then pouf . . . it would all have been for nothing." His other worry was his wife. She was actually beginning to like Israel, and the kids kept talking about it instead of Costa Rica as home. Unfortunately, I lost track of Hernandez in the early seventies, so I have no idea how he resolved his existential problems.

While I was at school in Finchley and debated Israel endlessly with my classmates, it was clear that another excellent reason for embarking for the Holy Land was to get away from home. Regularly my friends, such as Louis whom I've mentioned, would come up and say, "Just can't stand my dad, the old bastard. Refused to let me have the Jaguar again last night. Thinks because I'm his son he can walk all over me. I tell you. It's kibbutz for me. That'll teach him a lesson. He'll be sorry when I'm gone and he has to look after the damn business by himself."

In those days, it made sense. Hail and farewell. Across to Paris, tootle down to Marseilles in one of those decrepit, agonizing French trains, then five days on the blue Mediterranean till an unblemished Haifa hove into view. By that time, father, mother, brothers, sisters, the whole family were light years away. A letter would take six weeks to arrive, and a parcel, a year. Timbuktu couldn't have been farther away.

Unfortunately for my fleeing friends, progress has brought the 747 Jumbo and the UJA and Hadassah jet-streamed tour. Today, if you go on *aliya* (emigration to Israel) to flee your family, you are as likely as not to find your parents waiting for you on the doorstep as you step into your Haifa or Ramat Aviv apartment. Or if they're not actually waiting for you, they'll be over three times a year on the irresistible charter flight whose prices were too low to refuse.

Once you've settled in, it's worse. Then come the friends and the nieces and the nephews who, for a bottle of whiskey bought cheap at the duty-free, think they can stay with you gratis before going on to India or Katmandu. To top it all, they usually drink all the whiskey they bring. On second thoughts, maybe teaching Dad a lesson today and escaping from the family is no longer the great idea that it once was.

In the cozy suburban Jewish London I lived in in the fifties, it also seemed to me, beyond all argument, that one of the most frequent reasons for emigrating to Israel was to escape from the police. In fact, so vast was the British exodus, that I was surprised to hear there were any Jewish prisoners still inhabiting Pentonville or

Wormwood Scrubs. All this, of course, was prior to the Guiness scandals, Maxwell's revelations, and the take over of Marbella by the British underworld.

The news used to go in ten-day periods. First the *Mail* or the *Daily Telegraph* would announce that Mr. X, formerly of Hendon or Leeds, had disappeared from his opulent West End penthouse, to the complete astonishment of his wife, children, mistress, and business associates. A day later, the newspapers would add that Mr. X was suspected by the police of forgery, embezzlement, company fraud, currency speculation, and income tax evasion (but never, I'm happy to say, would the words *rape* or *assault with violence* be mentioned).

A week later, an investigatory report in *Sunday Times* would reveal that Mr. X had arrived in Netanya and was staying with his old friend from *yeshiva* (rabbinical college) days, Meyer Lansky. Furthermore, Mr. X wanted the world to know that he was a lifelong Zionist, and his deepest wish was to plough the Negev and sow the Galil and have his grandchildren surround him as he passed his declining years in the shade of an orange grove. As the Israeli government was, at the time, looking desperately for Negev plowers and Galil sowers, not to say anything of small party contributions, it was no surprise that Mr. X was accepted in the land of his ancestors with open arms.

If one remembers that at the same time that Mr. X was trying to get to Israel, Odessa and other right-wing German organizations were trying to smuggle Nazi criminals to Argentina and Paraguay, one has to wonder if there was any room left for normal travelers on those crowded southern routes. Did Bormann, Eichmann, and Mengele pass Mr. X and Mr. Y at passport control? Did they talk about the agricultural pursuits they would follow in their newly adopted homelands? All is possible.

Where does political Zionism come into all this? I must confess, after many years of thinking about the problem, I still find myself beaten. I don't know how to cope with or react to someone who calls himself or herself a fervent, dedicated, committed Zionist and claims to have come to Israel for ideological reasons.

Don't get me wrong. I admire passionate Zionists. I think they are fantastic, marvelous, beautiful people. I just don't know how to relate to their thinking. For me, fervent Zionism, as opposed to my own brand of luke warm, plodding, vaguely romantic Zionism comes into the same category as wanting to climb Everest or save Rwanda. Commendable endeavors, but let every sane person stay clear.

Now, I didn't always have this clearheaded approach. Fervent Zionism is like drink. You can afford to get blind drunk once in your life, so you know what the demon is like. Afterward, you can contemplate the devil forever from a safe distance. My period of intoxication came between the ages of fifteen and eighteen when I belonged to "The Movement," and nothing else in my life seemed to matter nearly as much.

Belonging to the movement meant only one thing, membership in Habonim (the Builders). This in turn meant for some two or three thousand of us youngsters a total seven-day-a-week commitment to the largest Zionist youth organization in the country. And this commitment and participation radically altered and reshaped the lives of a good number of us.

Habonim was founded in England in the late twenties by an ex-Cambridge student called "Wellesley Aron." He was a strange creature even for England, a Zionist who believed that Zionism actually meant living in Palestine. Thus against his parents' wishes, and to the amazement of his armchair Zionist friends, he abandoned Cambridge to become a teacher in Haifa. After a few years in the Middle East, he returned to England, older, wiser, but still a Zionist, and in between times helped set up Habonim.

Wellesley Aron's aim was to give the children of the Anglo-Jewish community some small realization of Jewish values and identity in a freer and more congenial setting than the *cheder* (small religious school) and synagogue classes. In structure and general pursuits Habonim often paralleled the Boy Scouts, except the Scouts lacked Zionism and the Jewish songs and dances that pervaded the movement. Furthermore, as in a good Hasidic wedding, the Scouts kept boys and girls apart, whereas Habonim prided itself on the free mixing of the sexes.

My brother Monty and my sisters Phylis and Iris had all belonged to Habonim before and during the war, and they showed me photos of weekend and summer camps that completely intoxicated me. There was Monty in shorts, straw in his hair, and his arms around two good-looking girls. There was Phylis, grinning shyly from a tent opening, next to a poetically handsome blonde youth of seventeen, destined to be her husband. And there was Iris, in the middle of a circle dance, pretending to be oblivious to the admiring glances of the boy on her right. Obviously, I was merely looking at "boy meets girl under marvelous conditions." Mistakenly, I took this for Zionism and rushed to join Habonim when a group was started at Kinloss Gardens synagogue.

Lured by the prospect of girls by the dozen, I joined on the same night as Bert and Bernie. Together the three of us had progressed from the further destruction of bombed houses to the pursuit of the fourteen-year-old girls at the local Catholic school. All at once Habonim seemed to promise the fulfillment of all our dreams, without interreligious barriers. No longer would we have to fake a knowledge of Communion and Absolution but could swap our solemn Hail Marys for a swift Hello Ruthi.

Our meeting place was in one the synagogue huts, which accommodated the overflow on Yom Kippur services and the dreary meetings of the synagogue study groups. Besides possessing a leaking roof, it was freezing and damp and had last been decorated before the Russian Revolution. Undaunted, this is where sixteen of us met faithfully every Wednesday from seven to ten to be indoctrinated into the ways of Habonim. Here, from a group leader only a few years older than us, we learned about Herzl, about Trumpeldor, and about the geography of Israel. Here we heard tales of the illegal ships that had cracked Bevin's policies to bits. Here we sang Hebrew songs, learned the latest Hebrew dances, and more important eyed the buxom beauties such as Helena and Isabel who had joined our group.

At that point in the early fifties, Habonim was at its peak. Enthusiasm for the new State of Israel was at its height, and I suddenly found myself caught up in a world of blue shirts, circle dances on street corners and in front of town halls, farewells to people going to Haaretz (the land; Israel), hikes, rows with parents, 2:00 A.M. discussions on Ben Gurion's policies, celebrations of Shabbat (Sabbath) with all my friends, and songs to drive you crazy. Songs about roads to Eilat. Odes to your beloved leaping over the mountains like a goat. Bass growls of encouragement to the cows to come home and camels to get a move on. Ditties to celebrate Simona from Dimona, red rocks in Jordan, and the bringing in of the harvest. And fragrant melodies whispering of cool nights over the sea, of Galillee. Above all there was a sense of total involvement, a firing of the imagination, a strange camaraderie, and a wonderful knowledge of belonging and feeling alive.

Though we met once a week locally, Saturday evening promised really fresh pastures and masses of new talent. Saturday we went to the *bayit* (house), the main Habonim center for northwest London. Here would be gathered at least eighty kids from all the other northwest London groups, and if you couldn't find a girlfriend from among that pack, you knew something was really wrong with you.

The ostensible reason for the Saturday evenings was to hear the latest news on Israel from one of the *chaverim* (comrades) who had returned from Israel. Suntanned and virile, he would relate how his kibbutz had grown, how Zelda now had three children, how they were now farming cotton as well as tomatoes, and similar world shattering events. Alternatively, the evening might be devoted to a lecture by a prospective Labor member of Parliament who promised faithfully to undo the perfidies of his predecessors. More happily, the Saturday evenings would sometimes be the occasion for one big Chanuka party, finishing up with everyone sitting cramped up on the floor, the beer being passed round, the accordion or guitars coming out, and Russian folk songs blending in with the latest songs of the soil. It was a wonderful time, when Paul Anka and the Beatles were still in kindergarten. Unknowingly, and blithely innocent, we were merely anticipating the hippie communes and atmosphere of the sixties.

Beyond the façade, the hikes, the songs, the weekly programs and the pursuit of the new one gradually sensed what was important about Habonim. At last, in a congenial atmosphere of deepening friendships, all the nascent burning questions of adolescence concerning self-identity, purpose, and goals were finally being given a meaningful answer.

When we met together midweek—sixteen-year-old Bert and Bernie; fifteen-year-old Jonny, the brightest of all of us; Danny, the would-be writer; and Helena and Isabel—we made a point of throwing questions at our *madrich* (group leader), Yoash, a blue-chinned student at the London School of Economics. Why anti-Semitism? What was wrong in becoming a businessman? Why war? What was wrong with staying in England and earning a decent living? Why couldn't the girls wear lipstick and all of us do ballroom dancing instead of Israeli folk dances, which . . . well . . . you know . . . they do get a bit boring after a while.

Yoash and Chanah, our pretty *madrichah* who was studying to be a nurse, brought order out of chaos. All the questions belonged to one of two categories: "What did it mean to be a Jew?" and "What was the proper relationship of man to man?" The first question was easily answered. We could accept Judaism negatively as a burden that would dog us throughout our lives or positively as a great cultural heritage. But full realization of our Jewish heritage was impossible in England. Only in one place could we live the "real" Jewish life, in the newly founded State of Israel.

Yoash and Chanah then went on to answer the second question. The proper relationship of man to man can only be found in a re-formed society created under the banner of socialism. For the world the possibility might be decades away, but for us, luckily, there was the immediate answer of the kibbutz, the Israeli communal farm, and the translation of socialism into a practical way of life. Thus after joining Habonim by accident, motivated by gross earthly plea-sures, Bert, Bernie, and I suddenly found ourselves being offered a key that unlocked the door to a rational, meaningful life based on Israel and the kibbutz.

Of course there was more. By chance it was our luck and privi-lege to be of the generation to be called upon to rebuild the home-land. Others had gone, and were already living in kibbutzim such as Kfar Hanassi and Amiad near Rosh Pina, and in Beth Haemek near Nahariya. So *chaverim* (comrade), arise and run! Haven't you read what Arthur Koestler says in *Judah at the Crossroads*? There are no half ways. It's either England and full assimilation or Israel and the chance to become a Jew in the complete sense of the word. Israel needs you, but for your own identity you need Israel. What more was there to say?

All around us, at the same time, we felt the frustration of English youth in the postwar years, which was eventually to find articula-tion in the writings of John Osbourne and other "angry young men." Where are we going? What are we going to do? This was the plaint of my non-Jewish school friends when I played football with them on lazy Saturday mornings or ate fish and chips with them while walking home after the muddy game. They were confused. By con-trast, in Habonim, we felt pretty smug. This doesn't concern us. We've found belief. Aim. A challenge to our world-building ener-gies. *Israel.*

Meanwhile, behind all this façade of theory we never realized that the romanticism of Israel was pulling us with a compulsion far stronger than any logic. Here was a land of rebirth, heroes, and vitality. Stirred by tales of one-armed Trumpeldor dying at Tel Hai and the campaigns of '48, and invigorated by the stories of the *shomrim* (Jewish guards of the early twentieth century) and that crazy Englishman Wingate leading the night raiders, we relived the battles and saw ourselves continuing the fight. We read of Israel and its people, and we identified entirely. We took the wild *sabra* (native-born Israeli Jew) as our ideal, changed our white shirts for the blue of the pioneer, and took on Israeli names. So, to the confusion and consternation of their parents, Bernie became Baruch, Shirley became Shulamit, and Henry became Chaim. My friend Basil, who had always considered his name effeminate, used to complain about his failures with women. "Who's going to look into your eyes and say, Basil, you're so manly. I adore you." In Habonim he was able to change his name from Basil to Arieh, which meant the lion, and according to his own stories never looked back.

Finally we were drowned and engulfed by Israel's rainbow vibrancy. Coming from the drabness of postwar Manchester, Liverpool, and Leeds, with their dirt, brick, soot, and fogs, their neon signs and Coca-Cola culture, we could only be amazed and enchanted by the dream of an Israel we had never seen in the flesh. It was our fairy land somewhere over the rainbow. It was a paradise of eternal blue skies, Van Gogh yellows, and dazzling white buildings, where every action from posting a letter to digging the roads was done to song. Of our contemporaries we alone had the chance to relive the glories and the myth of the pioneer. Out of all England only we could put off our jackets, tear off our school ties, and adopt the open-necked simple life in a land of glorious technicolor. We saw it, and we wanted it, or at least Bert did.

Although we went to different schools, and Bert was two years older than me, we had more or less grown up together two streets apart. We joined Habonim together, chased the same girls, even crashed our fathers' cars on the same day, when returning to Finchley on a wet evening after a friend's wedding. However, whereas I was always a bit wary, Bert bought Habonim, Israel, and the dream in their entirety. And naturally, that included kibbutz.

Habonim had always been vaguely motivated towards socialism, and the center in Kilburn was full of the famous red-jacketed covers of the Left Wing Book Club. Yet for my brother and sisters' generation it was never taken seriously. It was left to the years after the war to see kibbutz elevated to the principle dogma of the movement, a belief that was eventually to alienate as many as it enticed.

The champions of the dogma were to be found in the European immigrants who filled the Habonim hostels during the war with their fiery tradition of Continental youth movement socialism. In contrast to the English kids such as myself and Bernie, only interested in cricket and girls, they took their politics seriously. For them socialism was often a God, and Israel only the incidental place where the new society based on kibbutz was to be worked out.

I could see the culmination of socialism in the way of the kibbutz with its communal life and totality of sharing, but why communal life on the land? To me agricultural work seemed overrated, underpaid, and worst of all, horrendously soul killing and boring. I believed passionately that you had to be out of your mind and certifiably insane to get up at five o'clock in the morning and go and milk a foul-smelling, evil-tempered cow, even if her name was Doris or Daisy. My friends such as Bert and Shulamit saw it otherwise. Their prophets were A. D. Gordon and Borochov. While one stressed the redemption of the Jew through physical labor, the other provided the theoretical arguments for a reorganization of Jewish society with a majority on the land and only a fraction in the professions.

Life on kibbutz being the ultimate end of movement education, everything was geared to motivate you in that direction. At sixteen or seventeen you were encouraged to go on *hachsharat noar* (junior preparation), where you would spend a year on a training farm in England devoting half your time to work and half your time to study. This was to enable you to adjust to the physical and mental demands of the communal farming life. On completion you made real *aliya* and joined a Habonim kibbutz in Israel like Amiad or Beth Haemek. This was the path chosen by Bert and Shulamit. The result was hell and fury on the home front.

Bert's parents had dreams of him becoming a doctor, a lawyer, an engineer. This is why he had gone to one of the best schools in London. Now, at the tender age of seventeen, he was abandoning everything, to be a *meshuganah* (crazy) farmer in a distant, uncivilized land. The boy needed his brains tested. At least let him take school-leaving certificate. Let him train for something, get a skill, a profession. Bert! Bert! You're killing us. The pleadings were useless.

Bert was adamant. Ideals were ideals. Thus on a wet Sunday after-noon, he packed his bags, left his tight-lipped parents, and headed for the training farm in Sussex.

Bert's exit for the muck and mud and the life of a Tolstoy vision-ary was just another way-stone in the fragmentation of our group. Bernie, the breaker of windows, had unexpectedly left for Jerusa-lem the year before. His father had sold up the grocery shop soon after Israel was declared a state and gone off to drive a taxi in the Holy Land, taking son and family with him. Basil, a.k.a Arieh, had gained entry to London University to study electrical engineering and would later establish a record in taking seven years to finish his B.A. Another friend of mine, Jonny, the most brilliant of our group, had gained a major scholarship to Cambridge. His was to be a lin-ear path that went from Cambridge, to Columbia, to a full profes-sorship in Russian studies at the Hebrew University. And while Bert and Shulamit had gone to the David Eder training farm, I was daw-dling with my usual indecision, happy to drift along, watch Arse-nal on a Saturday, and not take life too seriously.

Though I didn't fancy kibbutz, I wasn't averse to the odd visit to see how Bert and Shulamit were doing down in the south. From what I saw they seemed to be enjoying life. The countryside around the farm was beautiful and green and ideal for walking and camping. Altogether this was rural England at its best, a long, long way from deserts and drought.

Besides Bert and Shulamit, there were sixteen other youngsters on the farm, all being trained by the non-Jewish farm manager into the ways and wisdom of animal husbandry and the agrarian life. Though there were a few moans, most seemed to be immensely enjoying the experience. Marriage hadn't come to break up the happy sense of group, and after tea and a shower, everybody got together for a sing song before supper. In the evenings there were the occasional discussions—where to go in Israel, which kibbutz to join—but mostly people sat in front of the fire listening to Beethoven's Seventh or Mozart. Later there would be the relaxed, warm half-hour in the kitchen, sitting on or lazing around the huge oven, eating toast or chatting over hot cocoa. There was closeness, and there was companionship, and it was marvelous. Life in fact could be seen as one perpetual Habonim camp, the only difference being that the eventual setting was to be Israel rather than the Gainsborough's and Constable's England.

The accumulation of a few years in Habonim produced some strange results. We came to worthwhile ends through a confusion of logic, romanticism, and group pressure. We created a vision of Israel that was too good to be true. At the same time, we became mildly anti-Semitic in the sense that we despised the Anglo-Jewish community and most of the things it stood for, which we believed to be hypocrisy and social Judaism. We also became blind to life around us. Centered on Israel, we divorced ourselves from the world and its problems, power struggles, and peace movements. Basil was a burning internationalist, and I can still recall the laughter that greeted his antiwar, antibomb poems. We were sympathetic, yes, but we had to tell him straight out that those kinds of problems just didn't concern us.

Bert had left his mother in tears. She just about understood the ideas of Israel, but why oh why couldn't Bert train for something first? Get a profession. Find a way to earn a living. Go to a polytechnic. Get some education. Because, well, you never know. The answer of Habonim was no, no, NO! Israel's immediate needs were for tractor drivers, potato pickers, and stone movers, and one should answer that call and abandon all thoughts of university education. And here, on the subject of university, was finally exposed the inner tension of Habonim and its blindness to anything outside its own needs.

Habonim in the fifties didn't just frown on the idea of university but at most times was completely opposed to it as a path for its members. The study of very practical mechanical or agricultural subjects might just about be tolerated, but law, literature, and the humanities could not. Thus as a potential law student I had to keep my face very low and mumble unintelligibly when talk turned to the future.

The reason given by the anti-university faction was that Israel's most immediate need was for kibbutzniks. Many of us, in opposition, felt there was more to be said. The truth was that pure thought, pure science, and abstract discussion and questioning were alien to the Habonim pattern. The realization was strange because Habonim prided itself on turning out "intellectual farmers," but instead of encouragement one only saw a latent hostility to the luxury of the arts.

The second, mainly unstated reason for opposition was the fear in Habonim that at university a person would find much of the same camaraderie and satisfaction that the movement offered and would then be "lost." This was one of the reasons why the age for going on the training farm was lowered to seventeen and sixteen.

Till about the age of seventeen or eighteen, the fissures, cracks, and divisions in the way we all thought could be covered over. By the age of eighteen, the choice between the way of the movement and different personal wishes could no longer be evaded. Some accepted the ideology unquestioningly and went off to kibbutzim in the Negev and Galil. Others, like Bert and Shulamit, were more critical but went on to Kfar Hanassi or Beth Haemek in order to test the myth against reality. Jonny went off to Cambridge, and I went off to do two years' national service in the air force. Some of us forgot Israel. For others it was an idea lying dormant that would reemerge when the time was right. For all of us the idyll was over.

And yet the bond is never entirely broken for the person who was thoroughly immersed in Habonim. The years leave a pattern and set of attitudes and values that are hard to throw off. Something stays with you: an attitude, an outlook, a yearning for something more than just making a living. And of course, the friendships go on.

Nowadays Habonim seems to have changed. It's expanding in England, and the narrow dogmatism seems to have gone. Zionism is acknowledged as the prime moving force, and though kibbutz is encouraged it is a secondary issue. Also, *university* is no longer a dirty word. There are still the rows with parents. There is still the dancing and singing, but now Cuba and Clinton are discussed as much as Marx and the Moshav. So the movement evolves.

For years I criticized Habonim for its narrow look, but now I wonder. The triumph of the movement is that in spite of its faults, a high proportion of its members from those years did eventually make the decision to live in Israel even if not in kibbutz. The result is that anywhere you go, from Arad to Kiryat Shmoneh, you are likely to find someone slapping you on your back and saying, "Hey, shalom. Isn't your name Rosie, or Fishy, or Zvi, and weren't you in the movement in . . ."

All these are, of course, later reflections. At the age of eighteen, I didn't bother too much about all this because I had got into Oxford to study law. The only problem was having to do two years' national service first, in the Royal Air Force. Though the time dragged, it passed pleasantly enough. I became an aircraft radio and radar mechanic, played a lot of cricket and darts, and, like all national servicemen, counted the days to freedom.

When my father visited me at Oxford, one of his first questions concerned the age of my college, which was Lincoln. With pride, I told him it dated from about 1350. Dad then examined the drains and peered at the old baths in the cellar and at the rusty pipes along the windows and shook his head. "1350. When I see this plumbing, I don't doubt it for a minute."

Both my father and Monty had thought Oxford would be a sheer waste of time. Who needed all that intellectual rubbish when a good business beckoned? My mother thought otherwise. She believed it might smooth the edges, give me polish and grooming, make a man of me.

Though my father had commented negatively on my college's drains, my mother had a warmer attitude to my home from home. Looking at the ivy-covered walls, the stained-glass windows of the chapel, the neat squares of grass in the quad that had been growing undisturbed since the time of Henry VIII, she had only one main comment: "It's *heimish*," meaning—it's small, it's cozy, it's warm, it has spirit, and you could have done a lot worse for yourself. When I took her into the great hall with its marvelous sixteenth-century oak roof, what caught her attention were the oil portraits of the great, the near great, and the totally forgotten festooning the walls. She took this all in and pondered a while, obviously reflecting on her own roots in the East End of London and her father's journey from Warsaw. Finally, she hugged me and said, "Alan, I'm pleased for you. And *kein ahora* [exclamation to avert misfortune], you should hang here as well."

My mother was right. Lincoln was *heimish*. It was one of the smaller Oxford colleges but still maintained a very good academic and sporting record. It took about eighty students a year, and within a short time you knew everybody. Above all, it allowed you to be yourself and unlike many other colleges was almost totally free of snobbery or class prejudices, important for so many of us who were scholarship boys from ordinary city grammar schools.

If the RAF had been a study in avoiding work and time wasting, such lessons were well put to use at Oxford. Apart from one discourse on crime, I don't think I went to a single other lecture my first year at Lincoln. One reason was that almost everything you wanted to know about law could be obtained straight from the text books. But more important, Oxford was too interesting to waste time studying. That could all be done in the vacations. You had to get your priorities right. Term time was for eating, drinking, talking, playing, and maybe a little bit of reading.

Well, if the energy didn't go into work (and it certainly didn't go into sex, as there weren't many girls around in a university where 80 percent of the students were men), where did it go? Mainly into "becoming." It went into establishing a self-portrait. It went into creating an image of yourself as the person you'd like to be in the future.

In your mind, you could see everybody standing in line proudly establishing society positions. I'm going to be the lord chancellor. I'm going to be the conservative foreign secretary. I'm going to be the next Labor prime minister. No you can't. *I'm* going to be the next Labor prime minister. Well, after you then.

And many became exactly who they wanted to be. I breakfasted with a silent, saturnine thinker, who had the next room to me in my second year. Later he turned into Dennis Potter, author of wonderful the television series *The Singing Detective*. I played the guitar in a review with an excruciatingly funny music student whose merest gesture could make the audience laugh. Taking me aside afterward, he told me that, with luck, he thought he could become Dudley Moore.

All this "becoming" business was fine, and even a certain tentativeness and uncertainty was accepted. If you weren't sure you wanted to become President Roosevelt or Winston Churchill, that was OK. It was acknowledged you needed time to develop. What was not accepted was that you wanted to become somebody ordinary. To state that was to become a leper, a social outcast. What! You want to become an income tax inspector? Phew! Get away from me before you contaminate me.

I was one of the "don't knows." In the RAF, I had spent page after page in my diary trying to figure out whether I wanted Judaism, agnosticism, England, Israel, or even the South Seas and was still no closer to a solution. For a while I thought I might act as well as be a lawyer and appeared in a Ugo Betti play, *The Burnt Flower Bed*. My role was that of a spy. Since at that time I'd never heard of method acting, I decided to base my approach on the style of Peter

Lorre. I would lisp a little, act oily and ingratiatingly, put on a German accent, and talk out of the side of my mouth. Eventually, a review appeared in *Isis*, the main university magazine. What I remembered from it was a sentence which ran, "All the actors are bad, but Rosenthal is ghastly. Nothing quite so putrid as his performance has been seen in Oxford for many a year."

Abandoning acting, I took up the guitar. My speciality was Israeli music, which I sang with my pal Elkan, who earned his holiday bread by acting as his synagogue's relief cantor over the High Holidays. Most of the songs were pinched from Israeli records made by groups with inspirational names such as the Sons of the Desert or the Wilderness Trio. But that was something we never let on about. As far as our audience was concerned, these were the songs of our forefathers, handed down as a precious legacy from generation to generation. We called ourselves, naturally, "The Sinai Sinners" and sang for various reviews and at college parties. In a small way, we were a hit. Unfortunately, the music almost got me thrown out of college.

One afternoon, Elkan and I were rehearsing a potential winner in my rooms. The song was called "Hasela Haadom" (the red rock) and tells of Israelis trying to get to Petra, in Jordan, and perishing in the attempt. It was banned by Israeli radio, and each chorus ends with a wild scream of the dying men. Sung with passion, the song could make chandeliers quiver and windows vibrate. It could also easily invoke the wrath of the powers that be.

In my enthusiasm for the song, I had forgotten my rooms were directly over those of the college chaplain, who was also the history tutor. Normally he was the mildest of men. When I was summoned to his room, I saw a different personality entirely.

"What on earth was that racket going on in your room?"

"I was singing, sir."

"Unbelievable. And in what language?"

"Hebrew, sir. The language of the Bible."

"Oh! Were you singing a song of praise, a message of praise to the Good Lord? If so, he must be deaf."

"No sir. It's a modern Israeli song. It's about being lost in the desert and looking for a red rock. That's the style of these songs. Powerful. Dynamic. Bold."

The chaplain filled his pipe and looked at me very slowly, as if I had only just come into focus.

"Rosenthal, I have to tell you something that has been puzzling me for years but is now crystal clear. When I hear these wild Israeli songs, I now understand, for the first time, why Pharaoh let the Children of Israel go."

The cynicism and querulousness of the chaplain was luckily balanced by the enthusiasm that greeted us in the Oxford Israel Group. The club was never very large and only attracted twenty or thirty students to its meetings. Of those who came, a few were dedicated Zionists. Others, like myself, had grown up in Zionist youth movements and couldn't get the experience out of our heads. Most of us came because the group attracted the prettiest visiting Israeli girls, had good parties, and occasionally produced interesting speakers, such as the Israeli cultural attaché or the Tiger of the Negev.

The Tiger was aged thirty-five, had a square, rocklike face, and wore his black shirt open almost to his waist. This had the effect of revealing a dense nest of tightly curled black hair. The Tiger's eyes were intensely blue and gazed deeply and penetratingly into the orbs of the three prettiest women in the room. His English was fluent but guttural, and between his sentences there would be long pauses as he drank from the bottle of Chivas at his elbow.

According to the introduction, the Tiger had single-handedly evicted the Egyptians from the Negev in the 1948 and 1949 battles for Israel's independence. Well, maybe not single-handedly, because, as he admitted, Yossi had loaded the machine gun and Dudu had repaired the jeep. Besides clearing the Negev, the Tiger had lifted the siege on kibbutz Yad Mordechai, had flown relief planes into kibbutz Ruhama with a bandage over one eye and his arm in a sling, had crawled on his belly for fifteen miles to save a dying comrade, and had raised Israel's flag in Eilat after a fierce fight in which he had killed five of the enemy with his bare hands.

We males knew we were beaten. There was nothing in our lives that could compare to those exploits. We thought getting a scholarship to Oxford was hot work, but how could that compare to killing five men with your bare hands in the dark? No wonder he needed the Chivas, the poor guy. As for the women, they were grouped around the Tiger, lost in reverie, and for the first time in my life I understood the phrase *heaving breasts*. All around the room breasts were straining at buttons, pressing, pushing, and inviting. As the sensual temperature of the room rose, most of the men made their exits, unnoticed. I too left, thus missing the story of how the Tiger had impersonated General Montgomery and freed five of his friends from a British prison.

The Tiger must have told all his friends about his success because a few months later we were visited by the Lion of Jerusalem. Basically, they were two peas in a pod. The only difference was that the Lion was a few years younger and drank Johnnie Walker instead of Chivas. Like the Tiger, his shirt was unbuttoned, and like his predecessor, his body hair would have made a sheep dog wild with envy.

Whereas the Tiger had saved the Negev, the Lion had single-handedly saved Jerusalem. He had put reinforcing plates on trucks in the dead of night. He had put on disguise and penetrated Abdulla's legions for information. He had built a new supply road to Jerusalem while battling Syrian irregulars and had been the last man out of the besieged Jewish quarter of the Old City.

Once more we men felt inferior. Once more breasts heaved in unison, and silently I wondered where it would all end. How many more members of the animal kingdom were coming to visit us? Would we get a Bear of Beersheba or a Gorilla of the Gallil? The prospect was appalling.

Yet beyond the jealousy, we were also conscious of a profound admiration because we realized only half the stories were exaggerated. These men *had* risked their lives. They *had* done remarkable things. They *had* saved the Negev and Jerusalem. And the cost had been appalling because they had lost friends and loved ones by the hundreds and the thousands. And if they drank, it was because they needed it. And if the women fell for them, well they deserved it. In short, we knew only too well that it was because of men and women like them that the State existed. What we didn't know was that the lone heroes of '48 were soon going to be joined by the men of '56, of '67, of '73, and so on as war followed war in an endless sad succession.

The first premonition I had that the Tigers of the Negev would soon fade into history was on opening the paper one cold October morning and seeing the headline "Israelis Invade Sinai." There had been increasing guerrilla raids and Israeli reprisals, but we were getting used to that. Nasser had nationalized the Suez Canal, and there had been hot words by Britain and others. But we reckoned that was all diplomatic talk. Again, the Soviets were initiating a massive new arms deal with Egypt, totally altering the balance of arms in the Middle East, to Israel's fury. All the world had seen these things and accepted them as the mere to and froing of the usual military and diplomatic games. No one knew another secret game was being played out among Israel, France, and Great Britain, whose result was the Israeli invasion of Sinai.

For the next few days, most of us were either glued to the newspapers or stuck in front of a radio or television as events unfolded. The Israelis were advancing at a fantastic pace. Britain had warned both sides to stay ten miles away from the canal, even though the Israelis were nowhere near there and had parachute units trapped in the Mitla Pass. The Israelis had reached Sharm El Sheikh and had captured most of Sinai. They were advancing on the canal. Shock followed shock, with the greatest one yet to come. Britain and France were sending troops through the Mediterranean in preparation for an assault on Egypt.

For once, England put beer and football aside as the events divided the nation. Watching TV one night, I saw Labor politicians attacking the Conservative government policy as if it was literally the work of the devil. In defending this policy, Prime Minister Antony Eden almost cried on camera, while his wife announced that she felt as if the waters of the Suez Canal were running through their living room.

In such an atmosphere it was impossible to work. All one could do was listen, watch, argue, read, wait, and argue some more. No one was neutral. Everybody had a passionate opinion, and my own staircase at college was typical of the way people divided up.

Besides myself, three others had rooms on the same level. Binks Montgomery, another law student born in Rhodesia who had the room next to me, took it all as a game. His life's main interest was rugby and whether he would be picked for the varsity side. What happened in some obscure place called the "Suez Canal" was only of very minor interest to him. Jean Paul, on the other hand, couldn't sleep for excitement. He came from Paris, had graduated the elite civil service college, and was doing economics at Oxford to polish things off. For Jean Paul, there were no doubts. Nasser was a second Hitler and had to be removed as soon as possible. I concurred with most of this, and we drank midnight champagne to the success of Israel and to Nasser's downfall.

Peter, the inhabitant of the fourth set of rooms, almost regarded Jean Paul and myself as the anti-Christ. Peter, who was studying for the church, had been at Harrow school with King Hussein and was a strong supporter of the Arab position. He was also a fervent Laborite (as I was, normally) and regarded Jean Paul and myself with loathing. A few days into the war, and seeing what our attitude was, he refused to speak to us except for one comment: "May God forgive you and pardon your sins." This was no joking gesture but came out of the depths of his fury at what he saw as our support for a Godless, sinful, imperialist venture. In later years, I came to move toward Peter's position that Nasser had every right to nationalize the canal. But I still considered his intentions toward Israel murderously provocative and so continued to welcome the Israeli advance.

After the Sinai campaign, my thoughts turned more and more toward Israel, and a visit in the summer vacation of my second year strengthened the hold. It seemed, even after my father's dire warnings, that it might be a place for me. Not definitely, but possibly. However, if that was the case, it was hard for me to see where a degree in law might fit in. My understanding then (which has changed drastically with the years) was that the last thing Israel needed was lawyers. Engineers. Soil conservationists, yes. Even accountants. But lawyers—they just didn't fit the pioneering picture. And even if I stayed in England I was beginning to have some doubts about becoming a solicitor or a barrister. Clearly, what I needed was time out to think. More and more I began to see the solution was to study for a graduate degree in America. At least it would buy me a period of grace. What I didn't know was that it would lead me into film and into a four-month daily confrontation with Adolf Eichmann that would change everything.

4 - Eichmann on TV

On 17 April 1961, I was sitting in a crowded, dark room over a Jerusalem bank watching four television screens, or monitors. In front of me was a row of television-camera switching controls. My task was to cut between the cameras at the command of the TV director. It was my second day on the job, and I was still nervous. While all the screens had pictures, it was the third monitor that held me. It showed a small, bald, intense man in long black legal gown, his arm outstretched like an avenging fury, pointing a finger of rage and passion at three silent judges sitting on a raised podium. The man's pose denoted a deliberate reaching for effect, but it was the voice that held you.

> When I stand before you, Judges of Israel, I am not standing alone. With me are six million accusers. But they cannot rise to their feet and point an accusing finger toward him who sits in the dock and cry, "I accuse." For their ashes are piled up on the hills of Auschwitz and the fields of Treblinka and are strewn in the forests of Poland. Their graves are scattered throughout the length and breadth of Europe. Their blood cries out, but their voice is not heard. Therefore I will be their spokesman, and in their name I will unfold the awesome indictment.

Such was my introduction to Gideon Hausner, attorney general of Israel and chief prosecutor at the trial of Adolf Eichmann. After a few more words he turned to the man sitting in the dock.

> Never, down the entire bloodstained road traveled by the Jewish people, has any man arisen who succeeded in dealing it such grievous blows as did Hitler. And it was his iniquitous regime that used Adolf Eichmann as its executive arm for the extermination of the Jewish people. In this trial we shall encounter a new kind of killer, the kind that exercises his bloody craft behind a desk and only occasionally does the deed with his own hands.

On the words "a new kind of killer," I switched cameras so that Eichmann was seen in close-up. He was totally expressionless, his face twisted slightly to one side in a look of quizzical indifference. So, for over 112 sessions sat former Lieutenant Colonel Eichmann, the man charged directly and indirectly with causing the deaths of over six million Jews in the Second World War.

My involvement with the trial came through a set of circumstances that even today makes me wonder about fate and predestination.

On completing Oxford, I had gone to Stanford University in California to study for an M.B.A. Israel was still vaguely in my mind, and I thought a degree in business administration might be more useful in Israel than law. Unknown to me when I had applied for its lush pastures, Stanford also had a small department of film. This discovery, after a month at the university, was a source of great delight. The result was that I started studying TV, film directing, and script writing alongside finance and statistics. The School of Business was distinctly unhappy about this turn of events, but I was in heaven. I could fool around endlessly and pretend I was working. My justification was that one day Israel might have TV, and who knows, my studies might lead to new possibilities.

When I returned to England after Stanford, my parents accepted these new developments with their usual equanimity. At least they had two sons with decent jobs, and if their third son was a butterfly, well that was the way things were. What jolted them was when Ray told them he was going to Israel for a year and asked me to join him. This was not a good scenario for my parents, but accepting the fact that they had five other kids in England, they finally reckoned they could part with two for a year or so.

After I agreed to go with him, Ray bought a small red Austin mini

Minor, which we loaded up with our possessions and promptly drove from London to Marseilles. From Marseilles we took a boat to Israel and two weeks later found ourselves sitting in a classroom in Jerusalem learning Hebrew with about twenty other potential new immigrants. And this is where fate stepped in.

As was usual in these courses, at some time or other you had to step in front of the class and tell who you were, what you did, and why you were in Israel. When my turn came to make a fool of myself, I let go a bit on television and my Hollywood experiences so that the class could appreciate that they had Cecil B. DeMille in their midst. Unknown to me, a rather pleasant Australian girl called "Judy" bought it hook, line, and sinker. Her memory of the occasion would have far-reaching consequences.

At the end of the three-month course, I was again at the crossroads. Ray had taken a job as an accountant, but I wasn't sure where to go. As I had told my parents I was coming to Israel to make a film about children of the kibbutzim, I thought I might as well familiarize myself with the territory. Bert and Shulamit were by this time both living on a kibbutz called "Kfar Hanassi," but that was too English for my liking. Instead I chose another kibbutz, Yehiam, where I had many friends and which rather quaintly was built around the ruins of a crusader castle.

At Yehiam, I realized my father's worst fears had come true. I was about to work in cowsheds, wallow in manure, get my hands dirty, be bored out of my skull, and all in the name of Zionism. But after ten days there was a phone call that indicated fate had taken pity on my plight. It was Judy, the Australian girl from the Hebrew course. Had I been serious about my TV work? What a question! Of course I was serious. Of course I had worked with Hitch and Ford. Reassured on my credentials, Judy asked me to come to Jerusalem to see a mysterious Mr. Fruchtmann about a TV job. However, if I preferred life on the kibbutz or was too busy . . . ? Busy! I was back in Jerusalem that same evening.

Milton Fruchtmann was one of those bright, relaxed, languid Americans who always give you the benefit of the doubt. He liked my Oxford and Stanford credentials. He even accepted my few minor TV jobs in California and New York as having some worth. For himself, he was thirty-four and a shrewd New Yorker who had gotten various jobs in Hollywood, working with Rita Hayworth among others. After Hollywood he had returned to New York and risen high very quickly. At the time I met him, he was second in command to Lowell Thomas, head of Capital Cities TV.

Besides being a top professional, Milton was married to an Israeli and had become deeply involved in Israel. The upcoming Eichmann trial had been on his mind for some months when he realized one damning fact. A world-shattering trial was about to take place, but though people would hear about it and read about it, no would see it because no one had thought of filming it. At least, no one till Milton.

Grabbing a flight from New York, Milton had flown to Israel to persuade the Israeli government to let his company film the trial and distribute it free to world television. It was a brilliant idea that faced many obstacles. First, there was no television in Israel and hence no TV cameras or recording equipment. Second, there were the issues of decorum and custom. Cameras were normally banned from courtrooms, and Israel was already so sensitive about the trial that it wasn't sure if it wanted to get involved in another row. Luckily there was one famous precedent that argued for coverage, namely the filming and recording of the Nuremberg trials.

In practice Milton was pushing at an open door. Israel wanted to *show* as well as tell the world that a fair and open trial was taking place. Again everyone knew that the main (but usually unstated) point of the trial was to tell the story of the Holocaust to the world in the most powerful way. If this was true, then TV would be a stronger weapon than radio.

Persuaded by Milton's arguments, the government had agreed to let Capital Cities go ahead with the exclusive filming, on condition that a copy of the tapes was left with the state archives and that world distribution was arranged. However, it was still necessary to get the agreement of the court on the matter. Here there was trouble. Whereas Hausner, the attorney general was very much in favor of recording the proceedings, Dr. Servatius, Eichmann's counsel, was totally opposed to the use of TV. His main argument was that filming might induce witnesses to express something less than the truth. This might be done from fear or from the desire to play act before world audiences. His second line of persuasion was that television broadcasts might lead to a distorted presentation of the proceedings, for example, leaving out the arguments of the defense.

Both Hausner and Servatius presented their views before the judges, with Hausner winning the argument. The decision of the court still makes interesting reading today, particularly the following quote:

> There can be no doubt that direct visual and sound recording will render the proceedings in the courtroom with complete faithfulness far more accurately than the written word. We therefore hold in view of the aforesaid considerations—widest possible publication, for the benefit of every person desiring to be informed and exposure of the court to the judgment of the public—a television broadcast of what happens in the courtroom is not only *not* objectionable but serves important interests of justice.

All this was explained to me by Milton as we sat in his office, pictures of his wife and two small kids before him on his desk. Finally we got down to business and the reason for Judy's call. Milton needed a personal assistant. Maybe I could do the job.

With the permission of both the government and the court, Milton had gone ahead and brought Marconi television cameras and equipment into Israel from Europe. He had then set up four concealed cameras behind small netted windows that let on to the courtroom. As the cameras worked under ordinary lighting and made no noise, the court was satisfied that the dignity of the proceedings would be totally preserved. To keep the equipment running smoothly, Milton had brought in ten American technicians. While his four cameramen were all Israelis, directing would be done by a fifty-one-year-old U.S. veteran documentary director, Leo Hurwitz.

So the equipment was in place and the team ready, except for one thing. Milton needed an able right-hand man—someone who'd worked in TV and who could do any job that came up from camera switching to emergency directing. In the United States there would have been hundreds of applicants for such a position, but not in Israel, where television was still far in the future. Suddenly Judy, who was Milton's secretary, had a brainwave. "There was this guy I knew when I studied Hebrew—said he'd worked in TV in the States. I think he's now making a film on a kibbutz." Judy had phoned, and the rest was history.

Luckily Milton had accepted me at face value and hadn't inquired too much about my experience. This was just as well, because my

TV directing had been limited to three short courses and a few days' experience at KQED, San Francisco. Clearly it was a case of taking a big breath, plunging in at the deep end, and hoping I didn't screw up on the job.

Eichmann's capture by the Mossad, the Israeli secret service, had been one of the major news stories of the previous year. I'd been at Stanford at the time and had read of the capture in the *San Francisco Chronicle*. The headlines had been sensational: "Major Nazi War Criminal Apprehended and Taken Secretly to Israel." This we all understood, but who was Eichmann? He wasn't one of the known major Nazis like Dr. Mengele or Martin Bormann, so what had he done, where did he fit in, and why the excitement?

Eichmann had been a lieutenant colonel (*Obersturmbannfuehrer*) in Division 4 B4 of the Reich security head office. His job entailed overall responsibility for the disposal of the Jews. Expressed bluntly, his task was to put into working operation the decisions of the Wannsee Conference to annihilate all the Jews of Europe. His name had been mentioned at the Nuremberg trials, the most famous reference to him coming from his deputy, Captain Dieter Wisliceny. On being questioned by a U.S. officer, Wisliceny had quoted one of the last remarks of Eichmann: "He said he would leap laughing into his grave because the feeling that he had 5 million people on his conscience would be, for him, a source of extraordinary satisfaction."

Born in the Rhineland in 1906, Eichmann joined the Nazi Party in 1932. His promotions through the SS were rapid. By 1939 he was a captain and was made lieutenant colonel in 1941. The speed of his promotions may well have been due to his specialization in a rather nonmilitary subject, Jewish communities and their organization. The real start of his career as direct administrator of Jewish affairs came after Hitler's occupation of Austria in 1938. Posted to Vienna in August of that year, he immediately started seeing how he could rid Austria of its Jews. From there his career took off at incredible speed. As author Moshe Pearlman remarks in *The Capture of Adolph Eichmann*, "His was the fastest promotion of any of his contemporaries. He had certainly been 'perceptive' in his choice of a subject."

In January 1940, Eichmann moved into the Berlin headquarters of the RHSA. His task was to take care of the Gestapo's Jewish Affairs Office, section 4B. It was this bureau that became the orga-

nizational headquarters for putting into effect "the Final Solution"—
the plan for the total extermination of European Jewry. By the end
of the war, the horrifying success of the plan was attested to by the
death of over six million Jews. But Eichmann, one of the instruments
of the plan, had disappeared.

The search for Adolf Eichmann started in 1945. Though many
Nazi criminals had been captured and put on trial at Nuremberg,
hundreds of others, including Eichmann, had evaded that net. After living for a few months under a fake name in a prisoner of war
camp, he escaped and made his way to lower Saxony. Here he lived
an anonymous existence for three years, working as a lumberjack
under the name of Otto Heninger. In 1950, using the services of
Odessa—the Nazi underground organization—he finally made his
move to start a new life. Using a refugee passport under the name
of Richard Klement, he obtained a visa to Argentina and arrived at
Buenos Aires in mid-July 1950. Europe and the past were behind
him. Here he hoped to take up a new life.

By 1959 the dream of escape and freedom seemed to have become reality. Eichmann's wife had joined him in 1952, and for several years they lived peacefully in the remote town of Tucuman. In
1960 Eichmann went to work as a mechanic, and later as a fore-
man, at a Mercedes Benz factory in Suarez, a suburb of Buenos
Aires. The actual headquarters of the family was a one-story rundown house in Garibaldi Street, in another suburb at the edge of
the city. And it was here, close to the family home, that the Mossad
finally captured Eichmann.

The possibility that Eichmann was in Argentina had been passed
on to the Israeli secret service in 1959 through a Jew friendly with
the Buenos Aires German colony. Immediately Israeli agents were
sent to Buenos Aires to shadow the suspect. Intense surveillance
seemed to indicate that the mechanic of Garibaldi Street was indeed
Eichmann. When Eichmann's identity seemed 95 percent certain,
plans were generated in Israel for his capture.

The actual seizure took place on Wednesday, 11 May 1960, very
close to Garibaldi Street. Soon after Eichmann got off the bus on
his way home, he was captured by three Mossad agents and bundled
into a car. Once the secret custody place had been reached, the Israelis started examining their captive. Was he the fugitive SS officer
or someone else? While checking him physically, they found a scar
under his armpit, the place where the SS usually placed their iden-

tification tattoos. Only when the examination was complete did the captors ask the most important question . . . in German.

"Who are you?"

"Ich bin Adolf Eichmann. . . . I am Adolf Eichmann." Then, though the captors had not spoken Hebrew or identified themselves, he added, "I know. I am in the hands of Israelis." The fifteen-year hunt was complete.

Eventually, a drugged Eichmann was taken surreptitiously to Israel aboard an El Al plane "conveniently" visiting Argentina. On Monday, 23 May, David Ben Gurion, the prime minister, convened a special meeting of the Israeli Knesset (parliament). To a packed house, he made one of the most dramatic announcements of his career. "One of the greatest of the Nazi war criminals, Adolf Eichmann, who was responsible together with the Nazi leaders for what they called the 'final solution' of the Jewish question . . . is under arrest in Israel and will be put on trial."

The man responsible for the killing of millions of Jews would now be judged before the courts of a Jewish state. The forces of light seemed momentarily to have prevailed over the forces of darkness.

That phrase *the forces of light will triumph* was mentioned to me by the rabbi in charge of the Stanford University Hillel Group, when we first heard about the capture. No doubt he had grabbed the expression from some rabbinical circular. Or maybe Ben Gurion had used it in the Knesset. I don't know, but the phrase certainly seemed appropriate to me at the time. I was therefore surprised, as the weeks went by, to see how extremely mixed were the reactions to the capture, particularly in reference to Israel's position in the whole matter.

A few of my friends at Stanford, mostly my non-Jewish lawyer friends, thought Israel had no right to try Eichmann. He had been forcibly abducted from Argentina, and Israel hadn't existed when Eichmann's crimes were committed. These points were actually raised by Eichmann's counsel, Dr. Servatius before I joined Milton's TV team but had been dismissed by the Israeli court. A number of others maintained very forcibly that there was no way Eichmann would get a fair trial in Israel. The trial would become a vendetta, a lynching. This I totally disputed. It seemed to me even then that there would be so much publicity surrounding the trial that the judges would bend over backward to be fair. A more serious comment was that the trial was really an excuse for publicizing the history of the Holocaust. I thought that comment was pretty fair. But so what! The world had turned its back on the fate of the Jews in the war. Now let it hear about the consequences. Now anti-Semitism itself would be on trial.

There were also a number of comments from groups of Quakers and others, who preached sermons of forgiveness. They argued that like good Christians the Jews should turn the other cheek and let Eichmann go free if he said he was sorry! Others thought Eichmann should not be tried but should give public lectures on the dangers of totalitarianism. Possibly the most bizarre reaction was that of the British publisher and convert to Christianity, Victor Gollancz. Gollancz, too, thought Eichmann should not be brought to court. Instead let him be branded with the mark of Cain and make his way through the world as a lesson to others.

That was one side, the side of the purists. For myself, I thought there was only one group who had the moral right to decide these issues . . . the survivors of the Holocaust itself. And if the ones I knew were representative, then most of them believed Eichmann should stand trial . . . and what better way than before a Jewish court?

Though the usual center for local trials was in the Russian compound in downtown Jerusalem, the government felt the existing courts were too small and shabby for such a world-focused event. Instead a new building, close to Ben Yehudah and King George Streets, was chosen as the trial venue. This was the Beth Haam (People's House), which had been built to serve as a new municipal theater. Its attraction was that it held 750 seats and the stage could easily be fitted to accommodate the judges' bench, a witness stand, the various lawyers, and the accused himself. The main hall was also conveniently provided with angled walls, behind which the cameras could operate in secret yet still maintain a good view of the proceedings.

Our television control room was actually about sixty yards down the street from the Beth Haam, on the top floor of a small branch of the Igud bank. Contact with the cameras was maintained by huge cables that swung from our building, across the road to the Beth Haam. At odd times, it occurred to me that if anyone wanted to stop the filming, all they had to do was sabotage the cables. But although there were eruptions throughout the trial, that nightmare never came true.

The three trial judges were Moshe Landau, Yitzhak Raveh, and Binyamin Halevi. Generally, they acted as a tremendous counterpoint to Hausner. Whereas the prosecutor was flamboyant and melodramatic, the judges were quiet, composed, and thoughtful. By coincidence, all of them had grown up in Germany and could understand Eichmann in German, without the benefit of translators.

The witness stand was placed to the right of the judges whose high podium dominated the proceedings center stage. In front of them sat the two legal teams, while Eichmann was placed on the left. All this simplified things for the telerecording. One camera could be used for the judges, one for the prosecutor or defense counsel, and another allocated to Eichmann. In addition, we had one camera that could show us the witness stand or swing round and give us the reactions of the public. All four cameras registered the pictures simultaneously on four monitors in front of me, but only one camera was being recorded at any one time. If a witness's testimony was proving to be highly dramatic, then the cutting would usually be witness, back to prosecution, back to witness, then a short take of an Eichmann reaction. It was this edited version that was ultimately held for the record.

Eichmann himself sat in a bulletproof, boxlike glass dock, specially constructed for the trial. There he was—a small man with a thin neck, a sharp foxlike face, gaunt cheeks, a high forehead and balding black hair. Sometimes a small tic crossed his face. From time to time he ran his tongue around his mouth or seemed to suck his gums. Heavy glasses partially concealed the cold eyes, while large ear phones obscured part of the cheeks. In front of him lay piles of papers; behind him stood two Israeli policemen.

Like everyone who came to the court, I stared endlessly at him. For most Israelis there was a peculiar letdown. They had expected a monster, a man whose outward appearance would clearly show the inner evil. They wanted the distorted image of Dorian Gray's picture, Frankenstein's creature, or the wolf man. Instead all they got was a gray bureaucratic mouse in dark business suit. All of us wanted more and were asking the same questions: Who is he? What is happening inside him? Does he have any feelings, any remorse? How can he have done what he did? How was it possible?

Writing about the trial in the *Atlantic Magazine* in February of 1962, Martha Gellhorn had a very interesting observation to make on Eichmann: "The normal reaction to a man alone, in trouble, is pity. One man however odious his wrong doing, becomes pitiful when facing society in all its power. . . Yet this man in the dock arouses no such feelings, not once, not for an instant. . . . No single gesture, no passing expression of his face lays claim to our sympathy."

Eichmann's continual passivity and the expressionless quality of his ferretlike face are riveted in my memory. Only once can I recall any emotions seemingly crossing his features. It was late in the trial, and the prosecution was showing documentary pictures of naked bodies being bulldozed into pits after the liberation of Buchenwald. To do this, a small screen had been set up on the right of the stage and the lights dimmed so we could see the pictures. For once attention was not on Eichmann but on the ghastly film images. In fact Eichmann could hardly be seen . . . at least by the public. For us in the TV control room it was different, and even in the dim light I could see Eichmann very clearly in close-up on the second monitor screen. To my surprise, Eichmann appeared to be smiling and laughing at the sight of the flickering black and white images on the small courtroom screen. For a moment there was a ghoulish image of Dracula laughing at his victims.

The scene only lasted a few seconds but was caught very clearly in our recordings. Later in the day, after work, I went back to review the videotapes. There was no doubt, something like a smile or a laugh was crossing Eichmann's face as the corpses were manhandled into the trenches. Was this the real Eichmann? What I think happened was that knowing that attention was off him, Eichmann had allowed himself to relax. As a result, his nervous facial tick was for once out of control, and it was these facial grimaces that we had all interpreted as laughter. Whatever the reality, it was a chilling moment.

From April till August, I led two lives. One was the life of darkness, memories, shadows, and death. The other was a life of brightness, children's voices, fragrant smells, warm evenings, and the sighs of a Jerusalem night.

My entrance to the netherworld began at nine, when I went in to check on the cameras and the day's arrangements. Already the crowds were lining up outside the Beth Haam and showing their special passes to attend the days proceedings. Three hundred yards away I knew another two hundred people were waiting patiently at the Ratisbonne monastery to watch everything on closed circuit television. On top of the court building, the border guards with their green berets were settling down to their day's patrols and security duties. Farther down the road, the kids were going to school and their parents to work. So it went on, day after day for four months.

It was soon clear the trial was not so much about Eichmann, but about a process. It was the first massive telling of the whole story of the annihilation of the Jews before and during the Second World War. At such times Eichmann became almost incidental to the narration. His guilt and his connection with events was always stressed, but not in the same way as the later trials of Klaus Barbie or Maurice Papon. In the French trials it was always the accused himself who stood at the center of things. At the Eichmann trial it was the story of the Holocaust, the unfolding of twelve years of planned murder that stretched from the Baltic to the Mediterranean, that counted.

Day after day, as witness after witness mounted the stand, the devastating heartrending story of the destruction of Europe's Jews was revealed in detail after detail . . . a city ravaged here, a small village massacred there. And as the story moved from country to country, from Poland to Hungary, from France to Belgium, from Latvia to Greece, the documents piled up . . . over three thousand of them. Some gave names. Others talked of train schedules. Many were couched in bureaucratic formalities. Many talked of supplies, gas canisters, rolling stock, hardware. And a few were last letters, cards, pictures, thrown from trains and windows expressing love, hope, despair, confusion, and above all a desire to be remembered.

The shock of the proceedings was the quietness and decorum with which the witnesses told their stories. "My mother was shot. My sister was killed. My husband was clubbed." One wanted fury, rage, passion, but rarely did a witness raise his or her voice. Rarely did they cry. Often it was too overwhelming and numbing for the audience to grasp, but here and there a man wept or a woman sobbed. One heard words, a hundred killed here, a thousand killed there, but the meaning didn't sink in.

This coolness and distancing was also created by the voices of the translators. Even when a witness broke down, the voice of the translator would continue in that peculiar emotionless tone that is the standard trademark of translators everywhere.

One of my concerns as the months drifted by was how the world saw the trial. Was it following the proceedings? Was it interested?

Or, as I suspected, did the sports and gossip pages have much more meaning? In trying to figure this out I realized I had very mixed feelings about the caliber of correspondents covering the trial.

Many were excellent and grasped every nuance of the trial: the legal complexities, the breadth of the story, and the emotions behind the incidents. I knew this because many of us swam on Saturday afternoons at the President's Hotel, and discussed the trial while we dried off by the pool. Of them all, Ted Koppel, then a young correspondent for ABC, was the most impassioned and determined in his quest to get the story out in all its details. Another correspondent who made an impression on me by his authenticity and feeling was Hugh Nissenson. Hugh would eventually write not just a news report, but a very telling and emotional memoir of those long days for *Commentary* magazine.

Occasionally we were joined in swimming by the "parachutists." This was the name given to those journalists who flocked to the trial, stayed a day, and reported home as "experts." They usually did their stand-ups during the lunch break. While the court was empty they would stand in a dramatic pose before Eichmann's glass cage, mike in hand, mouthing platitudes, which seemed to me to be devoid of any real understanding of the case or the issue. But for the folks back home they had been there, they had appeared, and that was what was important.

In my own opinion, the worst correspondents were the TV network team. As I often had to prepare a TV summary of the day's events for them, I got to know their views reasonably well. The arguments of the trial, and the recitation of stories of destruction and death seemed to leave them cold. This was boring and passive. What excited them was when an uproar broke out in court, when a spectator started yelling, or when a witness hurled abuse at Eichmann. This was drama. This is what TV was made for. In my naivete I thought television could do more than that.

The best day for the TV correspondents was when the author Yechiel Dinur took the stand. Dinur had written extensively on Auschwitz under the pen name of Katzeknik, his most famous book being *The House of Dolls*. Dressed in a white suit and wearing dark glasses, Dinur was clearly disturbed and sweating profusely. He had met Eichmann in the camps and was asked by Hausner to describe what life was like in Auschwitz. His answer has haunted me ever since.

I was in Auschwitz for about two years. Time there was not like it is here on earth. Every fraction of a minute there passed on a different scale of time. The inhabitants of this planet had no names, no parents, nor children. There they did not dress in the way we dress here; they breathed according to different laws of nature; they did not live nor did they die according to the laws of this world.

I believe with perfect faith, that just as in astrology the stars influence our destiny, so does this planet of the ashes, Auschwitz, stand in opposition to our planet earth and influence it.

As I watched the TV monitor, it seemed to me that Dinur was in a trance. His body trembled. He seemed unaware of the court, his eyes fixed instead on some distant scene. Realizing this Hausner tried to put another question but was ignored as Dinur tried to continue. As Moshe Landau, the presiding judge, called sharply for Dinur's attention, Dinur rose from his seat, left the witness stand, and collapsed on the platform. For a few seconds there was shock, before Landau called for an adjournment. In the end Dinur never returned to the stand, and a general description of Auschwitz was given by someone else.

Over the years the incident has stayed in my mind for many reasons. One is the excitement the incident caused among the correspondents. Finally, at last, here was action, incident, something suitable for television. More important were the words of Dinur, which finally answered a question of mine. Throughout the trial I had been trying intellectually and emotionally to understand the nature of the Holocaust, the camps, the attitudes, and the feelings. Finally Dinur had shown me the impossibility of such understanding. Auschwitz was the other planet, the dark, evil planet that bore no resemblance to anything on earth. And unless you had been there, you would never understand.

Emerging from the darkened control room after work, and from the heaviness of the trial, into the blinding white light of Jerusalem was always a shock. Here was a world one had almost forgotten—a world of blue skies, summer birds, red spring flowers, babbling children, crazy traffic, kerosene smells, and yelling newspaper sellers. It was a world that affirmed life, not death.

Friday was always a short day for us because of Shabbat. As soon as the trial ended, about one, I would rush down to Ben Yehudah Street to meet friends and grab a coffee in Atara. At the time it was the café of choice of most of the press corps, and on a good day scores of European journalists would be hunched over their espressos and Vienna cream pastries while discussing everything from baseball to Wimbledon. Today Atara's glory is gone, its crowded buzzy bright atmosphere having given place to a gloomy, dark green branch of Burger King.

After Atara I would wander down Jaffa Street, continually wondering about the distance between my English fantasies and the reality of Israel. Instead of the camels of my dreams, filthy Eged buses belched out of a small side parking lot to totally block Jaffa Road. Instead of folk music records, all the music shops boasted recordings of Frank Sinatra and Frankie Laine. And final insult in the land of glorious citrus, the orange juice available in the hundreds of street kiosks tasted like the rusty deposits from a car's cooling tank.

Only here and there was there any resemblance to my exotic dreams. In the dusty interiors of the antique shops on King George, one could still find crusader helmets and Saracen swords. If you ventured into the open-air market of Machaneh Yehudah, the peacock-bright dresses of the women, and the swarthy beards of the men, plus the noise, plus the pungent smells of tropical fruit might easily convince you you were in Tashkent or Uzbekistan. And if you wandered over to Abu Tor at sunset and looked down on to the golden domes and walls of the forbidden and unreachable Old City in the distance, then for a moment you might believe you were in the Holy Land, and past and present would join into one.

Because of the war restrictions, the walks couldn't take you far. Jerusalem was a peculiarly hemmed-in, crazy, claustrophobic city, with exits only on its western side. Bethlehem was only five minutes to the south of the metropolis, but as it lay in Jordan, guards and barred wire halted you at the end of Bethlehem Road. From the kibbutz of Ramat Rahel, however, you could easily get a glimpse of Christ's birthplace on a clear day. To the north lay a broad strip of no man's land, leading on to refugee camps and the West Bank. And in the very middle of town, at the end of Mamilleh Street, where Iraqi immigrants used to congregate midday in their striped pajamas and smoke hookahs, massive, hastily erected concrete walls shielded Israelis from enemy snipers only a hundred yards away.

Jerusalem, of course, was so small and confined that after a while you knew everyone. If you walked down Ben Yehudah Street a friend from Habonim would suddenly call you to join him and his girlfriend. If you searched in Hillel Street for film for your camera (almost nonexistent in Israel at the time) an acquaintance from your Hebrew class would bang you on your back and ask for a loan. If by some fluke you were lonely and hadn't bumped into anyone, then you could always go for afternoon tea to the King David Hotel, where at least ten people you knew were sure to be hanging out.

The King David was not only the best, but in fact the *only* luxury hotel in Jerusalem. The President could boast of a small swimming pool, but for class it came nowhere near the King David. Fifteen years before, when it had acted as British headquarters, the King David had been bombed by Jewish terrorists. Since then that claim to fame had been replaced by the legend of Otto Preminger and the filming of *Exodus*. Only a year before, Preminger had filmed in and around the hotel and had used the magnificent palm-shadowed exterior balcony for a meeting between Paul Newman and Eva Marie Saint. So on Friday afternoons, when you gathered on the balcony and sipped English tea from white porcelain cups, at least four locals would tell you how Preminger had made them roll up their trousers, recruited them for his film because of their muscled thighs, and promised them a job in Hollywood once they obtained a visa for the States.

Most Friday evenings I either played the guitar at Bachus, went to Fink's, or drifted over to my girlfriend who lived at Notre Dame. Bachus has long since disappeared. In 1961 it was Jerusalem's closest approximation to a nightclub, student dive, and folk music spot. It was raucous, smoky, and crowded every night, and anyone who had any pretense to a voice, or facility with a guitar, mouth organ, or accordion would finish up there. I used to appear following another British singer, Judith Goldbloom, and since she did Hebrew songs so well, I would confine myself to Irish ballads and bawdy Scottish songs. The drink was free, the pay nonexistent, and the Israeli girls fantastically good-looking. As I toasted my old tutor from Oxford, I realized I'd never enjoyed myself more.

On evenings when I had been paid, I would slip into My Bar on Hillel Street or Fink's, just off King George. Fink's was the supreme journalist hangout but so concealed and so unobtrusive you could well stumble past it and never gain entry. Inside there was a narrow bar and a minuscule restaurant that could just about handle ten people if they all sat on top of each other. Posters, photos, autographs, and sayings cluttered the walls, and old man Fink himself ruled with an iron hand. The prices were exorbitant, the steaks fair, but you couldn't call yourself a member of the journalistic fraternity till you'd eaten or drunk there.

Many evenings, feeling rather depressed after work and in no mood for a drink, I would simply slip off to see my girlfriend. Yael, was French and lived in Notre Dame. This was an old multistoried Christian pilgrim hostel that stood opposite the walls of the Old City. It had been a base for an Israel machine gun nest in the '48 war and a target for snipers and light artillery, and its battered stone exterior still showed evidence of the massive shelling it had received.

It was always a weird feeling entering Notre Dame from Shivtei Zion Street. Though many Hebrew University students lived there, the feeling one had was of entering a medieval monastery. Hooded Carmelite monks would appear out of the shadows. Gregorian chants would waft up from some distant cellar or hidden chapel. Dark corridors would twist in and around themselves, and faceless strangers would hurry into whispering rooms. And everywhere there would be the oversweet smell of magnolia and hyacinth blossoms.

After a quick coffee, Yael and I would take a blanket and explore the bombed wing of Notre Dame. Here, where the shells had done their work, you could find a few rooms with their outer walls totally blown away. This was the spot Yael and I chose to practice since she had a wonderful voice and we had started singing duets together. A candle would be placed on the stone floor, the dust brushed away, and soon we would be trying out our latest effort.

If Notre Dame was strange, then this was totally surrealistic. Behind us were the three dust-caked walls of the shattered hostel. In front of us a gaping hole gave way to the blackness of the night. If we leant over the broken window frame and gazed right, we could see the bright neon lights of Jewish Jerusalem and hear the noises of the downtown traffic. In front of us, almost within hands' reach, lay eastern Jerusalem and the Old City, all under Jordanese control and totally inaccessible to Jews after the '48 war. And while the lights blazed in the west, in the Old City all was darkness and quiet. In practice, I suppose we were only a few yards' distance, but in reality we were an eternity and universe away.

Israel's Independence Day occurred a few weeks after I arrived back in Jerusalem, and I was invited to a few parties to celebrate the occasion. The one I chose was given by Judy and held at her small apartment in Katamon. About forty people were there, including a few people I knew from the language classes, but most were strangers. The unusual thing, however, was that unlike most parties I had been to up to that point, there was also a fair gathering of Israeli students.

Although I'd been in Israel a few months, I had, in fact, met very few Israelis. My colleagues at the TV were mostly Americans, the students in my Hebrew class had been foreigners, and I hadn't been long enough on kibbutz to make any real friends. So Israelis were still a strange species for me.

What characterized the ones at Judy's party was a certain aloofness and diffidence and an incredulity that anyone would want voluntarily to come to Israel.

"You must be out of your mind," one of them called "Rafi" told me. "For me, as soon as I get my degree, I'm off to the States."

His friends backed him up. Israel was a backward Levantine apology for a country and one had to be crazy to come here if there was an alternative. For a moment he sounded very much like my father. Some of the Israeli girls thought otherwise. Israel would be all right in maybe ten or fifteen years, but it wasn't much joy at the moment. A few inquired why I had come when I could have stayed in California, the real Garden of Eden. My old Habonim murmurs about being Jewish and a Zionist and the necessity for building a land amused them. Except for the few of them who had belonged to Israeli youth movements like the Tzofim, it all sounded very strange. They had been born in Israel. It was their country. They liked it, but they weren't about to spout crazy slogans in its honor.

When they heard that I worked at the trial not many of them showed much interest, and this startled me.

"Aren't you paying any attention? Doesn't this concern you?"

"Not really. Eichmann was dealing with ghetto Jews, European Jews. They went along meekly and did everything he demanded. No wonder they became *sabon*. We're different. We're Israelis. We would have put up a fight."

The purported indifference was, I learned later, merely a surface response, as thousands of Israeli youngsters were avidly following the trial on the daily radio. However this was the first time I had heard anyone use the expression *sabon*. It meant "soap" and was a slang term derived from the story of the Nazis making bodies into soap. I was shocked, but the Israelis laughed. "Look, tonight's independence night. Thirteen years ago there was a fight for this country, and we won. We didn't back down or give up. That's what the Jews should have done in Europe. Now drink up and enjoy yourself."

About two in the morning I walked Yael back home to Notre Dame. Along the Valley of the Cross, a hundred bonfires lit up the night, all in celebration of Independence Day. Here and there sparks shot upward, and songs drifted toward us from the valley. Tomorrow proud paratroopers in red berets would march up King George Street. Beautiful girls in white naval uniforms would march alongside them, carrying Uzis, and breaking a thousand hearts. In front, the sergeant major, probably a brother or cousin to my old Tiger of the Negev, would twirl his mustaches and flash his medals and white teeth at all the girls. And overhead a thousand Israeli blue and white flags would flutter in the breeze, as Eichmann was forgotten and a new power celebrated.

The trial resumed after Independence Day. As witness after witness took the stand, we were once more back in hell, a hell where every detail was relentlessly spelled out. Here was the story of the son who could not abandon his father and was likewise shot through the head. There was the story of the boy who was hung twice in front of the camp. Long before *Schindler's List*, we heard of Amon Goeth's shooting sprees, and long before *Sophie's Choice*, we heard of the mother who had to choose between her children. In the mornings we heard of the battered heads, the bayonetings, the scattered blood, and the clutching hands on the barbed wire. In the afternoons we heard of the ditches, the nakedness, the SS machine guns, the half-dead bodies. Unable to turn away we heard of the showers, the Sonderkommando, the ashes, the girls being shot and pushed straight into the crematoria fire, the eight kilos of gold teeth being yanked from bodies and starvation leading to cannibalism.

This was not even hell or another planet, it was another universe. And through all the recounting, Eichmann kept shuffling his documents, adjusting his glasses, wetting his lips, and keeping his notes. He was outside it. This was not his concern, not his responsibility. Later he would say he had merely been a soldier doing his duty.

Occasionally, the witnesses had met with him, seen him in a camp, or run across him in some dark confrontation. Of these meetings the most bizarre was between Eichmann and Willy Brandt, a Hungarian representative of both the Joint and the Jewish Agency. Looking closely at Eichmann, Brandt recalled the meeting. "With hands on hips he bellowed at me. Do you know who I am? I am in charge of the operation. It has been completed in Europe, Poland, Czechoslovakia, and Austria. And now it is the turn of Hungary."

Hausner asked him why Eichmann had summoned him.

"He wanted to propose a deal. He was prepared to sell me a million Jews—goods for blood. That was his way of speech at the time. He said 'Whom do you want rescued? Women able to bear children? Males able to produce? Old men? Children? What do you want, goods or blood?' He was not interested in money. He wanted goods, foreign goods, not Hungarian goods."

Nothing came of this strange proposal. Instead hundreds of thousands of Hungarian Jews were taken to Auschwitz. For Eichmann, this was just another story.

One of the most chilling stories was that told by Dr. Aaron Peretz of the Kovno ghetto. "The children in the ghetto would play and laugh, and in their games the entire tragedy was reflected. They would play gravedigging; they would dig a pit and put a child inside and call him 'Hitler.' And they would play at being gatekeepers of the ghetto. Some of the children played the parts of the Germans and would get angry and would beat the other children."

More than once Hausner echoed the question I had heard at the party. Confronting witnesses, he would ask, "Why did you not revolt?" Some witnesses tried to describe the all-embracing fear that seized them when facing hundreds of SS men with fixed bayonets, a fear impossible to picture or define for anyone today. Others explained how if one resisted, ten others were killed. And others such as Abba Kovner related how in spite of everything, helpless and broken, there *was* resistance and defiance in spite of the most overwhelming odds.

In Auschwitz the Sonderkommando, the cleaners of the pits and the ovens, blew up part of the crematorium. In Sobibor there was a mass escape. In over a hundred ghettos there were revolts. In the Warsaw ghetto a few brave men under Mordecai Anilewicz and Yitzhak Zuckerman led an uprising that held the Germans at bay for months. And throughout Europe those who escaped the killings fled to the woods and the forests to join other partisans and freedom fighters. This resistance, like so much of the trial, was another of the stories the world had scarcely heard about.

Neither had the world heard much about the stories that gave
hope, moments of decency in the midst of the nightmare. There were
the Danes who ferried the majority of their Jews across the waters
to neutral Sweden and the Swedes who gave the newcomers instant
citizenship. Luxembourg opened its gates to the Jews. In Belgium
the underground derailed the death trains and helped Jews to escape. In Italy, in spite of the silence of the pope, thousands of Ital-
ians sheltered their fellow citizens.

Everywhere there were isolated acts of humanity. Of these none
was greater than the work of Raoul Wallenberg, counselor of the
Swedish legation in Budapest. Single-handedly Wallenberg saved
hundreds of Hungarian Jews by putting them into rented houses in
Budapest, which flew the untouchable Swedish flag. Later Wallenberg was captured by the Russians and died in one of their prison
camps—a tragic end for one of the true saints of the war.

The stories come and go, and through it all Eichmann sits unmoved.
Day after day, I see him on the screen. Day after day, all of us wait
for a reaction, but there is nothing. The dark winter clothes of the
police that guard him have been changed for light summer uniforms,
but in Eichmann there is no change. Today, however, he is due to
speak, and the courtroom is packed. In the television control room,
our team has swollen to ten, as everyone comes in to hear Eichmann.
Milton has taken over the directing, and all eyes are on the screen.

At the beginning of the trial, Eichmann had been arraigned on
fifteen counts, ranging from crimes against the Jewish people to
crimes against humanity. To all of them he had answered not guilty.
Now he was going to explain why.

After a short presentation by his defense lawyer, Dr. Servatius,
Eichmann began to speak. He looked different. The arrogance was
gone. Like a diffident suitor he began telling the court the story of
his life. He was a nobody, someone who by chance had taken up a
special interest in the Jews. He had even started to learn Hebrew. "I
could have grabbed a rabbi, locked him up, and had him teach me.
But no. I paid good money." This in a sense was his most revealing
statement. The SS man was still speaking. Jews were still objects to
be grabbed, threatened, imprisoned, and killed. Unwittingly, Eichmann had revealed the gulf between the normal man, the decent
human being, and the followers of the Nazi ideology.

After a few days the line of defense became clear. "I was merely a cog in the machine. I was merely concerned with transport. I was only a bureaucrat. I had no special position." Again and again he wriggled and turned. "I had no ideology. I was just a soldier. I was just doing my duty." Unfortunately, his record stood against him. Time after time, Eichmann had personally hunted out *this* Jew and had made sure *that* one didn't get away. There was a passion and zealousness that could not be denied, even by the biggest lie. Occasionally, the salvation of certain Jews was sought by Germany's allies. Eichmann discouraged such pleas for mercy. To the contrary; if the Jews could be found alive, they were sent straight to the gas chambers. But the faceless bureaucrat was only doing his duty.

He felt compassion for the SS men who had to do the killing. He hoped they wouldn't become sadists. Occasionally, his squeamishness came out. The screams of those dying in gas trucks unnerved him. The blood of the dying put him off. As a consequence, "I could never have been a doctor." Never ever, not once, was there a word for the slain. But then he was absolved of everything. As he put it, "The question of conscience is a matter for the head of state, the sovereign."

On 9 August, the lawyers started the summing up. The arguments were concluded five days later. Judgment wouldn't be given for months, and everyone started to disburse. Spring had slipped into summer. School was out. The heat was becoming impossible. A Russian had been put into space. The U.S. elections were getting close, and the journalists had long gone. For myself, I wasn't sure where to go, but Stanford had given me a scholarship to finish my studies, and for want of anything better that was where I was heading.

The verdict came out in December, and I read the details in the Stanford library. Eichmann had been found guilty on all counts. Later he appealed, but the appeal was turned down. Eventually, he was hung, his body cremated, and his ashes dispersed at sea.

Over the years, I have wondered what it all meant. What examples and what moral could be drawn from those days. I'm still confused. Clearly the world would quietly have passed over the story of the Holocaust if not for the trial. So that was something. I also naively thought the world would draw lessons, but we have since seen the bloody histories of Cambodia, Rwanda, and other places. The cog in the wheel theory has become acceptable, to be used by Barbie, Papon, and others. In postwar Switzerland, the courts have twice found police captain Paul Gruninger guilty of the crime of faking entry visas to save thousands of fleeing Jews from the savagery of the Nazis. Twice they have confirmed his sentence of dismissal with disgrace from the Swiss police, proving that one country's definition of a saint is another's description of a scoundrel.

I think, however, the Israelis learned something. Over eighty-four thousand people attended the trial, and it educated a whole generation. I believe that part of the reason for the Six-Day War was that when Nasser talked of annihilating Israel, the Israelis believed him. They remembered Eichmann and vowed that such murder would never happen again.

Finally, at a distance of more than thirty years, two memories stay with me. The first is the shock of that first day, seeing Eichmann being tried in a Jewish court, with three Jewish judges sitting under the menorah, the emblem of the state of Israel. If ever there was poetic justice, that was it.

The second is returning to Stanford, telling people I had worked at the Eichmann trial, and hearing them say, "Eichmann . . . who?"

5 - Six Days in June

When the Six-Day War broke out, I was working as a film lawyer in London. I'd finally finished my Stanford degree and had married an Israeli whom I'd met at Stanford. On my return to England, I'd qualified as a solicitor and was settling down to a rather dull but pleasant middle-class life, in which the connections with my large family provided one of the principal pleasures of existence. I was still making films on the side but wasn't sure if that was the way I wanted to go. And though still interested in Israel, I had gone through a period of severe disillusionment.

In 1964 I had returned there with a BBC friend to make a film about kibbutzim in the North and had hated the country. It had seemed to me noisy, ugly, pushy, dirty, and totally unattractive. The romance was gone. The bloom had faded, and I began to sympathize with all my friends who had lived there for a year or two and then come back to England saying, "Enough. It's not for me." So whether I admitted it to myself or not, I was trying to put Israel out of my mind and grow up. And then came the shattering days of May and June.

The news broke sometime in mid-May. President Nasser of Egypt had demanded that the UN withdraw its troops from Sinai. He was also putting a blockade on the straits of Tiran, in effect cutting off the Israeli port of Eilat. All this was contrary to various international agreements of 1950 and 1956, and for a few days we waited for a strong world response. In vain. U Thant, the president of the UN, capitulated without a murmur, and our television screens were soon full of pictures of UN troops leaving the desert peninsula. More ominous was the fact that we could see various divisions of Egyptian tanks moving in their place.

Every day as I read my paper on my way to work or watched the TV in the evening, the headlines got bigger and more ominous. Ahmed Shukeiry, head of the recently formed PLO, was promising to throw the Jews into the sea. Mobs in Cairo were raising their guns as politicians exhorted them to a final victory. In Iraq effigies of Jews were being hung from lamp posts. A Syrian minister had claimed there was only one solution to the situation—the eradication of the State of Israel. On the evening news, a young, smartly uniformed King Hussein was seen affirming a new military pact with Egypt. At an air base in Sinai, a smiling Nasser had invited Israel's chief of staff to try to change the situation if he could . . . ending ironically with "Ahlan Wasahlan . . . see you soon!"

The reaction of the great powers was muted at best, disgusting at worst. In Moscow the Kremlin was totally justifying Nasser's moves. In France the Foreign Ministry stated in the strongest terms that the Three-Power declaration of 1950 regarding the safeguarding of peace in the region could no longer be regarded as binding. Vague statements were made about the Maritime Powers running a flotilla to break Nasser's blockade, but few people believed action would be taken. In fact, as the days wore on it seemed more and more as if we were witnessing a new Munich, with everyone backing off from a confrontation with a new Arab dictator.

Of course, for a few liberals Nasser was still God. He represented the new wave of Arab nationalism. He had rightly kicked the British and the French out of control of the Suez Canal. And if he used gas in the Yemen War and ruled without any signs of real democracy at home, so what. He was the new Middle East, the new savior who would finally get rid of the colonialists and bring justice and socialism to his people. This, in slightly different words, was the line taken by the Labor Party's own paper the *Tribune* and that bastion of righteousness, the *Observer*. Other newspapers, such as the *Mirror* and the *Express*, came down solidly on the side of Israel.

In the middle of the crisis, we pinned our hopes to Abba Eban. We had heard that this wunderkind of Israeli politics, this suave

Cambridge-educated genius at diplomacy, was going to make the round of world capitals and plead Israel's case. But it was to no end. In Paris, Eban was totally rebuffed by de Gaulle, who warned Israel not to take the first step. In London, Prime Minister Harold Wilson was sympathetic, but no concrete help could be offered. A similar answer was forthcoming from Washington.

At home the telephone lines were busy. My wife, Miki, had a brother and a cousin in the Israeli reserves. We knew that they were being called up along with thousands of others. What would happen to them and the dozens of other people we knew and cared for? Along with pictures of Nasser's troops, we were now beginning to see pictures of Israel's home front on the TV. In Tel Aviv, shelters were being cleared out. In Jerusalem, people were rushing to give blood. On the kibbutzim, trenches were being dug, sand bags filled, and barriers erected. Gradually, it became clear to everyone that very soon, nineteen years after the declaration of the State, Israel might well be fighting for its very life.

One day, one moment among many, made that suddenly crystal clear. King Feisal of Saudi Arabia was staying at the Claridges Hotel and had deigned to give a television interview in his luxury suite. Clad in his white desert robes and talking through an interpreter, King Feisal told television viewers throughout the world that the only solution to the crisis was the extermination of the State of Israel. True to British tradition, no one turned an eye. No one followed up on his suggestion of genocide. No flunkeyed hand was raised in protest, and one can only assume the bowing and scraping went on as usual. But for the Jews of the world, the message was clear. Once more a holocaust was being threatened, and maybe Eichmann would get the last laugh after all.

King Feisal's speech had a profound effect on all of us, "us" being every single Jew I knew. Suddenly there was no "us and them," Israelis and other Jews. Instead, for a few days and a few weeks, there was a bonding the like of which I had never seen before. And I'm not just speaking of Zionists, but also people who never before in their lives had had any connection with Israel, had no friends there, had never thought of visiting there. Suddenly people were realizing that if something catastrophic happened to Israel, their own lives as Jews would never ever be the same again.

The problem was what to do. On the one hand, we could declare our sympathy and unity, but we also had to go beyond that and do something positive. In terms of sympathy and support, we could see that all over the place. In spite of examples of the *Observer* and the *Tribune*, the majority of English newspapers came out on the side of Israel. At the Albert Hall a mass rally was held in which a well-known Conservative politician, Lord Hailsham, stated that Israel had a right to live. In the *Sunday Times*, seventy of England's top intellectuals, many of them non-Jews, writers, filmmakers, politicians, and actors made an impassioned appeal on Israel's behalf. It came out on 5 June and read as follows:

> Israel is fighting for survival. The avowed intention of the Arab nations is Israel's extermination—nothing less than the annihilation of two and a half million men, women and children. General Dayan, Israel's Minister of Defense, has stated that he does not want British and American boys to die for Israel. This does not preclude our giving other forms of assistance. Our Prime Minister and all parties in parliament have pledged Israel's right to live.
>
> In the name of humanity, let us take positive and immediate action. To fulfill this pledge we, the undersigned, affirm Israel's right to exist as a free, independent, democratic state.

Other letters and other petitions hit the headlines. All affirmed Israel's right to live in peace, but few suggested how this could be supported by action. One could just as well have been affirming that the earth was flat for all the effect the declarations had on the situation. The real truth was that the affirmations were necessary for our own pride, for our own sense of ourselves as decent people, even though we realized that by themselves the words meant little. Nevertheless they had to be said. To be passive, to do nothing, was to go crazy.

At work I tried to raise money for Israel. This was fairly easy because it was an office with very strong Jewish and Zionist sympathies. I knew this because I could recall one violent incident when the senior partner, Louis Courts, had thrown a basket of stamps halfway across the room in disgust. The reason for his fury was that the stamps, commemorating the Battle of Britain, showed the emblem of the swastikas on some of the planes featured on the stamps. No swastikas, no Nazi emblems, and no memorials of Hitler were ever going to disgrace his office, not even in the most innocuous way.

So with Mr. Courts and most of the staff, I had no problem. They wrote out checks, they dug into their handbags, they promised to ask friends, and they promised more tomorrow. One of the partners, a lovely South African, Monty Cohen, also confided that he wished he could go and fight. Only one man refused. That was Tony, the thirty-five-year-old litigation manager. This surprised me. Tony and I had often had drinks together after work. I considered him a close friend, and we shared a common view of the world and the need for democracy and liberalism. But in this case, he was adamant. Israel was colonialist. The Jews had no right in Palestine. Nasser was the true socialist, and if he wanted to retake Israel, he had every right to pursue that course.

Apart from Tony, everybody wanted to give. This was the smallest thing they could do. A friend of mine, Hanoch Bartov, then Israeli cultural attache in London, wrote afterward of the extraordinary scenes that were taking place daily at the Embassy offices. According to Hanoch, one morning an odd, shabby, stooped man rang the bell and demanded to give an old cardboard box to the ambassador. As he looked suspicious, the man was asked to wait in the hall till someone else came down. By the time the duty administrator had arrived, the man had vanished, but the box was left. When the box was opened after taking due precautions, the Embassy staff found eight thousand pounds inside. Who was the man? Were they his life savings? According to Hanoch, the Embassy never learned. The man had emerged from anonymity, made his contribution to Israel, then vanished.

Another story told by Hanoch was of a group of taxi drivers who insisted on giving the proceeds of their mutual-aid fund to Israel. But that was just the beginning. The drivers then went on to organize a free-of-charge, twenty-four-hour-a-day service in front of the Embassy. Some of my friends went around collecting blankets. My friend Leah Hertz wanted to organize a rescue service for Israeli children and bring them to London till she realized nobody was running. In fact the reality was the opposite. Everywhere Israelis were pleading to be sent home, pleading to find a place on a plane so that they could rejoin their units. According to Hanoch specialist physicians phoned up the Embassy to offer their services, and Cambridge professors called, ready to volunteer for anything. One day one of my old friends from Oxford contacted me out of the blue. He had become a pilot while doing his national service in the RAF. How could he get to Israel and fly with their air force?

At my local synagogue in Kinloss Gardens, a meeting was held one evening on behalf of the Israel Emergency Appeal. For once the place was packed. People I had never expected to see in a synagogue in my lifetime were there. No one was absent. They came, and they came ready to give. For once they needed no exhortation. There were speeches, but who remembers the speeches? I certainly don't except for one. The rabbi had spoken, and the man from the Embassy had spoken, and the collection had been taken. And it had been good. Then someone on the *bimah* (the pulpit) got up and started speaking in a low voice. "OK, you've given. And you've given well. And now we are going to go round again. All we are asking from you is money. In Israel they will be asking for blood and lives. And you are going to give till it really hurts."

So in the hushed synagogue, the collectors went round again. This time not only the notes and the check books dropped onto the plate, but wedding rings and watches, earrings and bracelets. Some gave thousands. Some gave a few shillings. All doubled and tripled what they had given before. Many people were choked. Many had tears in their eyes. All realized unless they gave now there might not be a second chance.

The real chance to identify with Israel came on a Sunday, when there was to be a mass rally at Hyde Park Corner, followed by a huge march to the Israeli embassy in Kensington Palace Gardens. It was a blustery, gray day, but it seemed that everyone I knew or had ever known was there. There were school friends of mine who had gone on to become prosperous businessmen. There they were, a little bit older, a little bit grayer, but they'd come. Two of the partners from my office were there, plus a few of the secretaries. My dentist was there, plus the boy who delivered our newspapers. And of course there was the Habonim contingent, blue shirts to the fore, doing the *hora* (circle dance) and belting out all the songs I had sung so enthusiastically ten years before.

When I talk to my American friends, the march they remember is the march on Washington to hear Martin Luther King Jr. talk of his dream. As an English Jew the march of my life was that one on Sunday, only a few days before the war. Like armies we took warmth and comfort from those by our side. We felt a band. For the first time in our lives, as Jews, we were publicly saying, "This cannot be. This cannot pass." It was a new sensation for us English Jews whose total education had been devoted to keeping a low profile and effacing ourselves in the background. It was a new sensation, and it felt good, at least on the surface.

Underneath, we realized we were participating in what might seem like a cliché scene from a bad war movie. The people were banding together to defy the Jerries. All that was missing was a cheerful cockney song, and we could be back in the blitz. What we were really doing was carrying out some necessary public acting and putting on a necessary but deceiving bold face. Underneath, if the truth be told, we were angry, depressed, and deathly afraid.

So, as if to deny reality, we talked. We marched. We linked arms. We sang. We gossiped. In the park the leaves were coming out, the babies were being wheeled, and dozens of people were staring at us, inquiring, and occasionally joining us. Along the way we stopped just once, to hear Harold Levy. Levy was an unusual man, a really down-to-earth rabbi who spoke eloquently and powerfully and had just the right sense of occasion. His text has vanished, but not his last words. Grasping the microphone, he surveyed the crowd, now swollen to some tens of thousands.

"I want you all to raise your right arm like me. Now I want you to repeat after me—*im eshkachech Yerushalyim, tishkach yemini*— If I forget thee O Jerusalem, let my right hand forget its cunning." And there, with the sun now bursting through over London, we vowed to remember Jerusalem and to think of the boys crouched down by the tanks, the women putting strips over the windows, and the children going fearfully to school. We remembered but also wondered what tomorrow would bring.

We knew war was inevitable, but it nevertheless came as a shock. I was upstairs shaving, when my wife, Miki, rushed into the bathroom and shouted, "It's started."

As usual the BBC was cool, calm, and indifferent.

"This morning, at 5:00 A.M., Israeli forces started moving into Sinai. So far no word has been obtained from our correspondent how far they have penetrated or the force of the Egyptian reaction."

Throughout the day other reports rushed in, none of them confirmed, all couched in the most alarming tone. The Egyptian air force was dominating the skies. Jordanian forces were massing on the West

Bank. Jerusalem had been attacked. Northern Israel was in flames. In desperation I tried phoning my friends at the Israeli embassy, but not unexpectedly all the phones were engaged.

That evening, in the lowest of moods, I went with Miki to visit two Israeli friends, Gaby and Rachel Warburg. They had contacts in the embassy. Maybe we could get a true picture from them as to what was happening. But they were as much in the dark as we were. The only thing they said as we sat there drinking whiskey and waiting for the news was that they'd heard that it wasn't all bad. But what did that mean? Only fifty tanks lost? Only five hundred dead?

The evening news confirmed my worst expectations. Egypt claimed to have totally repulsed the Israeli advance and inflicted heavy casualties on the Israeli forces. It also claimed to have bombed Tel Aviv and other cities with few losses. West Jerusalem had been shelled by King Hussein, and his forces had taken the Jerusalem UN post. Two Iraqi divisions had joined the Jordanians, and King Feisal had pledged to drive the infidels from the soil of the Holy Land.

Watching the news our faces got longer and longer, till one correspondent was quoted with a rather different story. His name was Mike Elkins. What he had to say was short and startling. According to Elkins, the war was over. In one fell swoop the Israel air force had totally obliterated the combined air forces of Egypt, Syria, and Jordan. This news flash contradicted everything we were hearing from Egypt. It was also greeted by total skepticism by the BBC military pundits. *Impossible* and *total rubbish* were just few of the epithets used. Hunched round the TV set with Gaby and Rachel, we didn't know what to think. There had been little official news from the Israeli side. If true the news was fantastic. It just seemed so totally unbelievable.

Elkins, of course, was right. And the following days brought more incredible Israeli successes. Three Israeli divisions were driving deep into the Sinai peninsula with relatively few casualties. Having repulsed a Jordanian attack, Israel's central command was sweeping across the West bank. By Wednesday the Old City had been captured, and for the first time in nineteen years, Jews were seen praying at the Western Wall. And on Friday we heard about the general who had telephoned his wife saying, "We are doing a lot of swimming." He had been trying to avoid military censorship, but the point was clear. The Egyptians had been driven from Sinai, and the Israelis had reached the Suez Canal.

A week earlier, before the war had started, I had gone to the senior partner of my law firm, Louis Courts, with a request. If war should break out, I wanted his permission to take leave of absence from the office to go to Israel. I just couldn't stick around in London knowing that Israel was under threat. It was an impulsive, emotional, irrational, unthought-out request that was answered with an instant "Yes."

I'd also talked over the possibility of such a trip with Miki. She was sympathetic but wary. Our son, Gil, was not even a year old, and in such a situation zooming off to Israel seemed just a little bit impulsive and immature. Nevertheless, after a few evenings of long talks, Miki agreed that I should go.

So it was because of Miki's and Mr. Court's graciousness and understanding that I found myself on the second day of the war standing on the doorstep of Rex House, in lower Regent Street. Rex House was the London center for the Jewish Agency and the obvious place to go to if you wanted to volunteer or help Israel. I was standing on the doorstep because it was impossible to get in. In front of me hundreds of young men and women—students, executives, hippies, and housewives, in everything from bright miniskirts to dark business suits—were queuing up to help Israel. I found out later that over eight thousand people came forward in three days.

Eventually, we got inside and passed from official to official. What skills did we have? Did we know Israel or speak Hebrew? Could we drive a tractor? Had we done military service? How did we think we could be of service? Were we willing to work on the kibbutzim or in factories? Most people's response was "We can do some of these things, and we'll do anything to help."

As we waited the news was shouted along crowded, excited corridors. "They've taken Jenin." But who the hell knew where Jenin was? "They've gone through Gaza and Rafiah. They're attacking the Old City and have gone in through the Lion's Gate. They've reached Sharm El Sheikh and spiked the guns. And they're through the Mitla Pass."

There was only one problem about the volunteering. There was no way to get to Israel. All the airlines except El Al had canceled their flights to the war zone, and the El Al flights were only taking Israeli personnel returning to their battle units. This was all a bit deflating as we wanted to be there now, not next week, not in a month. One of the officials whom I discussed this with had an idea. "Do you want to drive to Israel because there was a guy here a few minutes ago who wanted to leave in a few days, and he was looking for another driver. He's downstairs in room 303, and his name is Louis Lentin."

It seemed a long way round, but after consideration I thought it might be a quicker way to go than waiting three weeks for a plane.

After filling in numerous forms, I rushed downstairs, found a bald, stocky, and cheerful Louis, and persuaded him to join me for a coffee in Piccadilly Circus.

"How long will the drive take?" I asked.

"Four, five days. It's easy to the Yugoslav coast, then down to Dubrovnik, across to Salonkia, down through Greece, and we can take a boat from Piraeus."

"And what's your car?"

"An open Austin spitfire sports car."

Now it was Louis's turn.

"What do you do?"

"Well, I'm a lawyer, and I make films. And you?"

"I'm a television director in Dublin."

After that there was nothing more to be said. This was obviously a match made in heaven. So following a bit more discussion and a handshake, we decided to leave the following Sunday. That would give us time to sort out our business affairs, say good-bye to our families, and figure out a decent route that would eventually deposit us alongside a Greek ferry bound for Haifa.

Five days into the war, it was clear that the Israeli victory went beyond anyone's expectations, and we decided to have a party. About forty people came, but the mood was one of thankfulness rather than celebration. There were still too many unknowns to let off proper steam. Getting through to Israel by phone was impossible. We didn't know what had happened to our friends and our relatives. My wife didn't know what was happening with her brother Mordecai who was in an intelligence unit. And I hadn't heard from my brother Ray, who was somewhere in Jerusalem. We had also heard that earlier in the day Israel had made an assault on the Golan Heights opposite Syria. It was murderous terrain, and casualties were expected to be high. So all we could do was pray for those who were close, drink a toast to Israel, and thank God that it had survived the week.

Israeli Diary Extracts

Early in May 1967, I started doing something I had only done once before, while in the air force. I started keeping a diary. Below are some extracts from June and July.

Louis and I arrive in Haifa at 8:00 A.M., but at 7:00 the ship's sides are already crowded with those wishing to get a first glimpse of land. Gradually there is a line on the horizon, and Haifa breaks into view through the morning mist. Slowly I look for the old landmarks, the Bahia temple, the Dan Hotel. It is all unchanged. Too calm. I am waiting for something to occur to match the turbulence within, to give visible evidence of the shattering six days. Then two signs appear: a small tug with guns fore and aft and then an aged black submarine moving slowly across the harbor mouth.

It's three years since my last visit, but the chaos in the customs shed remains exactly the same. The porters still stand around in their old blue baseball caps and baggy shorts. The officials shrug and continue to search nonchalantly for contraband. One of them closes my case, using my quarter-inch recording tapes as string to bind my packages. I remonstrate. He smiles, doesn't say sorry, and moves on to another smuggler. The tin customs sheds smell of kerosene, and the wall posters still invite you to seek the hospitality of a myriad of women's organizations.

It's Friday, and I buy the weekend edition of the *Jerusalem Post*. Efraim Kishon is busy writing a letter of advice to Nasser. An advert states that the troops did their best and obviously deserve the best . . . which is Cohen's cooking oil. I'm glad to see that Ascot cigarettes taste better and *are* better. While waiting around I ask at the tourist desk for a map of Jerusalem and to my surprise am given two. One is the familiar pink map of the Jerusalem I knew, while the other is a newcomer to me, showing the Old City and captured Jordanian territory.

While making farewells of friends from the boat, I listen to the news on someone's transistor radio. It ends with the longest weather forecast I have ever heard. In the past all we got was the weather for Tel Aviv, Haifa, Jerusalem, and the Galil. Now we have the weather for the Golan Heights, Jericho, Sharm el Sheikh, and the Suez Canal.

Louis gets his car out of customs fairly quickly, and we drive to
Jerusalem in the early afternoon, taking the main road we saw so
often in all the television newsreels. Three weeks ago it was crowded
with lorries, soldiers, tanks, and jeeps. Now it is almost deserted,
just a golden Zionist propaganda drive with a red Hollywood sunset reflecting off the sea and eucalyptus trees lining the road. There
are no signs of war except in the dusty outskirts of Ramleh where
two massive tank carriers, beached amphibians, lie tired and dormant under a tree. At Hartuv junction we give a lift to a twenty-
year-old soldier who looks suspiciously at our foreign number plates.
He fought in Latrun and Jenin where fourteen of his group were
killed. In eight months he leaves the army to study, to resume "normal life."

We arrive in Jerusalem before Shabbat and head straight for my
brother's apartment in Neveh Granot, a new housing estate just
below the Israeli museum. The whole area was heavily bombarded
in the war, and Ray proudly shows me the shell marks in the walls
of his building and the posters giving instructions on air raid precautions and shelter drill. His windows are still heavily taped to
prevent splinters of glass exploding into the room.

While he makes tea my brother tells me of his arrest. Ray is an
inveterate note taker. On the fourth day of the war, as the tanks
rumbled through after capturing the West Bank, Ray stood on the
corner of Jaffa road taking notes. It seemed to him this was a scene
that had to be captured for posterity. Suddenly there is a hand on
his shoulder, and Ray is confronted by an alarmed army sergeant.

"*Atah meragel*. You are a spy." Why else would one be making
tiny notes on the corner of an English-language newspaper. Eventually Ray is taken to the police headquarters in the Russian compound, where other "spies" are waiting patiently for the third degree. These include a little Moroccan garage mechanic from Ein
Karem who explains to the police that no, he wasn't signaling with
his torch to the Jordanians, he was merely lighting his way to have
a pee in the garden since the house toilet was blocked. Eventually
the investigating officer gets fed up. What is all this *shtuyot* (nonsense), bringing these guys here. Why can't people just leave him
alone to listen to Moshe on the radio. At the mention of Dayan he
blows a kiss to the crowd and dismisses them all with a wave of
his hand.

So we talk for hour after hour. On the balcony of the apartment are flowers arranged in empty artillery shell cases. The evening darkens, and a plane, with flashing wing tips, comes in to land at Kallandia Airport. This is the first time I have ever heard aircraft over Jerusalem. Before 5 June they were completely banned from the area. Now there's a daily flight from Jerusalem to Tel Aviv, and to Sharm el Sheikh. Slowly one begins to sense the changes in the country.

Three years before, I made a film about the kibbutzim on the Syrian border and impelled by this memory, decide to head north at the first opportunity. The memories are still strong of the last visit to Tel Katzir, one of the most exposed of the settlements. I can recall the barbed wire marking the perimeter of the kibbutz, the armor plating over the heads of the tractor drivers, and the way one of the kibbutzniks told me how sick and tired he was of film crews who boasted of their efforts being seen by 10 million people . . . as if that made the slightest difference to the lives of those living on the edge of the abyss.

The barbed wire is still there, but the tractors move about in the disputed areas without any protection. In the distance the yellow-brown hills rise up from the deep blue of Lake Kinneret toward the Syrian heights. I borrow binoculars. With their aid one can clearly see the paths made by the Israeli tanks as they blasted their way up the slopes to take positions that had seemed impregnable for two decades.

In Tel Katzir itself one is overwhelmed by the damage. One group of houses is now just concrete lumps of rubble scattered among the flowers. Two other houses stand with the roofs torn off. A third is ventilated by a dozen Syrian shells. Yet much repairing and rebuilding has already been done. The worst has been cleared. All we are seeing are the last fragments of the destruction.

All around there are clumps of vivid red bougainvillea, which stretch to the entrance of the shelters. We go down and enter two dark rooms with curved concrete walls. The ventilation shaft brings only a narrow beam of light, but it is sufficient for us to see the children's drawings of flowers and animals that decorate the rooms.

We enter another shelter, this time adorned by transfers of rabbits. A telephone lies silenced next to a metal cupboard containing tins of food. On one side of the shelter there are six iron-framed cots for the babies. On the other side there are two rows of striped green mattresses for the elder children. It's all silent and musty now, like the deserted shelters we used to play in in London after the war. Yet less than a month ago sixty people crowded into these shelters, not knowing what would await them when they emerged.

Is it the end to such experiences? I thought so in England and am shattered to see two new shelters in the course of hasty construction. One is almost finished. The other has only just had its foundations dug and its floor put in. By the side are set out those immense rocks that, once covered with chicken wire, will cover the concrete roof. Maybe there will be more shelters. No one here intends taking chances.

Leaving Tel Katzir I pass the new dining hall. Inside the tables are covered with fresh crockery donated to the kibbutz after the war. Someone tells me how during the June fighting hot food was brought up to Tel Katzir from neighboring kibbutz Kinneret. They also sent roses, a typical kibbutz gesture. Outside the dining hall is a concrete path in which the children have traced designs of flowers, planes, and monkeys. There are also two symbols of this mad existence juxtaposed in almost cliché positions . . . a high concrete defense wall which in turn shelters the children's own toy rowing boat. Inevitably the boat is called "shalom" (peace).

I had, of course, telephoned Bert from Jerusalem to see how he was doing and to tell him I was going north. He was still at kibbutz Kfar Hanassi and had agreed to join me on a trip around the Golan Heights. The war had been easy on the kibbutz. No one had been killed, and the damage to the kibbutz, only a few miles from the Syrian border, had been relatively slight. Bert himself had been in the engineers and had spent much of the time looking for mines along the border. This seemed to me an extremely hazardous occupation, particularly for someone such as Bert, whom I remembered as being a little bit clumsy. The thought of him trying to defuse antipersonnel mines was enough to make you go weak.

"Nothing to it," said Bert, always optimistic, always smiling. "All in a day's work."

"Does your father know?" I asked, remembering his anxious father back in London.

"Oh, I simply told him I was on guard duty and left it at that."

Going into Syria from the Banias springs, we see more relics of the fighting. Upturned tanks lie beside the road like castrated turtles.

They have become mere exhibits, and one just cannot grasp the fact that men lived, fought, and died in them only a short time ago.

From the Banias the road winds up to the Golan Heights. Below us, in the valley, the Israeli settlements, out of focus in the heat mist, look peaceful and inviting. As we ascend the wind freshens, and a crusader castle comes into view. I know it because once I saw it in a photograph taken by T. E. Lawrence, before he became Lawrence of Arabia. Around the castle fantastic blue thistles grow out of stagnant black earth, scarcely cultivated for the past twenty years. The Arab towns through which we pass are miserable and deserted. Everywhere there is a strange mixture of beauty and desolation. In the hazy distance Israel looks like a dark green garden of Eden.

Kuneitra, our destination, has become a ghost town. The Syrian garrison has fled leaving behind Russian arms manuals, Chinese clothing, hard-baked wedges of tea that resemble cuneiform clay tablets, and a vicious collection of children's anti-Semitic school books. Battered olive shutters lean at awkward angles over most of the shops. A few have their fronts smashed in. I see only two premises open, selling vegetables and bales of cloth. There is a silence over all the town, only broken when a jeep drives past or a military policeman hails us from a street corner.

From Kuneitra the route leads back to Israel via the Bridge of the Daughters of Jacob. At this point the River Jordan is only a few yards wide and superbly unimpressive. For a moment I think of the lines "Roll, Jordan, roll" and am glad the author never saw this thin, sluggish stream. Before we cross the bridge we look into the old customs house, or what remains of it after being blasted in various air attacks. Scattered army greatcoats lie outside the shattered windows. There are burns all over the yellow walls. Unexploded mortar bombs are scattered by the side of the road. A few feet behind them fluttering white ribbons indicate the presence of mines.

In the garden stands the remains of an armored car, bent and twisted . . . a burnt-out case. Almost everything is black and scorched. At the back of the car empty Bren gun magazines lie buried in ash. Mercifully the cindered corpses have been removed. This is the first time I've seen the effects of napalm. At last the war jumps from the cozy newspaper pages and becomes a frightening reality.

Leaving Bert at the Rosh Pina junction and vowing to come up to the kibbutz in a week or so, I head south for Tel Aviv. Once there I spend a fruitless evening arguing with Israeli friends who spent the war in New York. Nothing makes sense to them. They are deeply disturbed because nobody talks of anything except the fighting. The war songs stink, including the anthem of the war "Nasser mechakeh le Rabin" ("Nasser Waits for Rabin"), which I quite like. Most of what they see is bad. They feel depressed about the future.

Afterward I try to puzzle out their attitude and realize that if you are an Israeli and missed the war, you are faced with two possibilities. You can try and swallow every story you hear, listen to your friends' gossip till two in the morning, read all the newspapers, devour all the photos, and try all the time to recreate vicariously the lost experience. Or you can rationalize that you missed a war, so what! It really doesn't mean that much. This way one submerges the thought of having lost out on what could have been the most significant moment of one's life.

For once I am content to listen. Now the human stories emerge that were so absent from the statistical reports. In particular I begin to see old friends, such as Bert and others, in a new light. Menachem, for instance, a teacher of philosophy, had stayed with me in England. I used to find him in bed at noon, smoking and wondering whether the world existed and whether there was any real point in getting up. His mood, of course, was encouraged after seeing *Oblomov*. Menachem, continually lost in the clouds. Hard to think of him armed with an Uzi, chasing through the narrow streets of the Old City and routing out snipers.

Koffee and Steve were nice English boys from northwest London. Both fought in Jenin and Syria, and both had narrow escapes. Koffee took his jeep out of the column to change a wheel. A few minutes later most of the column remaining on the road was strafed and blown to smithereens from the air. Steve swapped places with his driver only to see the latter decapitated in his place seconds afterward.

Amnon takes me swimming. We talk of our last meeting in the States where Amnon was studying for his Ph.D. in psychology. Inevitably we come to the war, and it emerges Amnon was a tank commander in 1956 and again a few weeks ago. Till he told me that, I thought he had driven nothing more dangerous than a Volkswagen nor touched any weapon more serious than a typewriter. Now he coldly and analytically describes the feelings of battle, but it is a different world for me.

There is also, luckily, the lighter side of things. Giora is a frogman, a member of the elite Force 13. Others tell you their stories;

Giora never, except for one. Sometime toward the end of the war, Giora came home from active service, dressed in his uniform, to find a group of soldiers lining up at the door of his apartment. When he tried to enter a chorus of protest greeted his *chutspah* (his cheek) at shoving to the front. Evidently all of them were waiting to use the shower, a simple but welcome treat made available to them by Giora's wife, Michal.

I call myself a volunteer but shamefacedly am doing nothing except watching, observing, and collecting notes for future articles. Who said "They also serve who only stand and write"? But the volunteers are everywhere. One sees them working on the kibbutzim, working with the army, working in hospitals. The bus stations are full of them, waving guitars, looking sunburnt, and hurrying back to their *moshavim* (co-operative farming village). So is the Jewish Agency in King George street where they collect at lunch time, looking for jobs, changing friends, making assignations.

By now they have their own radio program, which comes out every Tuesday under the guidance of a young English-Canadian volunteer who spends two days a week at the radio and the rest of the time slogging in the fields of kibbutz Haogen. There is also a special volunteer magazine run by Shlomo Ketko, which has already reached its third issue. I'm curious about the number of volunteers, and Shlomo, who does much of the organizing, shows me the official figures. By the beginning of July it looks as if over twenty-three thousand people have volunteered, of whom seven thousand have already arrived with the help of the Jewish Agency. No one knows the numbers who have arrived under their own steam, but they must account for at least another three thousand.

Of the official Jewish Agency volunteers in Israel, 1,500 are from England, 900 from South Africa, and 700 from France. American volunteers who had passport and red tape problems number about 550. Hundreds of volunteers poured in from South America. Costa Rica, with only 60 Jewish families, has sent 24 volunteers.

A lot of Israelis are now beginning to open their homes to the volunteers, particularly over Shabbat. The women's organizations, such as Hadassah and WIZO, are also active in making the volunteers feel welcome and in organizing home contacts for them. Sometimes, however, the offers to take home a volunteer are just a little too pointed. Thus I'm told of the woman who demanded that the volunteer be between thirty and thirty-five, handsome, a bachelor, and a professional . . . suitable for a *shiduch* (arranged marriage) for her unmarried daughter.

Everyone admits there are problems related to the volunteer situation, yet no one seems to have any real picture of the meaning of the movement or its long-term implications. Overall there seems to be a total failure of the imagination in dealing with the volunteer phenomenon. Meanwhile the newspapers publish daily attacks on the government for its lack of constructive ideas regarding "the overseas helpers." Typical of these articles is the one that appeared in the *Jerusalem Post* under the title "The Gray Men versus the Volunteers." Who are the gray men? They are the Jewish Agency officials who told the volunteers they were needed, who failed to come up with an adequate plan to deal with the rush of arrivals and now lack the courage to tell the volunteers that their "sacrifices" are irrelevant. That's true, but it misses out the other side of the equation. Most of us know quite well that we came because we had to and that we came for our own benefit as much as Israel's.

Over a few evenings and much coffee I try to get a few volunteers to tell me why they came and what they feel. Most find it difficult to verbalize these things, but one answer that sticks in my mind is that given me by a London photographer. "The reasons I may have had for coming," he said, "aren't really the reasons I have now. This experience has made me realize every Jew is part of me, and I am part of every Jew."

Another volunteer, this time a fairly sophisticated New York lawyer, put his feelings to me another way. "Staying . . . I really don't know. The thing is you've got to pay Israel back for all it does for you. It takes longer than a month. Ask me in two years whether I'm staying, and I'll tell you."

Jerusalem is emotionally overwhelming. The best view of the city is to be had from Mount Scopus early in the morning. The light from the east is still soft, and as you take in the panorama from the Temple Mount to the Binyanei Haooma on the horizon, it seems unbelievable that the city was ever divided. Yet for the sight-seers a mere two hundred yards' walk brings them to a new world. Thus, while the Old City swallows up the *kova-tembelled* Israelis, scores of Arabs in two-toned shoes stroll down Jaffa Street, peering into windows and shouting as they recognize familiar places.

Across from Notre Dame, where Yael used to live, they have torn down the massive protective walls. Now, beyond the concrete rubble that lies all around, you can see Suleiman's magnificent Old City walls. It's early, but crowds are already flocking to the Wailing Wall, to the Kotel (Western Wall of Herod's temple; most sacred of Jewish sites). I know I shall have to go there sometime, but I want it to be when the crowds have gone so that I can have my own private moment by those stones.

Louis has vanished in the last few days. He's as excited as a kid and can't absorb enough. His open sports car has become very popular, and whenever I see him he usually has a dark-haired beauty occupying what I think of as my personal seat. Most of Louis's energy has gone into investigating when they are going to start television here. He is one of Ireland's most experienced studio directors and could contribute a great deal here if things ever got moving. On the journey he told me one story that made me a little bit wary, however. Evidently back home he did a full-fledged recreation of the 1916 Irish troubles, including the burning down of the Dublin post office. The show was a great success, but in a quest for authenticity, he also set the studio on fire. I think he should keep that story in the background when he pursues a TV job here.

Actually both of us have had an interview with Elihu Katz, who's investigating what could be done about TV here in the future. I saw talk of Elihu and his work in the *Maariv* newspaper and phoned Elihu for a chat. He's an American professor of communications and may well be the head of television, if it ever gets established. The interview went well, though he didn't quite understand how I do law alongside film. Well neither do I, so that makes two of us.

I try to cross Zion Square to meet Giora and am nearly run over by a jeep that parks hurriedly to let a group of soldiers descend. All are bareheaded and casual and swing their Uzis and Belgian rifles as if they were drum majorettes' batons. I follow them in to café Atara where they sling their rifles over the chairs and dump their slim olive canisters of bullets onto the table next to the iced coffee.

Both the air force and the army weekly magazines have brought out memorial editions, and the latter is so successful it is also being sold in an English edition. Winston Churchill's paperback (the grandson, not the old man) is a best-seller and on all the racks, but equally in demand is Elie Landau's book on the Jerusalem battles. At the back of the café Giora is looking at the *Sunday Times'* effort entitled

The Holy War but puts it down in disgust after reading a few pages
and seeing the old hackneyed photos of forsaken boots and Egyptian dead. To Giora it seems an oversimplified travesty of the facts.
Too many of his friends have died in the fighting for him to accept
reports and photos that imply it was a walkover. The occasion pro-
vides an excuse for Giora to comment on English newspapers generally. "They talk such bloody nonsense most of them. Moralizing
and advising the whole time, and just totally removed from reality.
Well, the time for listening to such rot is over, thank God."

Later the two of us go to see a hastily compiled feature documentary titled *Six Days to Eternity*. Half the film deals with the pre-June
situation and shows for the first time to many in the audience the
Arab propaganda clips of commandos in training. Most of the clips
are greeted in silence except for the shocked murmuring that goes
through the audience when they see the Zionist effigies hanging in
the streets of Baghdad. These are the same photos that shocked me
in England a month earlier. There is also an undertone of hissing
when Indian troops appear quitting Sinai and taking down the UN
signs. However when Dayan and Rabin emerge on the screen, there
is wild cheering throughout the theater, and all of us rise from our
seats as the air force sweeps by in a Magen David formation.

The following afternoon Giora takes me to the Hebrew University amphitheater near the Knesset to see the units of the Jerusalem Reserve Brigade receive their medals. It's also the occasion
for a memorial service to the members of the brigade who fell in
the fighting.

We arrive at five to a packed stadium. The loudspeakers are playing all the war songs, and the crowd hums along with "Jerusalem
of Gold" and "We Have Returned to Sharm el Sheikh." The police
band sits waiting in khaki uniforms. Tubas glint in the sun. Children dash for the best positions. Flags flutter against a blue sky, and
the green of the stadium grass contrasts strongly with the brown rock
of the surrounds. We are all waiting, and I am quite prepared to see
two football teams come rushing onto the turf ready to give battle.

As the shadows lengthen I notice at one end of the stadium two
long rows of upended rifles, with each group of three rifles forming
a tripod to support a helmet. Giora tells me the helmets are full of
paraffin and will be used as memorial candles. We are all expect-
ant, and soon enough the loudspeaker starts announcing each unit
as it enters the stadium. The paratroopers march in, and there is

tremendous cheering. And there is more cheering for the tankists and the infantry. I cheer along with the crowd, hiding my surprise. I've been expecting uniforms, but only the section commanders are in khaki. The rest of the reservists are dressed in white shirts and dark trousers and file into position with a minimum of ceremony.

Yitzhak Rabin, the chief of staff and Uzi Narkiss, head of Central Command, arrive to a tremendous ovation. Quickly they pass by the Guard of Honor to take their places with other officers on the tiny saluting base. There is total quiet now, and as the flag is lowered someone recites El Moleh Rachamim, the prayer for the dead. Suddenly three cannon shots ring out, and for a few seconds the valley reverberates with booming echoes. At the same time a figure goes down the rows of helmets, and soon two lines of flames brighten the dusk. A passage is read out from one of the poems of Nathan Alterman, and as the brigade commanders receive their unit's medals a choir starts to sing.

All eyes are now on the saluting base as Rabin prepares to speak. "Jerusalem today is one unit. Wherever the Israeli army stands, there are our borders. You have finished what was begun in 1948. I know it is impossible to replace the fathers and the sons who have fallen, but they have not fallen in vain. *Asitem avodah niflah. Kol hakavod.* You have done a fantastic job. Congratulations."

A woman weeps behind me as the band starts to play the "Hatikva" (the Israeli national anthem). Many of us are too overcome to sing, but though our heads are bent, our ears pick up the sounds of the singing of the thousands of reserves. There is a moment of silence; then the soldiers break rank and transform the arena into a sea of white. Two minutes later and the center of the stadium is half empty as the soldiers join their relatives on the terraced banks. For a fraction of a second the scene stands still, and I begin to understand what is meant by a citizen's army. The time accelerates, and I leave a deserted stadium in which nothing moves except some dying flames in an upturned helmet.

Aftermath

It was strange getting back to England. Everything was too normal. Too subdued. Too calm. The days were gray, the summer long and boring. In the office there was a slew of property cases and rent agreements I had to deal with. Nothing could have been further from my mind. I waited for people to ask me about Israel, but all they could talk of were the cricket results.

One night I went with my sister Sylvia and her husband, Ronnie, to see *Fiddler on the Roof*. It featured Topol, the Israeli actor, as Tevye the milkman. After the show he got a terrific hand. Was it for his performance, or was it an indirect way of saluting an Israel that hadn't run from the cossacks and the czar's persecutions? I wasn't sure.

For a few months in June, we had all been family. But it didn't last. By September it was all back to normal. Those who had been making plans to emigrate quietly put them aside. The writers and intellectuals who had gushed about Israel found other causes to take up their time. In June 1967 it had been Israel. The following year it was the May student riots and Czechoslovakia. And of course there was Vietnam. That's the way it went. But there was something else in the air. A growing anti-Israel feeling that was to swell to massive proportions in the seventies.

Till the war, Israel had been the darling of the media. It had taken in thousands. It had made deserts bloom. The kibbutz was an experiment in utopia. Above all Israel was an island of democracy in a sea of despotism. After the war this all changed, not immediately but quite significantly over the years.

Part of the explanation was that Israel had won "too easily." People felt cheated. They had been preparing to offer refuge and sanctuary to a beaten people, and suddenly that people had achieved one of the most outstanding victories in the history of warfare. Subtly the language of the newspapers changed. The tanks were not has-beens, bolted together from ancient disposals of the British and U.S. armies but units in panzer divisions. The divisions didn't attack but "blitzed" their way through enemy fortifications. I had noted a civilian army, but for Michael Adams writing in the *Guardian*, this was an army of Spartans, ruthless warriors, razor efficient.

Maybe there was a more subtle reason for the change. For twenty years or so, the memory of the Holocaust and the death of six million had hung over Europe like a black cloud. The Eichmann trial had once more forced the story into the newspaper headlines. Implicitly the message had been, Why didn't you, the civilized nations of the West, do more to help? Because of a troubled conscience, much of the world had treated Israel with kid gloves. Now one could forget the Holocaust. Now one could throw off blame. Israel was just like everyone else, a Spartan-efficient, cold-blooded group of warriors who not only had put the Arabs to flight in '48 but had created a new Arab exodus in '67.

When I had left, the TV screens had been full of pictures of Israelis preparing hospitals and young girls volunteering blood. When I came back, these pictures had been replaced by Arab refugees fleeing across the Allenby Bridge. Every day there seemed to be another story about the plight and squalor of the refugee camps, every night, another story of dispersion, heart break, and broken families. Our family screen had once delighted me with pictures of orange trees, and blossom, and smiling Israeli girls. Now this was all gone. In their wake cold, hungry, barefoot Arab children, their eyes surrounded by flies, stared out at us blankly from makeshift huts. The center of gravity had shifted with a vengeance and speed that was unbelievable.

In Israel in June I had heard talk of a documentary film being done by Wolf Mankowitz, John Schlesinger, and Harry Saltzman. The film, very pro-Zionist, was going to show the new Israel, the new spirit. When I inquired about it in October and November, the reactions were negative. Hours of film had been shot and edited, but nobody liked the result. *Israeli*, as the film was called, was too triumphant, too out of keeping with the changed mood. It had a few showings and then passed into oblivion, while Schlesinger went on to finish *Far from the Madding Crowd*.

Almost twenty-five years later, I made my own film about those days and called it *Year of Decision*. The title was slightly incorrect and really should have been in the plural since it dealt with the years 1967 to 1973. But no one seemed to care, so we stuck with the original. The film was made very fast and was part of a series I was doing for PBS on the life of Abba Eban and the development of Israel. It wasn't a great film, but it wasn't bad, and it gave me a chance to rethink and relive the events of those distant years.

In 1967 Eban had almost represented God to us, and his speeches at the UN were generally taken to have been amongst the most eloquent ever given in that august assembly. What particularly interested me for film was knowing what had happened on Eban's rushed journeys to Paris, London, and Washington. According to Eban the worst discussion was with General de Gaulle.

Evidently, the French president was absolutely intractable. In no way should Israel take the initiative. It should wait and show patience and forbearance. If Israel moved alone, it could forget the backing of France. In the event, Israel acted and French-Israeli relations took a nosedive, with de Gaulle later making snide references to a proud, stubborn people. French arms deliveries were halted and mutual pacts put on ice. To teach Israel a lesson, France later refused to deliver to Israel missile boats that she had ordered and paid for and that were under construction in Cherbourg. Israel's answer was a daring raid in which the boats were secretly taken over by skeleton crews and sailed hastily to Haifa.

In Eban's eyes, Harold Wilson had been outstandingly sympathetic but powerless. The long shadow of the 1956 disastrous Suez venture still traumatized England, and there was no way she could take unilateral action. President Johnson also told Eban that America couldn't act but went on to transmit a very clear position. If Israel acted alone, the United States would understand, and if it captured territories, it might not have to give them back with the alacrity of '56.

While we were discussing the film, Eban told me he thought his journey had achieved two major diplomatic goals. It had gained Israel vital time to deploy its reserves, and it had ensured that if territory were captured, the United States would look on with sympathy to its temporary retention. Later I interviewed Ezer Weizman, who had been chief of military operations in '67. Weizman expressed a slightly different view. According to Weizman, the troops were ready for action after the first week of the crisis, and the delay was actually not good for Israel's military situation.

Besides looking at the diplomatic maneuvers of '67, I also wanted to throw some light on the actions of King Hussein. This seemed to me vital, given the troubled history of the West Bank since that era. Here Eban was very specific. Using General Odd Bull of the UN as a go-between, Eban had sent a very detailed message to King Hussein assuring him that Israel had no aggressive intentions toward his kingdom and requesting him to stay out of the fighting. The request was ignored, and Hussein started shelling Jerusalem. The rest is history.

In retrospect it's clear that King Hussein's actions were largely prompted by the misinformation being fed to him by the Egyptians. According to the propaganda of the Egyptians on the first two days, victory was only hours away. Every Arab I interviewed for the program repeated how he had been absolutely taken in by the triumphal tone of Egyptian radio broadcasts. The saddest story was that wryly related to me by one of the Arab doctors of the Augusta Victoria hospital in East Jerusalem. "We saw tanks in the courtyard of the hospital. So we rushed out to welcome them. We were sure they were Iraqi tanks. It took us maybe five minutes to grasp the fact that they were Israeli tanks. But how could this be? This was impossible. Only then did we learn the truth about the war."

In Beth Sahur I interviewed an Arab student who'd been a young boy at the time. How did he see the Israeli victory? "I was in my village, and everybody came out saying the Israelis are here. Quick, put up a flag before they kill us. Quick, everyone must go down and greet them. But I couldn't. I felt so ashamed. Later the Israelis gave out chocolates. But I couldn't take any. I felt so humiliated. What were they doing on my land, in my village?"

In making documentaries you deal with a hundred opinions, and the trap is to conclude that this one rather than that most clearly defines public sentiment. In the film I wanted to insert something about Israeli attitudes to the West Bank takeover but soon realized it was more interesting (at least to me) to look for those who were asking questions, rather than those who simply glorified in the victory. In the end I used an ex-officer to talk about the subject. "At first we wanted to travel everywhere. There was space. We could move. It was wonderful. We rushed through the West Bank on trips, in jeeps, in cars, looking, picnicking, wondering, exulting. We were euphoric. And we just didn't see that there was another population there, a silent, beaten population, and that unless we were very careful the victory would turn to ashes."

In conversation Eban made it clear that he felt that both Israelis and Arabs had thrown away fantastic chances for peace in those years. He sadly acknowledged the statement of the Arab powers in November 1967—"No peace. No recognition. No negotiations"—and summarized that attitude in his most famous quote: "The Arabs have never lost an opportunity to miss an opportunity." Nevertheless, he believed Israel could have done more. "We went crazy over the territories. But they were just cards in the hands for peace. We should have used them. But we didn't. And later we paid for our mistakes."

While making the film, I remembered Giora's comment about European journalists depicting the war as a walkover. With this in mind, I started interviewing soldiers about the battle for Jerusalem. Mike Ronnen, of the *Jerusalem Post* told me about the bloody hand-to-hand battle for the Jordan police headquarters. Over twenty Israelis died in the long night encounter. Today there is a small military museum near the scene of the battle. Every day a few visitors come, but for the most part buses pass the grassed-over spot on the way to the Hebrew University, with no one paying attention.

In preparation for discussing the course of the battles, I talked to a paratrooper who had been destined for the battles in Sinai.

> We were ready to head for the Mitla Pass, and then they told us it wasn't necessary. We were to head up to Jerusalem instead. But we had the wrong maps and no preparation. Anyway we came, in five buses. . . . At first we joined those attacking the police headquarters. A few hours later we went into the Old City with Motta Gur and fought our way to the Wall. Then someone grabbed a flag and put it on the top of the Kotel. I didn't even realize what he was doing. We just slumped at the Wall, totally exhausted. Two days later we went back to base. You ask about losses? When we came up to Jerusalem the buses were full. When we went back the buses were half empty. Those guys weren't coming back.

Yesterday was Shavuot, one of the main festivals in the Jewish calendar. During Shavuot Jerusalem becomes a madhouse. It is packed with visitors, and thousands of people make their way to the Western Wall, to the Kotel, to celebrate next to the sacred stones of the temple. This morning, reading about all the weekend's activities in the Haaretz newspaper, my eye caught two pieces of news. The first talked of a group of several hundred teenage Haredim (ultraorthodox Jews) totally refusing to let any mixed congregations of American and Liberal Jews get close to the Wall. Instead they yelled insults and hurled various objects at them.

The second article talked of a letter from two rabbis, Yosef Elyashiv and Aharon Steinman, published on the eve of Shavuot. The rabbis, both members of the Degel Hatorah party, were joining their leader Rabbi Eliezer Menachem Shach, in declaring that *yeshiva* students were absolutely prohibited from joining the army. Shach had also proclaimed that "if it is necessary one should sacrifice one's life for this principle of avoiding army service."

Suddenly I remembered the paratrooper's story of the half-empty buses leaving Jerusalem. I remembered the soldiers who had not written letters or made declarations but had sacrificed their lives to get to the wall. And it was one of those bad moments when you wonder what has been the point of all the struggles.

My film did not end triumphantly but extremely soberly. I took Israel and Eban's story up to 1973 and spent the last ten minutes of the film looking at the darkening story at the Bar Lev line and along the Suez Canal. Soldiers telephone headquarters to give warnings of massive build-ups along the canal, but the warnings are ignored. The chief of staff, General David Elazar asks for a general mobilization of troops, but Security Minister Moshe Dayan and Prime Minister Golda Meir turn him down. It is the eve of Yom Kippur. Crowds are seen at the Western Wall. The prayers float up, yet tomorrow will not bring absolution and forgiveness but one of the blackest days in the whole history of the State of Israel.

Alan's sons, Gil and Tal, and Gil's wife, Tzofnat. All three served in the Israeli army but were fortunate to miss the war in Lebanon. (Author's collection)

Preparing to do some helicopter filming for the series *A Nation Is Born*, 1992. Cameraman Yoram Milo is on the far right. (Author's collection)

Filming from a helicopter over Jerusalem for *A Nation Is Born*, 1992. (Author's collection)

Making up Abba Eban for *Out of the Ashes*, 1983. (Author's collection)

Filming at the main gate of Auschwitz-Birkenau for *Out of the Ashes*.
(Author's collection)

Filming at Auschwitz for *Out of the Ashes*. (Author's collection)

Abba Eban before a Holocaust memorial, from *Out of the Ashes*. (Author's collection)

Bert Wolfin, Alan's lifelong Habonim friend, 1956. Bert's parents wept when he decided to go to Israel. (Author's collection)

Bert (*left*) and his wife, Tamar, with Alan, 1989. After more than thirty years, Bert was still happily living on the kibbutz. (Author's collection)

Abba Eban and his wife, Suzy (*far left*), with Jordan's King Hussein and Alan's film crew, after the interview with Hussein at his palace in Amman for *On the Brink of Peace*, 1997. (Author's collection)

Abu Alaa (*seated, far left*) and Uri Savir (*far right*) signing the secret Oslo agreements between the PLO and Israel in 1993. (Courtesy Norwegian Government)

Abba Eban interviewing Yassir Arafat for *On the Brink of Peace*. (Author's collection)

6 - Selling Zion

Sometime in the spring of 1980, I found myself stuck in the editing room of the Jewish Agency. I'd been working on a film about the annual meeting of the World Zionist Organization (WZO) and had suddenly hit a major stumbling block. I had missed out the *macher* (big shot, someone of importance), and this was unforgivable. And not only was he the *macher*, he was the *ganser macher*, the biggest of the big shots, and in my naivete, foolishness, and unwisdom I had omitted him from the film. In the opinion of the producer, Al Potashnik, there would be hell to pay unless I could do something.

Perhaps I should explain that the film was a fund-raiser, outlining the activities of the Keren Hayesod and the WZO. For the framework of the film, we had chosen to show parts of the annual meeting of these august bodies, and to liven things we were telling four inspirational stories of Zionist triumphs. These vignettes ranged from the tale of a Russian family making good, to a farmer triumphing over adversity in the wilds of the Gush Katif area. On the positive side, the stories were interesting. In contrast the speeches at the Zionist congress were absolutely boring. But that's part of the burden of a filmmaker's life, how to spin straw into gold.

Anyway, it was all coming along nicely till Al spotted we were missing the *macher*. He was Australia's biggest donor. He was present at the assembly, and if he didn't see himself in the final film, his annual Zionist contribution was likely to drop by the thousands, if not the millions. For the good of Israel and for the honor of Australia, not to speak of my keeping my job, it was vital that we find this honorable personage and shove him in the film, come hell or high water.

Unfortunately, no one had told me till that moment that we needed that good man. I hadn't got a clue what he looked like, and I knew that if he did exist on celluloid it would be by pure chance and the foresight of God that we had grabbed him in the camera sights. Al was more positive. "He's so prominent, so conspicuous, you must have filmed him. Just look for the cigar." So I looked. I looked through twelve cans of film, or nearly five thousand feet and two hours of film. It was exhausting, but ultimately I found him. Actually, you couldn't really see him clearly because of the clouds of smoke. However his profile, which had been well described, was easily identifiable—hawklike, handsome, imposing, and domineering. I'd found the man, gave him a fast but convincing Hitchcocklike guest appearance in the film, and we were saved. Just. And along the way I'd learned another rule of Zionist filmmaking—always shoot the *ganser macher*.

I'd started making Zionist films soon after Miki and I decided to leave England and return to Israel in 1971. We'd been contemplating the move for some time, and an offer by my old boss, Elihu Katz, to take up a position at the Hebrew University clinched the decision for me. We also had a second son, Tal, by that time, and both Miki and I wanted the boys brought up in an Israeli environment.

Unlike some earlier academic work I'd done in California, teaching at the Hebrew University only took up about half of my time. This was an ideal arrangement enabling me to devote a few days a week to academia and the rest of the time to filmmaking. And since as an independent you took work wherever you could find it, I found myself working for the Jewish Agency as much as for the television.

I never really kept tally, but between 1971 and 1988 I must have made about fifteen films for all kinds of Zionist organizations, ranging from Hadassah to the UJA (United Jewish Appeal) and from Israel Bonds to the English UIA and Australian JIA. I also made three fund-raising films for the Hebrew University, two for the Technion, and one for Haifa University. All were different. All were made under very different conditions. But they all had one thing in common. In one way or another they were all selling Zion. So for fifteen years, in addition to making my standard documentaries, I became a salesman. Not quite Willy Loman, but a salesman all the same.

Luckily for my sanity and the quality of the films, the subjects varied enormously. For two years I was doing nothing but hospitals. A year later came a quickie about Youth *Aliya* (literally "ascent"; emigration to Israel), followed by a film on Israeli education. Then sometime in the late seventies, Menachem Begin introduced the idea of Project Renewal, and I started looking into urban renewal. Urban renewal in Ashkelon, in Tel Aviv, in Jerusalem, in Kiryat Shmoneh. You name it. Wherever they were renewing, I was there filming. Then, just when I felt I never wanted to see another building site, refurbished classroom, or shining new tennis court for at least another ten years, the hospital and Youth Aliya films started coming round again. When I was through with those, the Ethiopians started coming, and when that stage ran out, the Russians started coming.

The films may have differed, but they all had more or less similar rules, such as put in the big shot. The cardinal rule, of course, was be positive and constructive. You could discuss problems in your film. In fact it was vital that you discuss problems, so long as you showed that the organization in question was solving them or could and would solve them with the help of you good people at home who were watching the film and contributing so much to our worthy cause.

Another vital rule was to sanitize the film. You could show poor children, but poor children with smiles. You could show poverty, but in a sense it had to be nice, genteel poverty. Once I was showing a film on Youth Aliya to some clients from American Hadassah (the main U.S. Zionist organization for women). In one of the scenes, a young girl is hanging out clothes to dry on the line. Suddenly one of the examining committee raised a finger in protest. "You've got dirty washing in the picture. We can't have dirty washing in a Hadassah film."

Well, she was boss, so the dirty washing (actually very clean) came out.

Language was also very important. There had to be strong identification. "*We* are doing this. We are doing this *together*, you and I. Together we are making this country bloom." After a while you began to write inspirational phrases in your sleep. "Do you want two countries? A country of the privileged and a country of the poor? Do you want children of darkness or children of light?"

When the film was finished there was the problem of finding a suitable name. It had to be inspirational. Appealing. Upbeat. My favorites were *Miracle Hour*, *Choose Life*, *My Name Is Freedom*, *For the Good of All*, and *The Road Ahead*. Time and hope featured a great deal in the titles, which could be quite confusing. After a few films with titles such as *The Dawning Day*, *Yesterday Is Forgotten*, *Tomorrow Is Now*, and *Share Tomorrow*, you didn't know if you were coming or going. The word *bond*, as in closeness, togetherness, and money pledges also appeared frequently on the screen. Thus we had *A Certain Bond*, *Bonds of Hope*, and *A People's Bond*. *Vision* was also a good word to use, thus my film for the WZO was eventually given the title *Vision and Assembly*, though privately I was willing to settle for *Looking for Mr. Bigshot*.

When I observe features films I realize, however, that I shouldn't really complain that certain words are overused. After all we have *Love Story*, *The Young Lovers*, *Love and Death*, and *Love in the Afternoon*. We also have *Death and Glory*, *Death Wish*, *Dead on Arrival*, *Death in Venice*, and *Death by Hanging*. So why should I complain if Zionist film titles are so unimaginative? After all, they are merely following the norm.

Yet I do remember one film that had daring and chose to be different. It was a UJA film that circled the globe under the magnificent title of *I Gave at the Office*.

If I make fun of these films, it is hopefully only the gentle fun one has among friends and family, because at heart these films were made by organizations with passion, conviction, and a burning desire to help Israel. And for that I take my hat off to them. After fifteen years of working with these organizations, I am still amazed at the devotion and energy their members bring to whatever cause they are involved in. Let me give just one example.

My first Zionist propaganda film was made for Hadassah in 1969. It was *With These Children* and dealt with Youth Aliya, the voluntary association that brought children to Israel and attended to their needs afterward. It was not a subject I knew much about, so the picture became my education. To research it I traveled the length and breadth of Israel with my partner, Larry, visiting workshops, youth villages, training centers, and special projects. And two things happened. I got to know of the tremendous and vital work of Youth Aliya, and I got to appreciate Hadassah.

For me the women of Hadassah had always been seen as a group of elderly, blue-rinsed, wealthy matrons who had nothing better to do with their time than spend idle Wednesdays gossiping about their grandchildren and Israel. This was a patronizing, snobbish, totally mistaken view of which I am now thoroughly ashamed. It was simply so far from the truth. Most of the Hadassah women I met were intensely proud, and rightly so, of what they had done and were doing to help Israel. They had built hospitals and founded clinics and put Israeli health care on a firm basis. They had set up youth centers, founded children's villages, and established schools. And they had been among the first to help the Ethiopians and Russians who emigrated to Israel in the eighties and the nineties.

And what applies to Hadassah applies equally to WIZO, to the UJA, and to the dozens of other foreign organizations who helped build Israel for almost a century. Today the fashion is to deride that help and to scorn the organizations. This is all part of the modern process of separating Israel from the rest of the Jewish world. This seems to me both an ungenerous and a shortsighted attitude. But it is the prevailing one. My only hope is that this approach will pass, and common sense as to the real worth of friends, allies, and supporters will once more prevail.

Whereas Hadassah introduced me to the world of hospitals and youth villages, my films for Project Renewal took me into a world of urban slums, deprivation, and poverty. The idea of Project Renewal was to form links between foreign Jewish communities and various rundown Israeli towns or areas. Thus town A in the United States would adopt and care for town B in Israel. The hope was that such partnerships would bring in external money and help that would revitalize the communities. The partnership idea would also provide foreign groups with very specific projects that they could claim as their own, rather than have their money diffused over a dozen anonymous recipients.

I worked on about five Project Renewal films, mostly for the UJA, and all had the same requirement: Show us where our money is going and what changes it's making to the community. This general concept was often turned into reality by following one or two families in any given area and showing how they were benefitting by new schools, evening classes, a paint job on the outside of their apartment, and new sports facilities for the kids.

Project Renewal seemed to me one of the better ideas of the Jewish Agency and, at least on the surface, improved much of Israeli life. Where it worked best was in those cases where the foreign communities really got involved in the local scene and had their own representatives on the spot. Ashkelon was a good case in question. It was partnered by the English JIA, who sent a young Englishwoman, long resident in Israel, to see things and manage things on the spot. My impression was that this was very much appreciated by the local community, and in consequence it became one of the better examples of how Project Renewal could be put into action.

Sometimes I sensed the Israeli communities had, however, very mixed reactions to the whole idea. When I was filming in a very rough neighborhood in south Tel Aviv, the attitude of the people I spoke to was "They only give the money because they can boast about it back home." There was also a wariness by the Sephardic communities of being patronized by Ashkenazim. When I was filming the Hatikva quarter of Tel Aviv, my cameraman actually got into a fight over this question.

While I was setting up the lights in a community center dining hall, Rafi, my photographer, went to our van to collect the camera. When he failed to appear after ten minutes, I went out to check what was happening. I found Rafi spread-eagled across the van, being threatened by six teenagers.

"What are you doing here? We don't need you here. Hitler should have finished off you Ashkenazim in the ovens."

Alarmed, I went to get one of the community leaders. After he spoke with the teenagers, Rafi was released, scared but OK. Pinnie, the community organizer, tried explaining.

"They resent the outsiders coming in. They know it will all eventually help things here, but it hurts their pride. They want to be the ones to take care of things. And if they can't, then they prefer it all to stay as it is."

One of the objectives of Project Renewal was to get teenagers off the streets and stop them drifting into juvenile delinquency. Juvenile delinquency? Theft? Robbery? This was a side of Israel I hadn't encountered up to now. It certainly wasn't a subject we talked about in our normal propaganda films. But with Project Renewal a harder, tougher, and much healthier approach was being taken regarding information and education. Problems were admitted. Issues were discussed. And hopefully solutions were found.

Making films in areas where there was a high incidence of juvenile crime wasn't easy. At first I was extremely naive when I was warned I had better look out. Nah! You're kidding me. After we'd had our tires slashed a few times, I grew wiser. But my biggest lesson came in Ashkelon.

We were filming kids protesting police brutality and had a group of about thirty teenagers grouped around us in the street. One after the other, I asked them to tell me of their complaints.

"They blame things on us, plant drugs on us, accuse us of things we never did, rough us up."

To all this I nodded wisely in my polite, liberated, Western way. I wanted to show the kids I believed them and that I was on their side. When we'd finished I went to our Volvo station wagon, parked in the next street, to reload the film magazines. At least that was what I had hoped to do. But no chance. I found the Volvo open and all our gear missing. While we had been occupied and distracted filming one set of youngsters, another group had broken into the car and pinched everything.

Nothing like that occurred while doing the university films. The campuses were often islands of calm and beauty in the midst of urban sprawl. They also had guards, and they had order. So we never lost anything while filming around the colleges.

The public relations strategy of all the universities was unbendingly similar. Tell the public that Israel doesn't have minerals and geological wealth, but what we do have is brains. And in our college (put the name of the institute here), we develop those brains to serve the country. You then show the work of the graduates throughout Israel, in desert research, in economics, in planning new cities, and in government. It was a strategy that made sense, had an enormous appeal, and was also telling the truth. Thus when I did a film for the Hebrew University, I profiled graduates Aharon Barak and Michael Bruno. The first did a tremendous job as supreme court justice in insisting on democracy and the basic rule of law, often in the face of terrible attacks on the court. Economist Michael Bruno for his part became director of the Bank of Israel and straightened out the government finances in a period of great chaos.

The only problem doing PR college films was one of focus. The universities often wanted everything included, every department, every piece of research, and every famous professor. The secret was to persuade them that less was more and to cut out the laundry lists. Usually they understood this, but not always. Thus in one Hebrew University film I did, the authorities insisted that we show thirty-six donor plaques, one after the other. This building donated by Joe X. That laboratory constructed by the Y family. So we did a montage, covering the thirty-six donors in twenty-five seconds. If you blinked, you missed your name. I thought it was madness, but the university officials insisted. They knew what had to be shown if they wanted the donations to continue. So once more I was looking for the *ganser macher*, which is basically where I came in.

After years of doing Israeli PR films, I thought it might be fun to look at them in more depth. As a result, I proposed to Israel TV an hour film, which would examine the background, the objectives, and maybe the success of these films. The TV accepted the idea, and it was eventually screened under the title of *We Could Have Danced All Night*, my not-so-subtle reference to the obligatory folk dances that permeated these films.

I saw my first Zionist film at the age of eleven at our neighborhood synagogue in London. For my parents, gathered there for the annual Hanukah celebration, it was probably old hat. For me it was a wonder and a delight. Where was this place called "Israel" where the sun always shone; where girls in tight shorts sang as they plucked oranges; where cheerful, muscled boys put up building after building. Where was this land where everyone smiled and life was one long circle dance? Was this Dorothy's land beyond the rainbow? Already I could feel the attraction.

The messages of the film were potent. To me they said, "Come!" To my parents they said, "Give!" And both messages were part of one of the greatest cinematic propaganda enterprises of history: the attempt to sell the rebirth of a nation and a land. And this is what I wanted to investigate in my film.

Using film in the support of ideologies is, of course, not new. The Soviet cinema under Eisenstein and Pudovkin made quite a thing out of popularizing the Revolution and Communist achievement. In Germany Goebbels, Leni Riefenstahl, and Fritz Hippler made a hefty contribution to the dissemination of the Nazi message. And even in Britain John Grierson realized the importance of documentary might be in the *message* rather than in the *art*.

Like the Soviet directors of the twenties, the earliest Zionist filmmakers faced a country undergoing revolutionary changes. When *The Life of a Jew in Eretz Yisrael* was made in 1911, the Turks were still reaping the benefits of three hundred years of control of the region. When Yaakov Ben Dov made *Eretz Yisrael Awakening* in 1923, Britain had just established its Mandate over Palestine, and the Balfour Declaration had given hope to millions that a national home for Jews could be created in this neglected Middle Eastern backwater.

From the early twenties, film was recognized by the main Jewish organizations as a powerful tool for disseminating the Zionist message. The translation of this dream into visual reality initially rested on the back of three gifted cameraman-directors, Yaakov Ben Dov, Baruch Agadati, and Natan Axelrod. Hauling their cameras around deserts, swamps, budding towns, *kvutsot* (tiny agricultural groups of only a few dozen people), and nascent kibbutzim, the filmmakers recorded a turbulent land in flux and evolution. Tents are scattered everywhere. Drainage pipes dominate the landscape. Bearded men ride about on horseback, rifles slung across their backs. Flamboyant artists celebrate the opening of Bezalel art school. A smiling Einstein participates in an early Hebrew University celebration, and children push through swarms of geese to see an ancient train travel from Jerusalem to Tel Aviv.

For weeks I looked at the films of Ben Dov and the others in the basement of the Spielberg Film Archives at the Hebrew University. With the assistance of Maralyn Kulik, the head of the archives, and Hillel Tryster, a wonderful Australian scholar, writer, and actor, film after film was placed before me for sampling and analysis.

Many of the early films adopted a similar structure, that of the stranger who comes, sees, becomes a Zionist convert, and rushes to tell his friends back home all about it. In *Eretz Yisrael Awakening*, a wealthy American businessman stops for a day in Jaffa. Convinced by a guide that this is not enough, he spends a month touring kibbutzim and towns. He quickly falls in love with the country. When he leaves, he swears to return at the earliest opportunity.

Three things stand out about the film. First, there is its idealization of the country. Second, there is the question of its financing by the Keren Kayemet (the Jewish National Fund, the body responsible for the acquisition and resettlement of the land). Henceforth, 90 percent of the funding for documentaries about Palestine would come from the JNF or similar committed Zionist bodies. Third, there is the question of the target audience. It was the Jews of New York, Chicago, London, and Paris who had to be moved and affected . . . not the Jews of Haifa and Tel Aviv. And if they were moved enough, the hope was that they would dig into their pockets and fund the Zionist enterprise.

Looking at film after film from the twenties and the thirties, it was clear to me that the romantic basis of these early Zionist films was not very far from the mythic landscapes of the classic Western. There too—in the films of John Ford, Howard Hawks, and Raoul Walsh—lies the unknown West (read Negev or Galil) waiting to be conquered. There too the pioneer from the East waits to turn the desert into a Garden of Eden. There too the newcomer waits to show the Indian (read Arab) the meaning and benefits of civilization.

Yet there is a difference. While the Westerns were divided about the role of the Indian—was he the savage to be saved or the noble primitive to be emulated?—the early Zionist films show no such ambiguity. In the minority of cases, the Arab is either the enemy to be conquered or the peasant who has to be educated. But, for the most part, Arabs simply do not exist as members of the cinematic landscape, in spite of the riots in Hebron and Jerusalem and clashes with the British.

As I pursued the research for my film, it became clear that Zionist filmmaking could roughly be divided into three periods, each with its own distinctive style, subject matter, objectives, and approach. Although I intended to look at all three periods, the time period that most fascinated me was from 1920 to 1945, a period which might well be called "the high romantic era." Here—in films such as Ben Dov's *Springtime in Israel* (1928), *Labor* (1933) by Helmar Larsky, and *Built in a Day* (1939)—Zionist ideology is translated into the constantly occurring, easily understandable visual symbols that were so familiar to me from childhood: the changing desert, the muscular laborer, the dancing pioneers, and the image of hard-won water. Superficially, the gushing sprinklers and flowing irrigation channels might mean blooming deserts, but even the least intelligent observer knew the real meaning. Water was hope, fruitfulness, rebirth, and regeneration. No wonder it was one of the most beloved icons of Zionism.

All the films had to breathe confidence. To show anything negative was to jeopardize distribution. When Natan Axelrod's film *Oded the Wanderer* (1933), a very simple travelogue, was first screened, the representatives of the JNF complained that it lacked inspiration. "There is too much desolation . . . where is the pioneering spirit, the blossoming orchards, the sprinklers?" As a result the Jewish National Fund refused to handle the feature.

For my own film for Israel TV, I looked hard to find examples that would best illustrate that early feeling of optimism, hope, and the spirit of pioneering. Finally I found a great illustration in an early feature documentary titled *This Is My Land*, made by Baruch Agadati. In the film, a cloth-capped pioneer collapses in the fields, yelling to his comrades, *"Kadimah. Kadimah"* (Forward! Continue!). Which they do, by driving a horse-drawn plough over his collapsed body, the illusion created by superimposition. The pioneer is then seen in hospital. As a very pretty nurse weeps by his bed, the pioneer raises himself on one arm, waves into the distance, and with eyes misting declaims, "It is not so terrible to die under these conditions. But whatever you do in the future, you, my people, Israel, do not abandon Hadera!" Today Hadera is a rather neglected, uninspired town that you pass through as quickly as you can while driving from Tel Aviv to Haifa. Telling the country today not to abandon it has about as much appeal as an American president saying, "Do not abandon Oakland." Well, times change.

Another element I wanted to look at for my film was the representation of women in the early documentaries. Here I used a few scenes from Alexander Ford's *Sabra* (1933). In Ford's film, a small group sets up a farming community in the harshest of deserts. Suddenly the girlfriends come from town. Dressed in high heels and long dresses they clearly signify "the old decadent bourgeois woman." One enters the tent of a pioneer, unbuttons her dress, lies down on the hard bed, and invites him to make love and abandon the desert. In contrast we are shown a memorable scene with a very young Hannah Rovina. After having spent days digging a pit, five men are about to abandon their fruitless search for water. Rovina is furious at their lack of will. As she seizes a pickax and starts to dig, her words are scalding and prophetic, "You should be ashamed. If you men don't continue, we women will replace you." Here finally is the New Woman in all her glory, power, and resolution.

I also decided to use a further piece about the New Woman as heroic inspiration, which I found in another, and probably the greatest film of the thirties, *Land of Promise*. As we see women trundling bricks and pushing wheelbarrows, Maurice Samuel's script tells us, years before Gloria Steinem, the meaning of the sexual revolution: "The women pioneers of Palestine demand and obtain an equal share of the hardest work as plow women, stone breakers, road menders, masons, brick layers and builders."

Though the scenes of irrigation, stone breaking, and dancing mirror those of *Sabra*, the audience is treated to a fuller explanation of the meaning of the kibbutz and the communal society: "From these communal settlements may come new forms of social organization instructive to the rest of the world . . . and here a people, separated from the soil for two thousand years return to work with her in happy communion."

If my film started lightly and with a certain amount of humor, the second part became much darker. This I saw as the second period of Zionist filmmaking, the "post-Holocaust, post-State" era. Looming over everything is the Holocaust and the murder of six million Jews. Gradually, other events come to the fore. There is the battle against the British blockade of Palestine; the turbulence and struggle of the War of Independence; the ingathering of the remnants of Europe; the momentous immigration of the Jewish communities of North Africa, Iraq, Persia, and Yemen; and the dramatic story of the new state.

Viewing film after film in the small editing room of the archives, I was touched, moved, and saddened in a totally different way from my earlier screenings. These films were harder, more direct, more confrontational. They were more realistic, more dramatic, and much more news-based than the prewar films. They used far more witnesses, had much more personal narration, and presented a much more strident and passionate text. They said, "Pay attention. Don't tell us in the future that you didn't witness this, that you never saw, that you were not informed." Gone for the most part was the leisured commentary about a two-thousand-year exile. In its place came the demand for justice *now*, for the gates to be opened *now*, for a people to be freed *now*.

Most of the films of this era were dominated by the work of Hadassah, the Keren Kayemet, and the UJA. In contrast to Hadassah, the work of the last two tended to be harder in tone and wider in scope. Because the Joint Distribution Committee (the Joint) came under the aegis of the UJA, many of the latter's films of necessity dug deeper into the situation of postwar Europe than the films of Hadassah. Although Hadassah dealt feelingly and emotionally with children and immigration, it was usually left to the UJA to give a broader picture of *aliya* and indeed of general developments in Israel after the creation of the state. Then as now, the UJA saw itself as the main diaspora arm for raising funds for Israel, and its films left no doubt as to their *raison d'etre*. So seriously was the fundraising point taken that a 1947 UJA film even boasted the provocative title *The Year Nobody Gave*.

I very much wanted to say something about the work of UJA in my TV essay but wondered how to introduce the topic into the film. The mood of my piece was also getting very low, and I needed to take the film in a different direction. Suddenly I realized this could be done by talking about and showing the UJA's Los Angeles connection and the path it had beaten to the gates of the MGM and Warner Brothers' Studios.

To boost the appeal of its films the UJA simply turned to Hollywood. From 1945 through the early 1960s, star after star, both Jewish and non-Jewish volunteered his or her services to introduce a UJA appeal or provide commentary and backbone to a UJA picture. In one film that I pulled down off the racks, Charlton Heston sits and chats with Jane Wyman about Israel's needs. Well, who should know better than the most famous screen Moses? In a second film, Raymond Burr chastises Jeff Chandler for not giving. In a third picture, Lloyd Nolan tells his wife over breakfast in his suburban home that he's thought about the millions behind the Iron Curtain, and he knows it's up to people like them to save lives and help save democracy.

The list of participants in these films is impressive and includes such luminaries as Joseph Cotten, Lee J. Cobb, George Jessel, Lorne Greene, and Eli Wallach. Though their appeal looks limited to modern eyes, one assumes they were as effective in their day as Paul

Newman and Barbara Streisand in ours. Yet even allowing for
changes in taste one wonders whether some of the stars didn't look
faintly out of place even then. Agnes Moorehead, for example, who
played the mother in *Citizen Kane*, is at her most wooden and un-
convincing as she tells the UJA viewer: "We must not sit by help-
lessly. This inhumanity must stop." Nor is Eddie Cantor, the star of
Whoopee, believable when he steps forward in a dinner jacket and
bow tie and tells us that it won't be long now before Israel can
stand on its own two feet and that we are the ones that must bring
the sunrise.

The one actor who does succeed, even by today's standards, and
whom I decided to show at great length, is Edward G. Robinson.
In *Where Do You Get Off* (1957), we meet Robinson in a small UJA
office. He beckons us to sit down as he goes on with his telephone
call to a reluctant donor. Gradually, we join him in his annoyance
with the guy at the other end of the line. Can't that fellow see that
the arguments for donating to the UJA are irrefutable, especially
when illustrated with these moving pictures of Israeli children, new
immigrants, and kibbutz workers? And as Robinson concludes the
telephone call we, the UJA viewers, are almost in total agreement
when he tells us in his granite gangster voice that "the trip has taken
two thousand years. People have been willing to wait, to hope. But
they can't build the land without you. And in the end the Jews of
Palestine are not just fighting for themselves. They're fighting for
you and me."

When I proposed my film to the TV, my idea was not just to take a
lighthearted look at the past but also to reflect on the present and
our ability to take a hard, contemporary look at ourselves. This
deeper intent began to surface more and more as I dug into the last
third of the film.

The central belief of all Zionist filmmaking is that the future will
be infinitely better than the present. *Hope* and *confidence* are the
watchwords, reflected in titles where, as I've mentioned, *dreams* and
miracles predominate. No film is titled *Zionism Today* or *Tel Aviv
in the Nineties*. Instead we are treated to *The Dream Demands a
Struggle* and *The Future Is Ours*.

Yet it was clear to me as I pushed further and further into the
research that the titles did not quite fit the reality of the post-1973
Israeli world, or only fleetingly. In this third period of Zionist film-

making, the "postromantic" era, the dream has become more elusive and much more difficult to believe in and sell given the changing nature of Israel and its position in the Middle East. How can you make positive up-beat films when the economy is recession and when the kibbutz movement is being castigated by Menachem Begin as being an uncaring society of millionaires? How do you make films when you are deep into a war in Lebanon, when the Intifada explodes, when the world believes David has become Goliath? How can you make films when immigration is down, when people are leaving the country, and when the national joke is "Will the last person leaving Israel please turn off the light?"

If the changed facts made Zionist propaganda more problematic in the seventies, so did the circumstances of their coverage. Not only was the isolation of Israel broken by cheap flights so that people could see the new reality for themselves, but television coverage drastically altered the scene. After the Six-Day War over ten television networks established offices in Tel Aviv and Jerusalem. This meant that Zionist films no longer had a monopoly on interpretation and faced strong competition in the area of media information. In an era of satellite technology, the smallest event on the Israeli scene can be broadcast the same day on CBS, CNN, and ABC news. When, during the Intifada, a group of Israeli soldiers were photographed viciously pummeling an Arab youth, the event was shown four times in one day on CBS television.

The Zionist organizations answered the challenge by adopting two strategies. The first was to provide their members with short, hard-hitting but emotional films that provided back-up support for specific campaign objectives. These were the films on Project Renewal and Russian and Ethiopian immigration mentioned earlier. The problem was that while the stories of the Russians and the Ethiopians eminently suited the technique of the hard sell, there weren't many other subjects that generated a similar emotional uplift. I suppose one *can* get worked up about the diamond industry or building a new sewage plant in Petach Tikva, but it is not easy. Acknowledging this fact, the Zionist organizations adopted a new strategy. If emotion was not there in the original topic, then maybe it could be manufactured synthetically with ample doses of music, sex, and nostalgia. I thought it worthwhile commenting on this in my film and chose an extract from *Rhapsody in Green* as the best example of this trend.

Rhapsody in Green was produced by the JNF in 1978. Its story is familiar: the reclamation of the land, the blossoming of the desert, and the greening of Israel. The problem was how to invigorate the tired, old themes. The answer was to use Israeli dancers in stunning orange and black folk costumes to liven the scene. As the music plays the *krakoviak* or the *debka* (the first, incidentally a Polish folk dance), bare-footed, curly-headed men and nubile women weave in and out of cowsheds, throw hay to each other with a smile, and romp gaily to drum and flute as the sun goes down over the rocks of the Negev desert.

The pièce de résistance is saved for the end. Since water is the source of all life and all growth, what can be more natural than a *hora* (circle dance) performed in and out of the swirling water sprinklers? The abundant water soaks both the men and the women, but this only increases the pearl-toothed smiles and the radiant joy. Why are they so happy? Could it be they are rejoicing that they don't have to dig for water with their nails like Hannah Rovina did in *Sabra?*

Sexual innuendo pervades the film from start to finish. Whereas other films use fireworks as a sexual metaphor, here the bursting water jets are more explicit. And if the water running down the breasts of the women makes one think of a wet tee-shirt contest in Greenwich Village, well, that's just the way things are done when Zionist propaganda marries MTV.

Quite clearly, *Rhapsody in Green* was not really about desert projects and land reclamation. What it was saying, via the twirling skirts and the beaming smiles, was that Israel means youth, energy, vitality. It was a Coke advert in JNF clothes. It was telling us that although the way was still long, we had succeeded; the new Jew had come into being, and if we joined the happy band, we too could find the secret of eternal youth.

The thing that most intrigued me in trying to get to the core of Zionist propaganda was the use of symbolic images. Besides water there is one other image that for years pervaded most Zionist filmmaking: the dancing of the *hora*. Whether you are watching *Sabra*, *Land of Promise*, *With These Children*, or *The Song Goes On*, you know the moment will occur in which the workers, new immigrants, and young Sabras will link arms in a circle and dance. In one of the Hadassah films I looked at, *What a Wonderful Day*, Benjamin, the new immigrant from Germany, even goes so far as to say of the

people at his youth village, "Are they crazy? They never stop dancing." So pervasive is the image that it was quite clear the title of my
own retrospective film would have to be *We Could Have Danced
All Night*.

It was clear to me that the *hora* was the one image that most
succinctly conveyed the essence of Zionism. Here young and old
were linked together in a new spirit. Here the embracing arms were
the arms of uplift, the arms of fellowship, the arms of trust. When
Jew supports Jew no problem exists that cannot be solved, no burden is so heavy that it cannot be overcome, and no goal is so distant that it cannot be reached.

When I made *Danced All Night*, I decided to ask one of the
oldtime filmmakers how they saw this recurring image of the *hora*.
The director Natan Gross had a number of very interesting comments. While writing the script of *The Thirteenth Kilometer* (1953),
about the paving of the road to Sdom, Gross decided to include the
inevitable *hora*. To his consternation Gross discovered on actually
visiting the scene that "after a hard day's work the laborers had
neither the energy nor the slightest desire to dance the *hora*."

That was not the end of Gross's difficulties. He had also included
a scene in which the workers return exhausted and broken down
after a day of back-breaking work in the blazing sun. His camera
had captured the fatigue and then rested on the torn and broken
shoes of one of the workers. This realism was evidently too much
for the Labor federation officials who supervised the film, and Gross
was instructed to cut the sequence. As one of the advisers put it: "It
is impossible to show a worker in Israel with torn shoes. What will
the *goyim* say? What will the Jewish donors in America say? A
worker in Israel does not go around in torn shoes." So, like my dirty
washing, the torn shoes were cut.

As a filmmaker myself, I know and have always known that the
quest for idealization in Zionist films has, of necessity, bent the truth.
The degree to which it was done can never be known. It was an
ideological decision and demanded many things. In order to succeed,
idealization often demanded absence, such as exclusion of Arabs and
the Arab problem. It demanded careful subject selection, such as the
emphasis on the kibbutz and the blossoming desert. And it necessi-
tated obfuscation, concealment, the telling of the half-truth and the
portrayal of only part of the portrait.

The rationale for such filmmaking was best expressed by pioneer cameraman Natan Axelrod in "Axelrod Was There," a 1986 interview with director Renen Schorr. "I saw myself as a Zionist and only then as a cinematographer. My purpose as a Zionist, therefore, was to show the good side in building the country. . . . I made an effort so that vacant lots, unfinished streets, garbage and dirt would not be seen. I wanted everything to make a good impression" (*Bamachaneh*, no. 24, May 1986). Axelrod's words say it all, and I heard his views echoed by another pioneer cameraman I interviewed, Rolf Kneller. Zionist filmmaking was of necessity not about truth. It was about propagating ideology and disseminating a vision to those who were, for the most part, already convinced. And the response of the World's Jewish communities to the films, particularly prior to the creation of the State, was extraordinary. Hundreds of copies were made and sent, not only to America and Britain, but also to small Jewish communities in, for example, Abyssinia, Shanghai, Denmark, and Estonia.

After having surveyed the scene, chosen my extracts, illuminated the problems, and written the script, I was wondering what final message I could leave with the viewers. The conclusion seemed to me fairly obvious but not something everyone would agree with. It was this. Whatever the blurring of truth, and whatever the omissions, it is doubtful if the films would have succeeded as well as they did and for as long as they did had they not been based on some essential reality, had they not represented a relatively honest picture of the changing scene and events in Palestine and Israel. That the scenes depicted became after a while symbolic clichés is to miss the point. The clichés represented extraordinary events that possibly could not have been covered otherwise than in a mythic and heroic mode. The films were not meant to be a cold, objective record of a period. They were meant to represent a passionate evocation of the goals of Zionism. If the measure of their success was the winning of the hearts and minds of world Jewry, then they clearly succeeded beyond their wildest dreams.

When the film was finished, I came back to the question that had been pursuing me for years. Leaving propaganda aside, how is it possible to convey the reality of Israel to a foreign audience? How can you present the feel, the texture, and the complexity of this country to a stranger in a way that goes beyond the mere surface of things? I know few films that have done that, but I think the best of them is Claude Lanzmann's *Pourquoi Israel* (*Why Israel?*) made in 1975.

The three-hour film essentially follows a group of visiting Americans, new immigrants, and various other individuals around Israel. The film is very good, but not perfect, and Lanzmann's questions occasionally reveal that as a foreigner he doesn't quite understand Israeli culture. This is very clear in a scene shot in Ashdod where Lanzmann interviews a port worker. Lanzmann's questions invite the docker to agree with him that he is overworked, underpaid, underprivileged, and looked down upon by the rest of Israel. The docker gives a shrug and totally agrees with Lanzmann. When I saw the film at a screening at the Hebrew University, the audience broke out into raucous laughter on hearing this response. Everybody knew that the dockers were the highest paid workers in Israel, notorious for their many strikes and huge bonuses, and generally earned more than most academics and doctors. Lanzmann, in his naivete, had probably imposed his memories of Marseilles onto his perceptions of Israel and had got things totally wrong.

In general, however, Lanzmann got things right, often putting his finger on aspects of Israel that we locals overlook. His film also reveals a wonderful sense of humor and observation not usually revealed by foreign filmmakers. Thus in one hilarious scene he presents a montage of banners put up by various municipalities to welcome foreign delegations. In Jerusalem, for example, these ten-meter-long white banners are strung high across the road to greet you just as your car comes round the last mountain bend and into the city. In Lanzmann's film we see fifteen seconds of these banners, welcoming first Iowa UJA, then Kansas UJA, then a Mormon temple group, then the Southern Baptists, then Long Island Hadassah. The scene is very funny and makes you recall a similar sequence in the film *Sallah Shabati* where Topol keeps changing the names under JNF trees to accommodate different groups of donors.

Lanzmann's most perceptive segments have to do with the expectations and treatment of immigrants. These are spread out throughout the picture and are also filmed over the process of a few months. For his protagonists or stars, Lanzmann chooses to follow a young Russian couple from arrival through absorption, placement, and employment. Our first view of them is actually at Ben Gurion Airport. They have just gotten off the plane and are being interviewed by a Jewish Agency official.

"What do you do?" he asks the young immigrant.

"I'm an engineer."

"Ah, an engineer. Wonderful! We'll soon find work for you. And where would you like to live?"

"Very close by the sea. We love the sea."

"No problem. We have just the place for you. Arad."

"Is that close to the sea?"

"Yes! No distance at all!"

Arad is actually way inland, in the southern desert, miles and miles from any water, the closest sea being the unswimmable, oily, potassium- and potash-impregnated Dead Sea. But the closeness to the sea is just one lie amongst many put out by the official.

Later on in the film, we see the couple living in Arad in a hot, stifling one-room shack. A couple of old mattresses are laid out on the floor. The windows swing on their hinges. A mangy cat slinks by, and you can almost smell its urine. Sand blows in, and the listless wife and sweating husband sit on ramshackle stools as Lanzmann interviews them. The dreams and hopes have faded. OK, so Arad isn't beside the sea. One can put up with that. But the promise of an engineering job was totally false. Instead the husband was given work as a jobbing painter. And the litany of complaints goes on. They have been fed lie after lie and now wonder why they ever came to this place. While the Children of Israel a few thousand years before them yearned for the flesh pots of Egypt, they now in their turn yearn for the flesh pots of Leningrad and Tblisi.

Seeing all this the viewer begins to seethe with rage at the anonymous Jewish Agency officials. The lying bastards. Why do they always have to behave this way? What a corrupt, unscrupulous, scheming bunch of individuals. And then later in the film you see something that makes you wonder whether this harsh judgment needs to be modified.

Lanzmann is visiting Dimona, a small town in the northern Negev, mainly populated by the descendants of North African immigrants who came there in the fifties. It's a dusty flyblown town, originally built of cinder blocks and asbestos and could well serve as a setting for some low-budget Western. Lanzmann and his crew have come there with the American tourists and are being shown around by the mayor. Someone asks him where the name *Dimona* comes from.

"Well," he says, his brown eyes lighting up, "It could have come from *demaot* . . . 'tears.' But," and here the mayor smiles, "I prefer to think it comes from *dimayon* . . . 'imagination.' With imagination and perseverance, we will make this a great town."

When the reception is over, Lanzmann decides to interview the oldtimers in the town square. The youngest is seventy, the oldest a good rival to Methuselah. Nearly all have beards, give the impression of having been manual workers, and most of them are wearing *kipot* (skullcaps). All of them without exception seem to sparkle, as if they are sharing some joke about life. As with the Russian immigrants Lanzmann plunges in about their early beginnings.

"Most of us are from Morocco. A few from Tunis. And we came in the fifties." Lanzmann wickedly opens the stiletto.

"Where did you arrive?"

"Ah, we came into Haifa. What a beautiful place."

"And what did the Jewish Agency say to you?"

"They asked us where we wanted to live."

"And you said . . . ?"

"We all said Haifa. We all wanted to live in Haifa."

"So how did the agency official respond?"

"He said we were going to live in Dimona. So naturally we asked, is that close to Haifa? Oh yes, very close, he said. Maybe twenty minutes, half an hour from Haifa. Not more."

Today, with good roads, Dimona is maybe three hours from Haifa. In the fifties, it took more like five hours to get there. One story I heard about early Dimona was that when the immigrants got there they took one look at the place and refused to get out of the trucks that had transported them there.

Unperturbed by the answers Lanzmann gets on with the questioning.

"So what did you think of Dimona when you arrived?"

"Awful. Simply awful."

"And what do you think of it today?"

Suddenly all the eyes light up, the grins break out, teeth or what remains of them flash, and the broadest of smiles cross the men's faces.

"Wonderful. Wonderful. A pearl of a city. We wouldn't live anywhere else."

Suddenly, the scenes with the Russians come back to you, and you begin to perceive the subtle layerings of the film. Gradually, you begin to understand. Maybe this was the way it had to be. It's an unsettling thought, but suddenly all your previous certainties and assumptions are up for grabs. Maybe without the lying and cajoling there would have been no way to make the land grow and prosper. You are not sure. But Lanzmann has made you understand something about the Israeli process that few others have been able to do, and therein lies the greatness of his film.

7 - The Wars: Yom Kippur and After

We left Jerusalem about midnight. A thick, white mist covered the valleys all the way to Latrun, making us feel as if we were sailing through some inland sea. On the car radio the announcer's voice quietly gave news of blocking actions, reserve call-ups, and aircraft sorties before asking once more for people to come forward and give blood. By the Mevasseret Bridge we stopped briefly to give a soldier a lift and with difficulty crammed him in the back with the camera gear.

A few hours later, after heading south and west and getting closer to the front, we kept getting stopped every few miles by the military police. Besides our usual press passes, we also had special correspondents' passes issued by the army spokesman's unit. These helped, but it was clear that at some point the army was going to say, "This far, and no farther."

As we came through the desert and toward the canal, the inevitable signs of battle were everywhere: massive tank carriers waiting under trees; soldiers grouped around hastily erected tents; armored carriers being refueled; and abandoned ammunition boxes. And, more significant than anything else, in the predawn darkness we could see flashes of artillery fire straight in front of us. Unthinkably, we were once more at war.

When I had met with my friend Giora in the euphoric days of summer 1967, I had asked him if he thought the days of June marked the last of the Arab-Israeli wars. Giora had been one of the pessimists. "No. I think we'll see another two or three." I didn't believe him at the time, but he was right. In fact, only a few months later he was serving at the canal in that undiscussed but costly war against Egypt called the "War of Attrition." In 1971 the war was still going on as I clearly saw when I went down to Sinai to film *Battle Officer*.

However, in 1973 I think most Israeli would have agreed with me. Skirmishes, yes. But a major war, impossible! We had taught the Arabs a lesson in 1967 they would never forget. Golda Meir told us war was out and Moshe Dayan, our great hero general, told us we could all relax. Well, when Moshe tells you, you believe it. You put worries and doubts aside and begin to enjoy life.

For me, that meant exploring "the new Israel." Trying to find excuses to film in the wonderful scenic areas of the Judean desert, such as the fantastic gorges around Wadi Kelt and Mar Saba monasteries. For other friends, enjoying life meant taking an afternoon off and wandering around the glass factories of Hebron or dining on twenty piquant Arab salads in Ramallah.

June 1967 had brought a revolution. Physical. Mental. Psychological. Although change was happening all over Israel, I saw it most in Jerusalem. The quiet city I had known at the time of the Eichmann trial was fast disappearing under a rush of speculative building. A new bus station had opened at the top of Jaffa Street. A hideous fortified university was being built on Mount Scopus. Opposite the Old City walls the neglected student and artist quarters of Mishkanot Shaananim, which had once been right in the center of no mans land were now being turned into luxurious apartments, many owned by American expatriates. While new residential blocks sprouted on the outskirts of the city, hotels of all shapes and sizes mushroomed in the center.

Three other aspects of modern civilization were also beginning to make shy entrances. Thus traffic lights were beginning to appear everywhere to the delight of pedestrians and the consternation of Jerusalem's growing band of death-seeking motorists. A supermarket, possibly Israel's first, had opened near Terra Santa, and wonder of wonders, a new pizza shop was giving competition to the indigenous *shawarma* (grilled meat sandwich).

One evening sums up for me the delightful, untroubled tone of life of those years. It is the evening of Independence Day, 1973. I go out with my wife and my boys, Tal and Gil, to have an ice cream on Ben Yehudah. It is a hot evening. The flags are waving. Everywhere kids are hitting all and sundry with toy plastic hammers. Tomorrow Jerusalem is going to hold a massive military parade. Close to where I live soldiers are putting up tents for the night. In King George Street, blue lines have been painted down the road to show the tanks how to proceed on the morrow. It is a lovely evening, and as we walk along arm in arm everything seems pretty good, and for once I am deeply satisfied that I made the move to this strange land.

The war started for me, for all of us, at two o'clock on the Saturday afternoon of Yom Kippur. I had been to the synagogue in the morning, and at noon decided to lie down for a nap in my son Tal's room. It had been a stinking hot morning, and all I wanted to do was pull the blinds and sleep. Suddenly, out of nowhere, came the wail of the siren, deafening, ear splitting. Tal, who was three years old, woke up with a fright. "What is it, Abba [Father]? A fire engine?"

Putting on a few clothes, I rushed to the dining room window, which overlooks the Valley of the Cross and Herzog Boulevard. Outside the scene was unbelievable. Cars, trucks, lorries, and buses were zipping down the main road. This was impossible. On Yom Kippur, the most holy and solemn day in the Jewish calendar, nothing, but nothing moves. No one, not even the most irreligious Jew in the city drives. To use your car on Yom Kippur is, and was, unthinkable. And yet outside my window the traffic was moving in an ever-increasing and urgent volume.

There are also no radio programs on Yom Kippur as all the Israeli broadcast services shut down for the day. Nevertheless my wife, even more disturbed than me, turned on the radio. Finally everything became clear. "Today, at 2:00 P.M. Egyptian forces struck at our soldiers across the Suez Canal. At the same time, a large force of Syrian tanks have mounted a massive attack on the Golan Heights. We will update as and when we have more news."

Looking back, I realized the signs had been there the whole time, only I had failed to recognize them. First there had been the incident with the bus. Coming back from temple the night before, I had seen a truck, with parking lights on and radio going, standing idling in front of our building. My first response had been that the truck was picking up partygoers who deliberately wanted to flaunt their opposition to the holiness of Yom Kippur. The fact that the truck also said *"sherut bitachon"* (security services) should have warned me there was more going on, but my thoughts were elsewhere.

Then at midnight, with all Israeli news shut off, I had tuned in to the BBC. The headlines had talked of a mobilization of troops on the Syrian front, but there had been similar talk earlier in the year, so I paid little attention to the item. Finally, in the morning, I had noticed my neighbor, Dr. Rachmilewitz, rush out of his apartment in his army uniform. My smart aleck words to him had been, "You look absolutely great for Yom Kippur."

For the rest of the afternoon, after the radio announcements, I gathered with a few neighbors in one of the apartments of our building where we all tried to figure out what was going on. This was done by making frantic calls all round and keeping our ears to the radio. The news, in practice, was very sparse. Little was added to the early information about the attacks; instead the radio started putting out a series of code words such as *mavreg kiss* (pocket spanner) and *patish katan* (small hammer), all being call-up signs for different groups to join their units.

At first most of us were supremely confident and unphased. If the Egyptians and Syrians wanted to be beaten a second time, so be it. I'd seen the defenses at the Bar Lev line on the canal, and they were terrific, weren't they? And while I had been filming there a colonel had told me in confidence about the oil pipes leading into the water, which would allow the Israelis to set the canal on fire if the Egyptians were rash enough to cross. And we were also pretty strong in the Golan, since we dominated the heights, so why worry?

It took us about three days to realize how incredibly, devastatingly, and tragically wrong we all were. By 10 October, stories of the losses were beginning to come out. Over 20,000 Egyptian commandos and infantry had crossed the canal with relative ease. Most of the bunkers at the Bar Lev line had fallen or were about to fall. The Syrians were driving hard and fast into the Golan and had cracked through in two sections. Our losses were enormous. The Egyptians had an antitank weapon called the "sagger," which was wreaking devastation on our armored columns. Only the previous day Israel had lost 250 tanks in a disastrous counterattack against the enemy. Hundreds of our soldiers had been killed, and goodness knows how many wounded. And to top everything dozens of our planes had been brought down by Russian-made SAM missiles.

On television a gaunt Golda Meir and a gray-faced Moshe Dayan, current minister of defense, tried to assure us things would be all right. But it was quite clear they weren't. For the first time we were beginning to wonder how much of the real picture was being given to us. Only when I attended a press conference given by the chief of staff, David Elazar, did anything like the truth emerge.

Most battle units had allowed their soldiers to go home to celebrate Yom Kippur. As a result, nearly all the key Israeli positions were disastrously undermanned, including the vital Bar Lev string of forts along the Suez line. In consequence, Israeli forces were being pushed back from the canal and were being overrun on the Golan Heights. Equipment and ammunition were running dangerously low, and though more reserves were moving into place, the situation looked very bleak. That afternoon, for the first time I heard the word *machdal*. It meant "catastrophe" or "disaster" and would soon be used by every newspaper to characterize the first week of the war.

In such a confused situation, normal life ground to a total halt. It was a time of waiting, talking, wondering, questioning. Each morning we grabbed the papers for details. After dozens of phone calls, we would wander the streets talking to strangers, trying to find out if they had some news we had missed. And every hour on the hour we would turn on the news, hoping to hear of a breakthrough, a turnaround in the situation, just some small ray of hope.

At the time I was doing some teaching at the Hebrew University, but like most other academic institutions it had virtually closed down. The professors had gone to the front, the students to their battle units, and the women to various support jobs. When people did appear in their uniforms, there were surprises everywhere. Graduate students who you thought were fairly bright and promising now revealed themselves as tank majors or infantry captains. One of my colleagues, a mild teacher of visual education, turned out to be a lieutenant colonel in the paratroop reserves.

Temporarily jobless, the rest of us sought something to do, something to occupy us, something to make us feel we were helping in however small a way. For a few days I went to work in a pharmaceutical factory, manning one of their pill-making machines and sorting bandages. At other times I ferried soldiers back and forth from Jerusalem to Jericho. But this was all very frustrating. I wanted to be in there filming and wasn't sure how to do it. Finally a phone call to the Jewish Agency landed me a job as a kind of roving writer-director with one of their film crews. Nothing was laid down. It was just a matter of taking the crew, going out, and filming Israel at war.

For me that meant filming the home front. So I wandered into bakeries and filmed teenagers handling the bread pans and loading the newly baked loaves into the delivery trucks. I filmed sixteen-year-old girls painting everybody's car headlights blue, shot ex-army men driving garbage trucks, and recorded grandmothers coming to work in kindergartens. I went into homes where people talked about their sons and their husbands, and held back tears as they made me a cup of tea. I shot idle factories and empty workshops and then went to a few local kibbutzim to film women milking cows or desperately trying to get the fruit in. And I filmed the volunteers who, like in '67, were beginning to trickle in and help in whatever way possible.

And I filmed at night. I wanted to capture the silent, shuttered ghost town that Jerusalem had become. At night, with its lights extinguished, the city was bathed in blue darkness. Cars rolled by, their progress slow and hesitant as their dulled lamps struggled to find the way. Occasionally, couples appeared in streets, but as dark silhouettes. Occasionally, a light streaked out from behind curtained windows, but overall it had become a city of shadows and echoes, and, in a strange new way, a city of devastating and haunting beauty. With all lights extinguished the profiles of certain buildings stood out wonderfully against the sky. Notre Dame looked magnificent, and the Ratisbonne monastery felt as if it had been lifted straight out of a Renaissance painting.

After nine or ten days, the news seemed to change for the better. Supplies were being flown in from America. The Golan had miraculously not given way, and after some huge tank battles in Sinai, dwarfing many of those of the Second World War, the Israelis were regaining ground. Most encouraging of all, however, was the news that General Sharon had found a way through the center of the Egyptian forces, punched through all opposition, and had created an armored bridgehead on the western side of the canal. Given the improvement in situation, I once more applied for permission to go to the front. This time it was given, and shoving two cameras, film stock, and my crew into my battered Volvo station wagon I headed for Sinai, hoping to continue on later to the Golan Heights.

We filmed for three days continuously, but what we filmed remains a blur. Yet certain memories stand out. One is standing by the side of one of the southern roads at midnight close by a kibbutz. A bus full of reserve soldiers has pulled up, and the soldiers have piled out of the bus and dropped exhausted by the wayside. Within five minutes, the members of the kibbutz have brought steaming coffee, sandwiches, and blankets. The soldiers drink, saying little, but thanking with their eyes, a hug, a handshake. Our sun guns, our small battery lights capture the steam rising from the plastic coffee cups; the unshaven faces; the anxiety on the faces of the kibbutzniks, the dirty, stained, baggy uniforms of the reservists; and the embraces and the handshakes. Once more, as in '67 I am taken by the sense of binding and the sense of community.

At the canal I am shocked to see the broken, tangled girders of one of the concrete Bar Lev emplacements we had thought impregnable just two weeks ago. A year before I had filmed in this spot. Where are the soldiers now? Alive? Dead? Missing?

A hundred yards away from the bunker, a pontoon bridge leads across the canal, and jeeps and light armored vehicles rumble across every few seconds. The soldiers grin and wave their rifles. This morning the news has been good. The bridge head has grown. Sharon's tanks on the other side of the canal have been moving at an incredible speed, have totally surprised the opposition, and have begun a pincer movement around the Egyptian armies.

While other news crews head toward the fighting, I prefer to stay, watch, and talk to the men on this side of the canal. Many lie prostrate on the ground, shielding their eyes from the sun with newspapers or books. A few are writing letters, propping the paper up on the sides of jeeps and lorries. Seeing my crew they press the notes into our hands, and we promise to deliver them and phone relatives and tell them they are fine. I spend a lot of time talking to the tank crews as they dig in or prepare to cross the canal. Ambulances rush by. Almost everybody appears to be sleepwalking—almost dropping from fatigue.

From Sinai we head north. On the Golan Heights destruction and death are all around. The killing fields reveal themselves to the naked eye against a background of surrealist dawn skies whose garish reds and blues come straight from a savage Kandinsky painting. Dozens, maybe hundreds of smashed and pulverized tanks are everywhere, leaning at grotesque and impossible angles, their tracks torn off, their canopies blown apart, the earth scorched all around. As salvage crews save what they can of both friendly and enemy equipment, other tanks roar by, their aerials whipping back in the wind, each draped with an orange cloth which will identify them as friendly to Israel aircraft.

Heading deeper into the heights we come to a long, low bridge. On it, before it, and beyond lie the remains of a Syrian column. Caught in the open by Israeli jets, the whole column has been devastated beyond recognition. Getting closer we make out four or five black, charred bodies leaning out of what were once lorry windows. Other bodies lie burned beyond recognition on the ground. The only way to get through this experience is to pull down an emotional window that blanks out reality. That way you protect your mind from considering that these objects are really human beings and that a few hours ago they were alive, had families, wives, sons, and daughters. The experience also reminds me how far we journalists are from the searing impact of the real fighting. We see and record from a safe distance while others are in there, fighting, bleeding, dying. And if not dying, seeing their friends of years suddenly dying beside them.

In Safed we film in the main hospital. First we get the helicopters landing with the wounded. Various teams greet each helicopter and rush the soldiers into the emergency rooms. Around each bed another team of four or five green-coated doctors and surgeons cut away the clothes and investigate the wounds. Two of the soldiers are proclaiming they must go back; they are needed; they can't stay here.

Having talked to the head of the hospital, we get permission to film in one of the wards. Five soldiers, virtually kids, are lying down. Behind them, on the walls, their own children's kindergarten paintings and messages: "Abba, get well. Abba, we miss you. Abba, come home safely." The wives and girlfriends talk, and we try to be discreet and keep a distance. The usual questions, "How did it happen? How do you feel? What do you think of the war?" seem totally inappropriate. I prefer to watch and just take in the details, the pained grimace, the smile, the bloodsoaked bandages, the patch across the eyes, the arm suspended in a sling.

After a few minutes I go outside onto the balcony. A soldier is sitting in a wheelchair playing *shesh besh* with an orderly. His very beautiful young wife is wearing a blue print dress, smiling down at him and holding their baby. Beyond her blonde head a hazy green valley stretches out to the Jordan River. A flock of white pigeons races overhead. The wife smiles at me, and I hear her husband's last few words to her. "Don't worry, we'll come through. *Tachziki maamad*. Just hold on tight."

We leave as an awesome technicolor sunset sweeps over the hills. The clouds are flecked with red and gold, and as we descend to Tiberias, the Kinneret Lake looks wonderfully blue and inviting. Without thinking I start humming the kitschiest tunes I can think of from American musicals, "Oh What a Beautiful Morning," "The Surrey with the Fringe on Top." Behind us the war goes on.

The war ended on 22 October. In the North, Israeli troops had re-captured the total Golan Heights and were within striking distance of Damascus. In the South, Israel had dug in massively on the West Bank of the canal and had totally surrounded Egypt's third army. For Israel defeat had been turned into victory, but at a massive cost. Twenty-five hundred Israelis had died, and more than three thousand had been wounded.

Most of my close friends had survived, but not all. My best friends, Arieh and Yael, had lost their nephew with whom I had tracked in Sinai, and I discovered that the cousin of Yael, my old girlfriend, had been killed in the Golan. For days the television was full of funerals and the papers full of blackedged photos of the brothers, uncles, fathers, and husbands who had died. Only a few weeks had passed, but the victory tasted like ashes.

After the war I continued filming intermittently and also went back to Sinai and the Golan to do some articles for the *London Jewish Chronicle*. The university had still not reopened, and much of the army was still at the canal watching over an uneasy cease-fire. Now were the days of the waiting game with Egyptian-Israeli UN discussions going on at kilometer 101 and Henry Kissinger setting an all-time record for shuttles between Tel Aviv, Cairo, and Damascus.

Although I did a lot of interviewing, in the end I decided to base my articles on a series of letters I exchanged with two friends, Rafi and Danny. During the war we had all inhabited different planets. While mine had been the urban world of silent Jerusalem, Danny had spent his days (and nights) nursing his machine gun on a dust-choked hill overlooking the road to Jericho. And Rafi . . . well Rafi was in the hell of the Sinai bunkers and lost half of his unit.

After the cease-fire both Danny and Rafi stayed in the reserves till February, and in the long shadows of the guarded days both wrote me similar letters. Both talked of time standing still; of the lack of reference points; of the vagueness and haziness of anything outside their universe of guns, guards, sand, and sweat.

I was particularly struck by the change in Rafi. Before the war he had been the typical Israeli: tremendously outgoing, dynamic, a rough humor, and quite dedicated to his family. But things were happening inside. In January Rafi came home for a two-day leave, and it was disastrous. He and his wife fought, the baby cried, and in the end he was more than glad to get back to his unit. Something similar but less intense happened to Danny.

Both were suffering from a "re-entry" problem. Sinai, Jericho, and the Golan were only a few hours away by road but light years away in terms of living. Who suddenly was this strange woman confronting Rafi? Whose was this crying baby? What concern was it of his if the roof leaked, prices went up, or the car needed repairing. As Rafi put it, the only reality to him was the sand, the flies, the oppression of his tank, and the camaraderie and warmth of his men.

Danny came home more frequently. He had been in a different war, a waiting war. No action. No friends killed. A war bounded by dust, a stifling tent, long conversations, guard duty, and endless reading of light detective novels. Whereas Rafi was all pessimism, Danny was still a believer. Israel had done fantastic things. The army was better than ever. It had been a costly but glorious victory, and so on.

Where he had been hit was in his business. He'd ran a small engineering shop with his brother. Both had been called up, and business had vanished. Clients hadn't waited until his return but had gone elsewhere. This made him bitter, and he reckoned it would take him a year to catch up.

Rafi got his release when Israel withdrew from the West Bank of the canal, and Danny, a week later. All of us went out to celebrate. But to celebrate an end or a beginning—that we didn't know. For the first time since the war, Rafi appeared to be aware of his surroundings: the tourists, the pretty girl serving us drinks, and the laughing couple at the next table. I think it was the first time he realized something was over, finished, and that he had to move on. While his wife worked as a nurse, he was going back to the university to finish his doctorate. He'd missed a term, but arrangements were being made to help the soldiers. But he was going back without much enthusiasm.

Rafi had always been the true Zionist in my mind, the good Israeli, and I was shocked to hear him talk of leaving the country. "I've fought for it, but look at it now. The old guard as before: Golda and Dayan as complacent as ever; political horse trading; no change; no democracy; no movement. It's ugly, sterile, barren. Maybe I just want out."

Danny was also in shock, but like I've said, he was a believer. He admitted the faults but thought the possibilities existed for change. Unlike Rafi he had lived abroad and knew that the mess elsewhere could be as great as in Jerusalem.

And what did I think at the time? I had sent almost daily letters to my family in England, and one of those said everything: "Nobody here is an island. We share the warmth, and we share the pain. Slowly, gradually, we are discovering the price of the war, and inside it hurts like hell. Behind everything, however, there is movement. Beyond the physical pain we are all suffering a tremendous psychological shock, the shock of sudden weakness, abandonment, and total isolation. And because of the shock we are all having to revise our goals and self-image."

Looking back it is clear that like Danny and Rafi, we were all questioning. We knew we were entering a new period where the old verities had to be abandoned. But what would come in their place, none of us knew. Danny put it best in one of his last letters to me: "I'm alone on the hill, and all sorts of thoughts go through my mind. I know nothing will be the same, and I don't know where I'm going. But as I look around I still feel this is the right place for me to be and for me to bring up my children. We'll survive. Take care. Danny."

In 1990 I did a film for Channel 4/UK and PBS in which I tried to look back and describe those years after the war. Ostensibly it was a film biography of Abba Eban, but in practice it was a political and historical analysis of Israel from 1973 to the nineties. I titled it *The Dream Divided*, which I thought would tell the viewers immediately that I was dealing the fragmentation of the Israeli vision. In doing it I had once more to come to grips with the Yom Kippur War and its aftermath, and for me that was the hardest part of the exercise, reliving those days and realizing how little we knew of what was really happening.

For example, I thought our television had given a reasonable picture of the fighting. Only when I started going through the film archives of the army did I realize how severely censored everything had been. What we had seen on our living room screens had been pretty moving-wallpaper battles. Tanks moved in the distance. Cannons roared. Planes scrambled. Jets screamed overhead. Officers stood around in goggles and poured worriedly over maps. And now and then against the hills one could see the smoke of an exploding shell. The uncensored material showed something else entirely.

Here you were horrifyingly in the middle of the battle, with tanks burning everywhere. In one of the shots a tankist staggers out of his turret and collapses into a comrade's arms. In another shot a tank almost disintegrates before your eyes, its turret blown to smithereens. In a third the camera follows a plane down as it smashes into the ground seventy yards away. Everywhere there is smoke and confusion. This is surely the seventh circle of hell.

In another reel I pulled, we are with Israeli paratroopers trapped in a building by the side of the canal. The wounded lie around. Some of the men are firing out of the window. A few seconds later we see a desperate escape attempt. The men come out firing, and the wounded are dumped across a half-track. The reel comes to an end. Did they escape? This reel will never tell us.

At one stage I went to England for research and started browsing through the archives of Vis News and the BBC. What I was looking for were Israeli prisoners of war. I'd seen the shots briefly on Jordan television but wanted to look at them in detail. When I found them they were immensely sad: soldiers staring forlornly into the camera and others sitting on the ground, their hands bound behind their backs, their eyes covered.

Later I look in on the WTN, the British independent television news group. Here I'm looking for material of the Egyptians crossing the canal. When it comes I realize it is not authentic but a reconstruction in glorious color staged for British TV a few days after the real battles. Here soldiers call each other to move forward in classic Hollywood tradition. Boats slide into the canal as dinghy after dinghy makes for the other side. And finally, without the slightest opposition, the soldiers swarm up the sand walls of the canal to plant a victorious flag on the Israeli bunkers. Maybe that's the way it was. And yet in the middle of it all is one shot that is devastatingly authentic. It is in black and white and shows an Egyptian soldier ripping an Israeli flag to pieces. It is a shot I've seen a few times before, and one that always fills me with a profound sadness.

In 1973 in Israel there had been some major debate over the role of Henry Kissinger on the diplomatic front. Had he been a friend of Israel or had he merely manipulated the situation for American political advantage? And if he had been a friend, why had he seemed to delay sending supplies to Israel? They seemed good questions to ask, and I put them to Kissinger in his New York office.

Kissinger was affable, his accent as strong as ever, his humor very good. What did he think of Israel? "Well, Abba Eban once told me that Israelis saw objectivity as being a hundred percent in agreement with them. I thought that was a joke till I met Golda Meir. On one occasion she had eleven demands, and I only agreed to ten of them. She thereupon turned to Eban and said, 'Why is Henry betraying us again?'" Unfortunately, in regard to the war, his answers were totally guarded and unrevealing. No, he had always been a friend of Israel. Had he put pressure on Israel? Of course not. Had he deliberately delayed sending supplies? Absolutely not. Supplies were hard to come by, but he had pressured the Pentagon to send them as soon as possible.

A few days later Richard Nixon was interviewed for the film and gave a slightly different picture. Yes, Henry had been reluctant at first, but he, President Nixon, had battled against everyone to see that the supplies got through.

> At the Pentagon they were wary of an airlift. They thought the way to do it was to have Israeli planes come in. They would paint off the stars of David and then have them deliver the weapons. I said, "No way! It's got to be done by us." I consulted with Henry, and he said, "We have a plan. We'll send three C5s." I said, "How many do we have?" "I don't know. Maybe about twenty-five." So I said, "Send all twenty-five." Henry was dubious. He thought the Defense Department would go crazy. "That's more than the traffic can bear politically," he said. I said to Henry, "I'll take care of the politics. We'll get blamed as much for three as for twenty-five. I want you to send anything that can fly." And we did!

At one point, after his army had been surrounded, Sadat asked for joint Russian-American forces to patrol the cease-fire. When Kissinger said no the Russians panicked, with Brezhnev threatening to send in his own Russian troops to rescue the Egyptians. I remembered that as being a very hot moment, and Nixon was asked for his reaction. "We considered that message a most dangerous escalation. That's why we made a most difficult but necessary decision to tell Brezhnev that we would not tolerate Soviet unilateral intervention in Middle East affairs. We even called a Def Com alert, which involved the possible use of nuclear weapons. But we kept the Russians out. No Russian Middle East invasion."

The final, saddest part of the Yom Kippur survey came when I interviewed soldiers who'd been at the Bar Lev line about the first days of the war.

> We knew it was going to happen. Through the binoculars we could see them bringing up their heavy trucks, their artillery, and their reinforcements. And we kept phoning headquarters and telling them, and they kept saying, 'Don't worry. It's only an exercise, only an exercise.' Later, when our men died, they had nothing to say to us.
>
> We were in the bunker with twenty-one men when all hell let loose. Firing from every side. We tried to reply, but the power was too much for us. We called for help. They told us they were coming, but they never came. From the beginning there was a feeling of hopelessness. Eventually we surrendered. They let us surrender. When we came out of the bunker, the dead were all around. Everywhere. People I'd known and served with for years. They were lying there, arms outstretched, dead. It was like a slaughterhouse.

David, the man who told me all this, was one of my neighbors. He was one of the lucky ones at the canal. He survived and was taken into a prisoner of war camp in Egypt. After months of incarceration he returned, full of a bitterness, which is there till this day. "Who was really responsible?" I asked him.

"We all were. We were so arrogant. We thought we were invincible. After '67 we were living in a dream world. Who was responsible? Those who failed to believe the intelligence reports. Those who failed to act when the writing was on the wall. Who was responsible? Golda and Dayan."

After the war an inquiry board was set up called the "Agranat Commission." Its task was to look into the mistakes at the start of the war. While it faulted the intelligence analysis, it essentially failed to name names. Above all it failed to lay any blame at the feet of

Golda Meir, the prime minister, and Moshe Dayan, the defense minister. That was when the demonstrations began, particularly against Dayan, led by an angry war veteran, Motti Ashkenazi. In the hours before the war, the chief of staff, David Elazar, had called for a general mobilization. Dayan had refused to go ahead with the order. The result was disaster.

The campaign started by Ashkenazi soon grew in force and vehemence. I remember passing the Knesset on dark blustery winter mornings seeing a growing sea of placards with the words "Dayan Is a Murderer." "Go Down Moses [Moshe]." "Dayan Must Go." Eventually, yielding to public feeling, both Golda Meir and Dayan resigned and Yitzhak Rabin came in as prime minister.

In 1973 and 1974 we all talked of change but never suspected how fast it would come and how deeply the changes would cut into the flesh. The ouster of Golda Meir and Dayan were only the first signs of change. In retrospect it looks simple. The politicians failed; the politicians must go. But these weren't politicians; they were gods. Golda was the mother of the country, Dayan, the one-eyed hero of Sinai who symbolized the new Israel. If the old gods were being abandoned, what was there to believe in, and who and what would come in their place? The answer came two years later when almost thirty years of Labor and Ashkenazi ascendancy came to an end with the election to power of Menachem Begin and his right-wing Likud Party. This revolution was the final price that had to be paid for the Yom Kippur War. And after the revolution nothing would ever be the same again.

On the wall of my kitchen there is a fading colored newspaper photo. It shows Menachem Begin reaching across President Jimmy Carter to shake the hand of Egypt's president, Anwar Sadat. As I look at the photo, I can still hear the low, slow, and deliberate bass tones of Sadat's voice. "No more war. No more suffering. . . . We will beat swords into plough shares."

When Begin became prime minister, I was sick with disappointment. I and most of my friends saw him as a right-wing demagogue who would drag the country down to the lowest depths possible. In the end I think we were right. In the beginning we were 100 percent wrong, no more so than in November 1977, when I watched Sadat arrive at Ben Gurion Airport. Where others had merely talked of connecting to Egypt, Begin had succeeded. In Cairo, Sadat had suddenly talked of going to the ends of the earth to get peace, and Begin had taken him at his word. He had invited Sadat to Jerusalem, and miraculously the invitation had been accepted. So opened a chapter that changed the course of Middle Eastern history and dramatically transformed the whole political scene.

Afterward we learned of the tremendous preparatory groundwork that had been done in a secret meeting in Morocco between Sadat's envoy Hassan Tuhami and Moshe Dayan. Afterward every political journalist in the world started analyzing why, after 1973, it was so clear that Egypt would only recover land by negotiations and not by war. And afterward we all learned why Egypt had to move because it needed vast loans from America. Yet even after all the rationalizations were in, we still saw Sadat's arrival as a miracle and as a turning point in the history of the Middle East.

Occasionally, I have debated with academic historians on the quality and need for television history. Most serious academics scorn history as it is presented on the box. For them, the document and the word is all-important. But what would words say about the night of Sadat's visit? "President Sadat arrived to an enthusiastic welcome at the airport. Later he was driven to Jerusalem past happy crowds of well wishers, before settling in at the King David Hotel." Enthusiastic welcome? Happy crowds? What on earth are you talking about? We went mad. We went crazy. Banners were out. Egyptian flags flying. As Sadat drove into Jerusalem, all of us took to the streets, stretching out arms and clapping and crying. Strangers embraced. Policemen smiled. Fathers held out their children to greet a Sadat who only four years earlier had almost brought Israel to its knees. Tell me of any historical page that does justice to that scene. You won't find it. But it's all there on the television cassette. Wordsworth, talking of the French Revolution, wrote, "Bliss was it in that dawn to be alive / But to be young was heaven." Well, believe me, those words could be written of Israel that night.

And if you weren't in heaven, you were certainly at the center of the universe as journalists poured in from all over the world to capture those momentous days. This time I found myself working for Dutch television covering the breaking news and also doing the odd background interview. The latter consisted of finding people who could give an interesting slant on Sadat's visit like Elias Frej, the mayor of Bethlehem. When I saw him, Frej had already been interviewed so much that the words poured out of him like an automatic recording. "Yes, the visit could be good, but it depends if the Arab people get back their lands." This Frej doubted, knowing Begin's belief in a greater Israel. Others I interviewed included ex-prisoners of war. To a man they were enthusiastic about the visit and felt that only good things could come out of it.

For most of the time, I lived in the Jerusalem Theater, which had been reorganized into a tremendously huge and surprisingly effective media center. Here we watched on huge TV monitors as Sadat made a speech to the Israeli Knesset, reiterating his desire for peace. And here we watched Sadat being greeted by Knesset members and making his comment that Golda Meir was his favorite grandmother. Here also we saw television pictures of another sort such as the Libyan ambassador in New York burning the Egyptian flag in front of his embassy and the Syrian ambassador accusing Sadat of betrayal of the Arab dreams.

The only time I saw Sadat up close was at the ending press conference, also held at the Jerusalem Theater. With him on the platform was Begin. In front of them a blue baize table cloth. Flanking the platform huge bouquets of yellow flowers. Begin we had heard. Begin we knew. What we had all come for was to see and greet Sadat, to applaud him for his courage, and to send him on his way with our best wishes.

The speeches are mostly forgotten. The clever questions of the newsmen were buried with time. What remains is the image of a strong, upright man in a dark blue suit, standing alone, and telling not just Israelis but the whole Arab world that peace was possible. "Let us agree, whatever happens we shall solve it together by talks rather than going to war." And to be fair, what also remains is the memory of Begin declaiming, "No more bloodshed, no more attacks," and beginning to flex his muscles against his own internal opposition.

For my later film on those years, I looked for the images of Sadat departing Jerusalem. The green Egyptian flags still decorate the flagpoles as the diplomatic convoy rolls by. Police outriders roar past followed by black diplomatic limousines. Crowds line the streets to get a last glimpse of Sadat. Then the camera pulls back to reveal the magnificent panorama of the wooded Valley of the Cross as the cars head toward Tel Aviv.

At the press conference the main questions centered on *tachlis* (action). So the ice had been broken, but where would the sides go from here? The answer came later in the 1979 Peace Treaty and Begin and Sadat's handshake across Carter. But for my film that wasn't enough. I wanted to look at process and therefore arranged interviews with Ezer Weizman and President Carter and procured some footage of Boutros Boutros-Ghali. I also very much wanted to interview Begin, but by the time I made my film he was suffering from severe depression and had virtually excluded himself from the world. And Sadat, whom I had so admired, was dead, murdered by those opposed to the peace process.

Weizman, that strange maverick air force general turned politician, was the wild card on Begin's side. From '77 to '79, as defense minister, he had accompanied Begin on almost all his Tel Aviv-Cairo visits and during this time had achieved a tremendous bonding with President Sadat. As an ex-commander of the air force his word also had tremendous force when it came to discussing how an Israeli retreat from the Sinai air bases would affect the Israeli security situation. At Camp David he eventually came round to believing that giving up Sinai would work and made no bones about stressing that point. But it wasn't easy, and the trust he had built with Sadat did not necessarily reflect the positions of either the Israeli or the Egyptian legations at Camp David. Thus Weizman told me of the distance that was kept between the two delegations, so that they even ate separately. More seriously, Sadat and Begin, whose relations had so deteriorated between the Jerusalem visit and January 1968, met only three times, with the Americans acting as the intermediaries.

The most interesting part of my interview with Weizman was what he told me about the substance and mood of the negotiations, which were hidden at the time from the eyes of the media. Sadat may have put up a wonderful front in Israel, but at Camp David his first demands, basically calling for a total return to the pre-1967 position, were totally unacceptable to the Israelis. Even the Americans thought the demands extreme. Carter's entry into the negotiations were also fairly brutal, calling for Israel's withdrawal to the 1967 borders. According to Weizman, when Carter told Begin he had to accept these terms, Begin's answer was, "Mr. President, no threats please." Carter's promise of a letter to Sadat viewing Jerusalem as occupied territory was also not calculated to ingratiate him in Israeli eyes. Both Sadat and Begin at odd times threatened to leave Camp David, and the smiles that emerged at the end of the negotiations masked the tensions that more than once could have totally wrecked the negotiations.

For my interview with President Carter I traveled to the Carter Presidential Library in Atlanta. In preparation I had read Carter's memoirs about his Middle East journeys and among other things had been trying to fathom the nature of this intensely righteous, god-fearing man. In the Carter library you are surrounded by smiles and achievements: Carter smiling at Egyptian crowds, Carter beaming as he becomes president, and Rosalyn smiles at his side, and Carter enthusing at the signing of the peace treaty. The smile is indeed something, as I felt when we eventually got to film the great man. It is intense, movie star in its quality, backed up by the intense gleam of those so-blue eyes.

Reading Carter's biography, I had been moved by his passion, and following the peace process I had been taken by his dedication and energy, his visits to the Middle East in the cause of peace, and his constant pursuit of a resolution. Yet while appreciating his achievements, it was easy to be put off by the man. There was something cold about him, something too righteous. You disliked him in the way you dislike anyone who is always right and always knows what is best for you.

In Carter's version, though veiled in diplomatic smoothness, Begin was the villain, Moshe Dayan intransigent, Sadat the hero. At first it was a time of total despair. If Carter hadn't acted as a go-between, the talks would have packed up after three days. If Begin hadn't been so obstinate peace would have come sooner. And yes, Israel had to withdraw from the West Bank, give the Palestinians their rights, and generally learn to behave as a righteous people. I suspect, and this may not be fair, that had he not felt it was pushing things too far he would have asked the Israelis to behave as righteous Christians. This nagging impression, that in Carter's eyes Israel could do no right, was reinforced years later when I watched Carter castigate Israel for putting obstacles in the way of Arab voting procedures in the newly independent Palestinian territories.

Yet more than any other American president I can think of, even including Clinton at Wye River, Carter exhibited an immense moral will and passion for success. Without his journeys to Tel Aviv and Cairo after the American meetings, there would have been no peace. As he put it to me, "It didn't need much courage to go to Camp David. It was much more dangerous for me to risk the prestige of the White House and go on the Middle East mission." Well, he went, and he succeeded.

Camp David provided a framework for a peace agreement, not the agreement itself. That came later, calling for staged withdrawals from Sinai, abandonment of the bases, and a withdrawal from the Israeli settlements in northern Sinai. Again the historical document is not sufficient, and you need the photos, the movie camera, and the sound to understand history.

Sinai departure. It is shot from the air. Dozen upon dozens of lorries are moving east, their lines making long snakes through the desert. The band is playing. The Israeli flag comes down, is folded, and a white-uniformed girl soldier hands it to her officer. The green flag ascends as the Egyptian anthem is played. All is bathed in that golden afternoon light so beloved by Hollywood. The scene is not so romantic or nostalgic in Yamit, one of the Israeli settlements in northern Sinai that had to be abandoned in its entirety. Here the settlers battle with young Israeli soldiers. The clustered settlers stand on the flat, whitewashed roofs of the town in a last defiance. They are not leaving. In desperation the soldiers place scaling ladders against the houses and spray the settlers with dense clouds of fire-fighting foam. One by one the settlers are hauled off, two or three soldiers to each struggling settler. As they are carried by the cameras, they twist and curse. "Israel is being abandoned. The state is being destroyed." They are sentences that will now echo through the eighties and nineties.

I wandered into the Lebanese War by accident. In May 1982 I had been asked by a group in San Francisco to do a film for them on Project Renewal. This meant following a San Francisco group to Israel and then filming them in various centers, including Haifa and Kiryat Shmoneh, the latter being their adopted project city. We finished filming in Haifa late, about eight thirty in the evening and then bundled the gear into the cars and headed for Kiryat Shmoneh, about two hours' drive away. Suddenly, heading north, I found the roads blocked by endless columns of tanks, jeeps, lorries, and military police pushing everyone brusquely off the road. Again the radio gave the answer: troops were heading into Lebanon to deal with the PLO terrorist threat.

The attack didn't come out of the blue. I should have been warned but hadn't paid attention. There had been rocket attacks on northern Israeli towns earlier in the year, but for months there had been quiet on the northern borders. This was the result of a cease-fire negotiated by the Americans. But unknown to us, and unknown to most Israelis, Defense Minister Ariel Sharon believed he could clean up Lebanon. His belief was that Israeli forces could move into Lebanon, join up with the Christian Phalange forces, wipe out the PLO, and put in place a Christian government friendly to Israel. But all this needed was a pretext for attack. The excuse came when Shlomo Argov, Israel's ambassador to Britain, was shot by Arab terrorists in London. According to Sharon, if the terrorists wanted war, they could have it. And so the Israeli troops crossed into Lebanon.

Driving along the crowded northern roads, I felt extremely uneasy. It wasn't fear—how could you be afraid with so many visible signs of Israeli strength around—rather a queasiness as to what it was all about. A few years earlier Israel had pushed into Lebanon on the Litani raid, and that had definitely not been one of the most glorious moments in Israel's history. Was this going to be a repeat? Who knew.

When we reached Kiryat Shmoneh, only a few miles from the northern border, the hotel was packed with journalists and army officers. This was it. The big push. This is where the PLO would get some of its own medicine. But what were the objectives I inquired. Destruction of the PLO and its equipment were the vague answers.

Nothing was clearer the following day. In previous years Kiryat Shmoneh had suffered from countless Katusha attacks, and I had been up there more than once filming the damage and interviewing adults and kids about their experiences. I had also been up there to film the aftermath of a terrorist attack that had left seven people dead in a small apartment. So the reaction of the residents was predictable. As far as I could tell, they were totally behind this new army action. Everywhere they swarmed over the soldiers. Kisses. Hugs. Fruit. Food. Drinks. Here—you want it? Take it. It's yours.

After filming the tanks rumbling through the city and the soldiers queuing up to phone home, I headed for the northern outskirts. Here, slightly outside the city's perimeters, I found a number of huge, yellow, stubbly fields buzzing with activity. Hundreds of tanks were regrouping. Half tracks were set out in rows. Artillery cannons were being attached to tow trucks. And everywhere orders and yelling. Meanwhile, cobra helicopters and gun ships swooped overhead occasionally accompanied by larger transport helicopters.

Filmwise, I was in a dilemma. While my instincts were to go farther north and follow the fighting (though what fighting, where, and against whom were all unknown quantities), my responsibility was to film the San Francisco group. For once reason won over emotion, and I spent the day filming the not unconsiderable San Francisco contribution to the welfare of Kiryat Shmoneh. That, of course, was in between attending to the fears and the passions of the group. While half were frightened out of their wits about being caught in a war, the other half were having the time of their life, taking everything in and writing postcards and letters at every opportunity. In the end they all wanted to know what was happening. The answer was supplied on the evening news. According to government sources, Israel intended going a mere forty kilometers into Lebanon to destroy PLO weapons and bases. When that was done Israel would withdraw. No word then of Sharon's grand designs. All that would come later.

I returned to Jerusalem slightly euphoric, very up, and very much of the opinion of "Great! Let's give 'em hell." To my surprise most of my friends thought I was mad. In particular I remember sitting in the kitchen with Giora's wife, Michal, and two university friends Tirza and Shimon Zandbank, all of whom disparaged me for being naive, stupid, blind, and a political moron. None of them trusted the government's pronouncements. Speaking with tremendous sadness rather than anger all thought the government was lying, and that what was happening was catastrophic. All of them cursed this first Israeli initiated war as blind folly, and all predicted massive disasters.

They were totally right. And this was only the beginning. Sitting in the kitchen we couldn't yet envisage the flight of the Lebanese refugees, the attacks on Beirut, and the movement of the army officers against the war. We couldn't imagine the deceptions of Sharon, the hostility of the Lebanese, the length and futility of the war, the fury of the world, and the massive protest rallies in Tel Aviv. We could not dream that Begin would finish up broken and isolated, nor could we foresee the horror of Sabra and Shatilla. All this was to come.

Like many, I only grew up and came of age during the Lebanese War. It changed my vision of Israel. It didn't stop me believing in the place, but it cautioned the vision, sullied the dream, and brought a new and necessarily more realistic view of the country.

As the war continued, I found myself doing considerable filming for the UJA. Wisely they decided to stress the human cost of the war rather than its dubious politics. This meant that instead of filming the battles, I spent most of my time in the hospitals, among the crippled and the wounded. And it was the hardest filming I had ever done. What can you say to a beautiful boy of eighteen who sits in front of you totally crippled from a bullet in the back and yet still smiling. What do you say to a young doctor in Haifa's Rambam Hospital who has just had his leg amputated but tells you he will be out and about soon. And what do you say to the young American mother of six whose son was burned alive in a tank and who only has his tank insignia as a memory. In the best of circumstances, you say nothing. You can only listen. But what do you say when you believe inside you that it was all for nothing, all pointless, all to no end?

The Lebanese War, the war for "Peace in the Galil" as the government called it, stayed with us in one way or another for two years. It stayed with us in the headlines, and it stayed with us in the growing demonstrations outside the prime minister's house. But chiefly it stayed with us on the television as night after night we heard of another soldier killed in south Lebanon and watched yet another coffin draped with the blue and white Israeli flag being lowered into the ground while fathers collapsed in shock. Night after night the television showed the intimate family photos of the fallen. Here an eighteen-year-old bruised smiler. There an unshaven golden boy. Night after night we heard the names, the ranks, and the hometown. And night after night I blessed the fact that my elder son, Gil, just seventeen at the time, had not yet been called up.

But finally came the announcement. Israel was leaving Lebanon, and for the first time we saw the soldiers returning. They returned in the rain, against black skies, their lorries churning up the Lebanese mud, the rain pouring off their groundsheets, their faces soaked. But no one cared. They were returning. We could live again.

Soon after the Lebanese War, I went to Australia to teach at their national film school. This was great fun. I found the Aussies energetic, immensely likable, and totally open in a very un-British way. I liked their Hunter Valley wines, their forthright women, their beaches, and their parks. I found one or two great authors, such as David Malouf and Thomas Keneally. And, as they say, I learned to talk strine. I also learned how negatively Israel was regarded in the media, in the press, and by the universities. This wasn't totally new to me as the signs had been on the wall for years.

There had been, as I mentioned, the columns by Michael Adams and the *Tribune* after the Six-Day War. There had been the UN's vote equating Israel with racism, and there had been the UN Womens' Conference in Mexico that had again called Israel a racist state. In the seventies, in fact, I had noted how laying into Israel had become a national sport, but I never expected it in Australia. Maybe the reason was that the first time I had visited Australia I had arrived on 4 July 1976. That was the day Israel had freed the hostages at Entebbe, and the Aussie papers had carried headlines such as "Lechaim to Israel" (Long Live Israel). But by 1983 that had all changed. Thus walking down Flinders Street in Melbourne in July, I was faced by a horde of placards calling on fascist Israel to get out of Lebanon. Before giving a lecture at McQuarie University, I had to walk through corridor after corridor full of Arafat and PLO posters promising a democratic, secular state if only the world would get rid of the Israelis. The final straw came for me when, after a short talk on American documentary film at Melbourne University, I went to have supper with some lecturers and their wives. Unsure of my background they were fairly delicate with their questions, till one wife asked me brightly, "Isn't it difficult for you working in that fascist, racist country Israel?" I suppose in her eyes I was an Englishman, temporarily working in that strange Middle Eastern country run by strange people of Mosaic persuasion. As lightly as I could, I asked her whether she believed in women's rights, the vote, freedom of religion, and like matters. When she answered affirmatively, I asked her to tell me where these things existed in the Middle East outside of Israel.

When I talked to a friend about this encounter a few days later, he told me not to worry. The woman's attitude came from a desire to side with the underdog. In a country as happy and content as Australia, it was necessary to weep for some dire cause. At first it had been Vietnam. Later it would be East Timor. And now the flavor of the day was the Palestinian Arabs. In a sense, I could understand all this, and caring for something seemed to be highly commendable. But the sheer ignorance of what was really happening in Israel, and the distorted perspective of her and the students disgusted me. "Ah," said my friend. "Blame the media."

I think the pursuit of the Lebanese War was one of the greatest and most tragic mistakes ever perpetrated by Israel. The damage done and the suffering caused were and are, in my mind, unforgivable. But having said that let me also say that the overall media coverage of the war was one of the most biased and slanted pieces of sustained reporting I have ever come across.

First there was the ignorance of so many reporters. Time after time I would see TV reports of damage done by Israeli shells, clearly shot among ruins obviously dating back to the earlier civil war. Again, the flight of the refugees was heartbreaking, but to see their numbers exaggerated beyond credibility didn't help anyone's cause. In the television reports, Israeli shells were always landing in hospitals and schools. The fact that many of these places were also being used as PLO dumps for storing weapons was rarely mentioned.

There was the lying. When I had coffee with one Israeli cameraman in Jerusalem, he told me of the British correspondent whom he had filmed doing a stand-up outside a Lebanese hospital. The numbers of dead and wounded within being too few to make a good story, the number of casualties had been increased by the journalist so as to heighten the drama and the emotions. In a local editing room, I was around when a U.S. reporter was cutting his story on the bombing in Beirut. His words for every shot on camera were always the same: "Around me the bombing is increasing." Unfortunately, the quietness of the pictures didn't back up the story. On the fifth take a shell illuminated the background, and he had his story.

As part of his academic work, a colleague of mine at the Hebrew University's Department of Communications, Yitzhak Roeh, wrote several papers analyzing the language used by various U.S. TV correspondents, such as Peter Jennings. Invariably, the language was out of all proportion to the scale of the military actions; the bombings, for example, being compared to the horrors of Dresden and Hamburg. Not content with an exaggerated verbal description, the commentary would invariably be linked to some higher moral condemnation.

For me, the ultimate example of media manipulation came in the form of a BBC film on the Sabra and Shatilla massacre. Till the present day the massacre remains a stain on the Israeli conscience, being an event we might possibly have prevented or whose horrors we might possibly have lessened. Yet when all is said and done, the massacre was perpetrated by Phalangist troops on PLO members, many of whom had previously killed and brutalized the Christians. That is said merely to get the facts straight. Yet in the film the Israelis are the only villains, and to get this view out, the film is manipulated in every which way and becomes a role model in the use of propaganda techniques.

Ostensibly, the side of the Phalangists is given, explaining how they have suffered under the PLO. However, the Phalangist being interviewed is only shown in profiled silhouette, all human presence and believability thus being eliminated. By contrast. we see the very human faces of the women and children who will later be among the dead. Few PLO men are seen, the impression thus being conveyed that this was merely an attack of soldiers on women and children and not on opposing fighters as well. Young Israeli soldiers are seen in sympathetic close-up, regretting the action, the compassionate photography endearing them to the viewer. By contrast, the Israeli officer who is called upon to explain Israel's actions is shot distantly across the expanse of a plastic table. Everything about the framing of the scene dehumanizes him and makes us antagonistic to his point of view.

Occasionally while I was lecturing to UJA and Hadassah groups after the Lebanese War, three questions would always come up, no matter what the composition of the audience: Why does the media pitch into Israel in such a joyful way? Why can't the Israelis provide a better media response? And why are Jewish correspondents often so anti-Semitic? The first I answered echoing my comments on the aftermath of the Six-Day War. To see a country that has always talked about morality behaving badly is a wonderful story. Dog bites man is dull. Man bites dog is great! Israel behaving badly was man bites dog.

Why doesn't Israel provide a better media response? The key answer is that you can try all sorts of ways of disguising the truth, but eventually the truth will out. In the eighties we Israelis often behaved abominably, and that was a fact that could not and should not have been disguised. But there is a slight gloss on this. The networks and the TV news stations strictly control their own programs. Rarely do they accept the work of external producers in the news area. To do this, they say, would be to give up their independent status. Thus even if Israel or Israeli supporters had provided incredible pro-Israeli programs—or shall we merely say more-balanced reports?—there is no way these programs could have appeared on the major U.S. and British TV outlets.

Finally, why are Jewish correspondents so often anti-Semitic? Why does Thomas Friedman have to blast Israel? And why does Mike Wallace have to become a Syrian apologist? Well, first, I don't accept the thesis. Most of the Jewish international paper and TV correspondents that I know seem to do a great job. To accuse them of anti-Semitism is a great slur. Where the problem comes, if there is a problem, is that sometimes in their determination to be fair and objective, and not swayed by their Jewish ties, they give no benefit of the doubt to the Israelis, and perhaps unconsciously bend over backward in the other direction. At least that's how it seems to me in regard to the coverage of the Lebanese War.

However, in retrospect, one is almost tempted to say that the foreign coverage of the Lebanese War was almost a joyride. We thought it was bad, but by 1988 the foreign media had moved to such a confrontational stance as to make the coverage of the Lebanese War look like a paean of praise. The reason was summed up in two words: the Intifada.

The Intifada, or "the uprising" as it is known in English, was a spontaneous expression of rage by Arab youth against the Israeli occupation of the West Bank and Gaza. Its history is known, and I don't intend to go into it here. What is important is that it was a media battle that the Israelis never had a hope of winning and to the end never realized why. I think the answer lies in the way the media frames certain agendas. Till 1967 and maybe till 1973, the best media story was always framed as little Israel against twenty-two Arab nations. Hence the overwhelming sympathy for Israel's action in 1967. During the seventies, without Israelis paying close attention, the media agenda changed. The story was now Israel against the Palestinians or the PLO. Put this way, Israel's case was not quite so hot. When the Intifada burst forth in Gaza in 1987, the terms of the story changed once more, this time in the most drastic way possible. Now it was no longer even Israel against the PLO, but Israel against the Children. And this was one battle Israel hadn't a chance of winning. And the fact that the government totally misunderstood the nature of the change made things even worse.

Whichever way you look at it, it was a difficult story to tell in any way favorable to Israel. It was a story shot in searing white light among the depressing slums and refugee camps of Gaza and the poorest villages of the West Bank. It was a story that pitted the faceless uniformed armed Israeli, looking like Darth Vader, against pitiful undernourished children and weeping women. And it was a tale that placed small stones against rubber bullets, truncheons, and tear gas. It was an episode that at first the Israelis played down and then foolishly answered with Yitzhak Rabin's stupid policy of "breaking bones."

The most famous shot of the Intifada is exactly that. Taken by an Israeli cameraman using a telephoto lens, it shows four or five Israeli soldiers mercilessly pummeling a defenseless Arab. It is a ghastly shot and makes you turn away your face in horror and in disgust at what we, the people of the book, the proclaimed seekers after righteousness, have become. When Rabin said, "Break their bones," the soldiers did exactly that, and the shots from various Arab hospitals testified as to how well the commands were carried out . . . by some.

It is not a period we Israelis look back upon with joy. There are too many stories we have heard from our friends of breaking into Arab houses at midnight and facing frightened children as commands are given to hunt for weapons, too many stories of wanton destruction, brutality, and needless rage. Is there another side? One day, driving out of Jerusalem, I picked up a paratrooper, a strange man, angry, sullen, bitter. I asked him why. He had just come out of prison. He had been one of the soldiers filmed beating the Arab and had been traced, sentenced, and put in jail. I didn't need to ask him why he had resorted to blows. This just flowed out with everything else in a passion of resentment. Before the beating of the Arab, he had been in a confrontation. Young kids had thrown potatoes embedded with razor blades. One had severely gashed his commander. Another had almost blinded his friend. Seeing the Arab his rage had just overflowed.

In Jerusalem the mood became more and more depressed as day after day the same images graced the scene. Eventually, no matter what the day, all the programs merged into one. There were always the burning tires—then the soldiers framed low in the pictures, backs to the cameras firing tear gas or rubber bullets. In the distance the kids would be throwing stones, arming catapults, or fleeing. The soldiers would jump into jeeps, and the scene would end inevitably with a small boy giving the victory sign. Occasionally there would be variations. For the foreign media there would be the scenes in the Arab hospitals, showing the wounded and the broken—scenes rarely shown on Israeli TV. And at least once a week there would be the pathetic scene of Israeli soldiers trying to take down a red, green, and black Palestinian flag from a telegraph pole or erase an Intifada slogan written on someone's shutter or house.

For the most part, I watched all this from a distance, furious at the lack of any clear government policy, and saddened by the wretched plight of the Palestinians and the moral burdens put on our soldiers by the government. Then, out of the blue, I was asked by an old producer friend of mine, Arnie Labaton, to do some filming of the Intifada for WNET New York. Evidently WNET had painted themselves into a corner, and it was thought my filming might alleviate a touchy public relations problem.

The problem was simple. An independent woman producer, Joann Franklyn Trout, had done a very long film about the Intifada titled *Days of Rage*. PBS, the Public Television System, wanted to screen the film on its network but needed a presentation station. Unfortunately, because of its seemingly overwhelmingly anti-Israel bias, few stations wanted to take it. It was at that point, with what it possibly perceived as profound courage and screen-and-be-damned wisdom, WNET decided to accept the task of presentation. Applaudable as the decision might have been, it was also not the wisest decision for a station whose main viewers and supporters were Jewish. Hence the solution: produce a couple of reports that could be shown with *Days of Rage* that would soften the impact of Franklyn Trout's battering ram.

Actually, I thoroughly approved of Trout's idea of giving the Arabs a forum to express their grievances and wondered what all the fuss was about. Then I saw the film, and the penny dropped. It seemed to me pretty good as propaganda but savagely biased and wildly distorted as an investigative documentary. It failed to identify extreme points of view, seemed to distort some interviews, gave you no sense of majority opinion, was wildly sentimental in its use of women and children, had little sense of history, used the cheapest of editing tricks, and played the whole time with clichés and stereotypes. Worst of all, the producer herself would catch an Arab comment and then underline it and enlarge it in the most exaggerated way. Looking at the film more positively, Trout exhibited a certain flair for the latest silk fashions for desert wear; also in its favor, it was so devastatingly boring it was clearly a wonderful cure for insomnia.

It seemed pointless to go through Trout's film highlighting the mistakes and gross distortions. Instead, with WNET's backing and at Arnie Labaton's suggestion, I decided to do two short films, which could be used as bookends before and after *Days of Rage*. Together we decided that the first film would be about Israeli security.

This was fairly easy to do and was put together in less than two weeks. Basically, it was a look at how Israelis regarded their position and tried to explain their overwhelming paranoias and fears. Even today these things are difficult for an American or any foreigner to understand. Tell an American that Israel is tiny, can fit into New York State, and has less than six million people, and he will nod wisely and not comprehend a thing. Tell a New Yorker that the equivalent situation for her of deadly Katushas coming in from Lebanon would be someone firing rockets from Statten Island into Manhattan, and suddenly all is clear. For an American, the battle is either won or lost, and if lost he can always fight another day. Tell the same thing to an Israeli, and he will tell you there is no other day, lose the battle and the State ceases to exist.

These and other things, such as the nail-biting background to the Six-Day War, I tried to explain in the short time at my disposal in my first film. I showed the recent terrorist attack on a Jerusalem-bound bus, which was pushed off the road into a ravine, with great loss of life. I showed pictures of terrorist attacks on cars and interviewed terrorist victims in hospitals. These were hard pictures, but they were the scenes that Israelis saw and experienced every day. And the foreigner had to appreciate that. But above all I wanted the foreign viewer to understand the Israelis' view of history, the trauma of the Holocaust, the memory of Eichmann, the fear of rising Islamic fundamentalism, and the constant sense of threat because these were the things that, etched into the subconscious, motivated and still motivate Israel's actions.

The second film was much harder. Here we were dealing with the subject of human rights and had to make some sort of case for Israel's harsh responses to the Intifada. In a sense it was an impossible task, and we all knew that. Nevertheless, I thought certain things were worth saying that might provide a slightly different perspective on things. For example, I thought we should show that the voice of criticism was as strong in Israel as abroad. So I started the film with a number of Israelis expressing their very strong doubts about the official response to the Intifada. The important thing for me was to show that the sense of outrage and questioning began at home and that Israelis didn't need foreigners to preach to them about morality.

Second, I wanted to show that there was such a thing as the rule of law in Israel and that where a case could be made, perpetrators of brutality stood accused of their crimes. Thus I dug out archives of the recent trial involving members of the crack Givati unit, where four soldiers had been accused and sentenced for using excessive force. I also recounted that over two hundred men had been brought up for disciplinary trials before their unit commanders and two full colonels dishonorably discharged from the army because of their actions.

It also seemed to me important to show what in practice the soldiers were facing. The papers and broadcasts talked of small stones. Looking carefully through the archives I found plentiful pictures of axes, knives, small homemade bombs, and jagged glass being used. Ah, but you say, knives and axes against rubber bullets, you must be kidding me. What sort of a counterthreat is that? The answer is that in a narrow, dark, winding casbah all these things take on a menace and can kill.

The problem with the second film was also one of time. I wanted, in fact desperately needed, to get the voices and reactions of some young Israeli soldiers and show the problems they faced on patrol. To do this—to get permission to film a unit on patrol—I had to go through the office of the *dover zahal* (the army spokesman). Unfortunately, time was certainly not of the essence for them. Yes, they would get back in due time to say when I could go out with a unit. When would that be? Well, maybe in two or three weeks' time. But the film has to go out next week. Really? Well we'll see what we can do.

Permission was finally given two days before I left for the States, and we followed a unit round the Hebron casbah. Here we stopped to look at papers. There necks were craned to see that no building blocks were dropped from the roof. Luckily it was a quiet day. There were no confrontations, no episodes, no incidents. And on the positive side there was time to talk and to see the soldiers as individuals, not just faceless occupiers. All hated the job. All had tried to show restraint in the past, and I believed them. According to the lieutenant the good soldier was the one who waited, who held himself back, who remembered that the people he faced were ordinary family people. Was I being sold a bill of goods? Were these simplistic words for a simpleton director? I don't think so. The words tallied too much with everything I had been hearing from my friends, my students, and all the young people I knew.

To end the film, I tried to get an interview with Brigadier General Amnon Straschnov, advocate general of the defense forces, that is, head of the army's legal division. This again went through immense delays at the army spokesman's office. Eventually, permission was given, and full of questions I turned up early one morning in Straschnov's modest office in Tel Aviv's main army headquarters. Straschnov, a darkly handsome man in his early forties, heard all the questions patiently. Then one by one he took me through the dilemmas I had raised, giving me chapter and verse about army rules and numbers of men and officers put on trial for infringing basic human rights. Again it is the impression of the man rather than the answers that stay in the memory. If my judgment meant anything, I was facing an honest man, for whom the question of human rights and human dignity mattered as much as to any foreign journalist— mattered more so. For the journalist, and maybe I am being cynical here, these Intifada questions and stories were matters that sold papers and raised audience levels. For Straschnov, and others like him, these things raised grave moral dilemmas that unless answered in the correct way would affect the very fiber and personality of the state they loved.

I spent an hour with Straschnov and eventually used one of his answers to end the film. I used it because it seemed to me to totally sum up the situation:

> The problem is the clash between the needs of security and the civil liberties and the necessity to safeguard the human rights of the local inhabitants. Human rights are a very important thing and should be very carefully observed, but as Justice Jackson of the Supreme Court of the United States once said, "the Bill of Rights should not be a suicide pact." Again one of our liberal justices of the Supreme Court of Israel also said, "Human Rights should not be a device for self-destruction, and democracy should not commit suicide in order to prove its vitality."

So the films were made, put out, and made their points. Did they have any effect? As usual, no one knows. Thankfully for me that would be the end of filming "the enemy wars" for a long time. But life is never simple. Next time I would be filming clashes, it wouldn't be soldier against child but Jew against Jew.

8 - Of Heroes and Treasures

Sometime beginning in the late eighties, I realized I was in danger of doing heavy political, Zionist, and historical films and nothing else. Suddenly I felt an urge for something different, a few lighter, funnier, and more quirky films. As if in answer to a maiden's prayer, three films of this type came along one after the other. The first, *Special Counsel*, dealt with a lawyer. The second, *Waves of Freedom*, dealt with sailors. And the third took me on a treasure hunt.

Special Counsel starts with the signing of the Israeli-Egyptian peace treaty. After introducing the major participants, the commentary proclaims dramatically, "But there was one unknown player in that story who helped bring about that incredible breakthrough—Leon Charney!"

The camera then cuts to President Jimmy Carter at a book-signing ceremony in Atlanta. By his side stands a dark-haired, smiling man in his late forties. After a few words, Carter turns to the man, and with his widest Jimmy Carter grin says,

> In regard to the peace process, Leon Charney and Bob Lipschutz had areas of friendship and confidentiality and connections in the Middle East, which someone in an official capacity such as myself, or Secretary of State Vance, or Brezhinsky could not have had. And they channeled to me information and messages that ultimately proved to be very significant. Leon is the kind of person who really understands the complexity of international politics.

What Carter did not say of the other man at the podium, whose book he was celebrating, was that Leon was fascinating, extremely likable, and—at least in my eyes—more than a little crazy, a trait that very much endeared him to me.

I was asked to make a film about Charney by Arnon Zuckerman, the chairman of Tel Aviv University's film department. When I said, "Leon who?" Arnon looked at me in disgust. "Everyone knows Leon. How could you not know Leon? He's better known than the pope." When I still pleaded ignorance, Arnon gave me Charney's book to read and sent me off to meet the great man himself in New York.

Now, doing a film biography of someone of note is one of the great challenges of filmmaking. And usually the stranger the person, the better. It is the old story, that tales of sinners work better than tales of saints, and the weird is much more interesting than the ordinary. So, give me a choice between the pious and the peculiar, and I will always take the peculiar, and this was definitely the category that suited Leon. At least, so I thought on our first meeting.

This initial contact was arranged by John Bernstein, a young screen writer and Tel Aviv University teacher, whom I arranged to meet in the Lexington Hotel on Manhattan's East Side. John, who looks like a dead ringer for Tony Perkins in *Psycho* was a little diffident about Charney. As we drank scotches in the Lexington's bar, jostled on all sides by scurrying El Al crews and teeming Asian hordes of businessmen, John told me I would like Charney. "He's different. He's fresh. He's bright. And he's an extrovert." What John might have added was that Charney was an extremely engaging and warm madman.

We met at one of those New York restaurants where, if you breathe, you already owe them fifty dollars. But I wasn't worrying, because Leon was playing host and taking care of the bill. At the time, in deference to the surroundings, he was wearing a suit, though I chiefly remember him in a dark blue polo neck, or an opennecked, short-sleeved Izard shirt. The first impression was of warmth, openness, and an engaging smile. He didn't drink but made sure the rest of us in his party of eight were adequately supplied. After doing this he got down to business.

"OK, Al. I hear you've won a few prizes: Emmy, Peabody, Pulitzer. Great! Well, what do you think? Can we win an Oscar on this one?

Mind you, there's a problem. Where could we put it? John, where do they normally put the Oscars? I don't want to be like those *putzes* [idiots or pricks] who put them in the kitchen. Maybe we could place it on an elegant stand in the living room. What do you say?"

After we all agreed that a stand for the Oscar for this unmade film should be created from mahogany or teak, I started asking Leon about his past. I wanted to get to know the man. After all, we'd be working in harness for about four months at least. In the biography Leon had mentioned paying his way through college by acting as a synagogue cantor on the High Holy days.

"Er . . . Mr. Charney . . ." In the beginning I am always very deferential. "Er, Mr. Charney, in your book it says you sing, that you have a wonderful tenor voice, that your singing helped support your family. Is that true? And do you still sing?"

"Do I sing . . . ?" Taking that as cue Leon pushed back his chair and broke into a magnificent rendering of Sulzer's "Keddusha," followed by the stunning opening section of Lewandowski's "Halleluja," where the notes go through the roof. Pavarotti would have been proud. Placido Domingo would have been envious. And Beniamino Gigli was probably applauding from the grave. Meanwhile, I and the rest of the room, which consisted of blue-rinsed millionaires' wives, pin-striped suited bankers, and upwardly mobile starlets, started applauding. The waiters looked stunned, but the manager smiled. What did he care? He knew that Leon was richer than anyone present and if he wanted could probably buy the whole restaurant.

The following day I met Leon downtown in his opulent Wall Street office, which boasted a stunning view of the Hudson River and the Statue of Liberty. Around the walls were pictures of Leon with every Israeli and American of note you've ever heard of. Impressive!

I wanted a private talk so that he could tell me more about himself and so that we could explore where we were going with the film. But Leon was in no hurry. Feet up on his desk, he was castigating some unknown Israeli politician. "Listen Mr. X. You've got to tell the ambassador to get off his bottom. We've got to do things. Move. Act. Now. Tell those pen pushers and sycophants to get with it. If not, fuck 'em. We'll show them how it's done."

We didn't accomplish much that morning, but I knew one thing. We were in for a merry ride, maybe even an enjoyable one. Leon might well be, as one of his friends, Don Tanselle, told me, bizarre, off beat, and strange. But that was all to the good. That made for great television. And of three things I was sure: Leon had charisma, took shit from nobody, and had a great sense of humor. I was sure we were going to get on fine.

What interested me in Leon's book, and obviously interested Tel Aviv University, was what it had to say about the nature of political negotiations and the Israel-Egypt peace process. Leon's thesis was that very often ideas cannot be publicly expressed because of the known opposing positions of the two camps. Sometimes these negotiations need to be discreet, hidden, and tentative. And sometimes a facilitator is necessary who can secretly carry ideas between the camps and who, because of his position of trust can also add his own observations and suggestions in providing solutions. What Leon maintained was that during the Camp David meetings, which dealt with the Egyptian-Israeli peace process, and in the difficult months that followed, he and his lawyer friend Bob Lipschutz provided a secret channel of discussion between Israel and the U.S.A. Via this channel, ideas were broached that could simply not be stated in the open.

It was a strange idea, at least in regard to the peace negotiations, and I had never ever heard of Charney's name mentioned in any discussion on the subject. Here was an unknown man playing a very mysterious role in history. But who was he and how did this situation come about? The basic facts were in Charney's book, but the reality was much more interesting.

Charney came from an immigrant Jewish family, had studied law in New York, and on graduation started to specialize in show business. Here he quickly managed to snare some of the more interesting clients around, including the boxer Joe Louis and comedian Jackie Mason. Sammy Davis Jr. was also one of his clients and was brought to Israel on a quick visit by Charney, who tells the story this way. "When we arrived, Sammy hugged me. 'Boy, oh boy. It feels so good to be in the motherland,' he said, kissing the Kotel [Western Wall of Herod's temple; most sacred of Jewish sites]. 'Sammy,' I said, 'You're not in Nigeria.' 'Leon, Leon, I've converted. This is my homeland.'"

In one of the photos in Leon's album there indeed is the tiny

Sammy, his arms around two soldiers and smiling for all he's worth. Maybe he did see it as his homeland.

From show business, Charney moved into real estate, developing land in both Suffolk County and Manhattan, quickly becoming a multimillionaire. As Manhattan's *Metropolitan* magazine said in one of its articles, "His rise was meteoric even by Manhattan standards." Charney is seen on the cover of the same magazine and certainly looks happy. His chubby face glows, the brown hair is swept back, and he seems not to have a care in the world.

Besides advising American banks, such as the Merchant National Bank of Indiana, Charney also started making forays into the Jewish world. General Motti Hod came to him for advice on making a film about the air force. Yitzhak Rabin came to him for help regarding publishing his memoirs in the States. Bar-Lev included him among his close friends. And Ezer Weizman met him in a bar. "I invited him for a drink, but Leon doesn't drink. But as I got to know him I realized Leon was a very shrewd and wise man." It was this connection that was to open the way to the secret negotiations of later years.

The other man mentioned by Weizman, and also by Carter in his recollections of those behind-the-scenes dealings, is Robert Lipschutz. Lipschutz was an Atlanta lawyer who had helped Carter campaign for president. On gaining office, Carter appointed Lipschutz his presidential counsel. Charney was introduced to Lipschutz by Wolf Blitzer, then the *Jerusalem Post*'s representative in Washington. Both men hit it off very fast. Unwittingly, an alliance was formed that would have important repercussions later. Charney would have the ear of Weizman, Begin, Rabin, and others. Lipschutz would have the ear of Carter. In combination, Charney and Lipschutz could provide a secret conduit that could move information in either direction. Eventually, their friendship would be known throughout Washington and the duo referred to affectionately as "the Odd Couple."

Some of this background was already there in Charney's book, but a lot more was supplied to me when I visited Lipschutz in Atlanta. Lipschutz is a very sweet and open man, totally lacking that hardness and brutality that the media has taught us to associate with presidential personnel.

At first, he told me, his conversations with Leon had just been friendly and exploratory. Then, one day, Leon had flown to Washington relaying news from a secret Sadat confidant, that Sadat was willing to talk to the Israelis. The information also laid out the basic terms. This information had then been passed on to Carter, confirming other rumors of the talks between Dayan and Tuhomi. Gradually it became clear that a major channel of information was opening up between Charney and Lipschutz that might be of major importance.

Lipschutz gave me access to all his files, and for a day I went through them, sifting memoranda and letters on all manner of subjects. The impression I came away with was that Charney and Lipschutz had helped, or maintain they had helped, at three critical political turning points. They had been among the first to give a hint of Sadat's peace intentions. Second, and maybe much more important, they had acted as an informal link between the Israelis and Americans during the Camp David process. This was done with calls coming from the Israelis at Camp David to Charney in Washington and going back from Lipschutz to Carter at Camp David. Third, both had been of major assistance to the two sides when President Carter had visited Israel after Camp David, and the whole peace process had been in imminent danger of collapse.

After my meetings with Lipschutz, I went to Indiana to meet with Senator Vance Hartke, who was also mentioned in Leon's book. Charney had been a special adviser on Israel to Hartke in the early seventies, and I thought the bluff senator might shed some more light on Leon. Seated under enough flags to equip the whole of the United Nations, the senator filled me in on other odd bits of the story. First, he and Leon had worked very hard in the seventies to free Russian Jews, with Leon traveling to Russia to pressure the Soviets into granting exit visas. Second, at their joint initiative, Leon had gone to the Middle East at the start of the Yom Kippur War to see if the Russians were re-equipping the Egyptians. This information was then relayed to Hartke, who in turn started pressuring the Senate to re-supply Israel. What was emerging was that even prior to Camp David, Charney was willing to push in all directions to help Israel and to help Jews in distress.

After a few weeks in the States and copious interviews in Israel, I was ready to begin the film. I thought doing it as a straight documentary would be too dry and instead opted for a docudrama or dramatic reconstruction of the Charney story. Leon asked me who would play the Charney figure in the film, maybe Gregory Peck or Paul Newman. When I told Leon I wouldn't dare think of using anyone but himself, he seemed very pleased. But then he had already played an actor at various times, most notoriously in an Israeli Western.

This I knew from talking to Weizman and also from some photos I had seen in Leon's apartment. The story was typical Charney. On one Israeli visit, Charney had been asked to advise Herzliya studios about some film contracts. While drinking coffee in the studio canteen, Leon had been spied by a German director who was about to shoot a Western in the Negev desert. Leon was evidently the answer to the German director's dreams. He was just the ideal guy, according to the director, to play the part of the Mexican bandit in the film. Was Leon interested? Interested! You bet! So for six weeks the law practice in New York was put on hold, while Leon, looking like a slightly plumper version of Marlon Brando in *Viva Zapata*, snarled, grimaced, and roared around the Mexican cantinas of the Israeli desert.

Looking at the photos from the film, I can understand why it was easy for Leon to succumb to the grueling rigors of filmmaking. There he is. The cowboy hat set at a jaunty angle. The string waistcoat unbuttoned to the waist. His dark eyes are flashing, the black hair swept over his brow. And he is smiling. And why not? Wouldn't you, if you had one arm around Anna Karina and the other around Geraldine Chaplin, and they both looked as if they totally and utterly adored you?

Taking Leon to play himself made a lot of sense. Leon was unique, a phenomenon, and it was hard to think of anyone else bringing out all Leon's *chutzpa* and bravura. Getting Hartke, Lipschutz, and a few others to play themselves also wasn't too difficult. The only one who balked was Ezer Weizman, but even he in the end agreed, albeit reluctantly, to appear. In practice, we only used two actors. One was Barry Langford, who played Karl Kahane, an Austrian Jew who was a confidant of Sadat, the other a beautiful Polish actress, Lilliana Komorovski.

The casting of Lilliana came out of a conversation with Leon in the Hilton Hotel in Tel Aviv. I had finished the script and went with the producer Arnon Zuckerman to show it to Leon and get his approval. After giving Leon the script, Arnon went for a drink, and I went for a swim, all of us agreeing to meet in an hour.

When we reassembled, both Arnon and I waited nervously for Leon's reaction.

"It's genius, sheer genius. You've captured my life, my spirit, my hard times. It's all there on paper, a work of art. Genius."

Both Arnon and I gulped. We were used to Leon's hyperbole and waited for the inevitable "but."

"But there's one thing missing."

"Yes?" I said, wanting to get the agony over and done with.

"Well," said Leon. "There's no sex in the film."

Arnon and I looked at each other warily.

"No sex? Well there was no sex in your book. But tell me, what are your girlfriends like?"

Leon thought for a while, pondering my question, while I suddenly recalled the photos of a stunning Anna Karina and a youthful Geraldine Chaplin.

"Well, they're mostly nicely endowed air hostesses."

"Fine, no problem," says the quick-witted screen writer, up to all challenges. "I'll write you in a girlfriend. How about that?" And that's how the beautiful Lilliana dropped into the film.

The film was actually great fun to do and shot in three months, mostly using a Tel Aviv University crew. It was clearly a much more expensive production than Arnon Zuckerman, the producer, had ever envisaged, yet his support was always there 100 percent.

What surprised me was how my most outrageous demands were usually met with positive reaction and enthusiasm instead of the more sane retort of "Get out of here, you must be mad." For example, one day had us whizzing around the Atlanta airport, shooting from jeeps and lorries, trying to recreate Leon's mad rush from Israel to the U.S.A. "You want more planes?" said our airport contact. "No problem. Taking off. Landing. Taxiing. Tell me what you want, and you've got it."

Another day, we got entrance to the U.S. embassy in Tel Aviv, no small feat, so that we could show Leon using their secret phones. Another evening, we closed off the whole lobby of the King David Hotel in Jerusalem so that we could show Leon sprinting from his room in order to grab a taxi and rush to see Ezer at the Hilton. And, on a further occasion, a rather bewildered Israeli banker let us film him and Leon discussing some bank scandals of the sixties.

Ezer Weizman, who was pivotal to the story, didn't quite know what to make of everything. At first he had refused to appear in the film. Then I guess he had probably said to himself, "Okay. Some more of Leon's craziness. Well, why not?" Since he had a number of recreated scenes with Leon as well as straight interviews, this was quite a concession.

Leon, of course, is the one who made the film come totally alive by giving 150 percent of himself whether before the camera or by showing a tremendous generosity to the crew. Instead of being stand-offish, which is very easy for the talent to do in these kind of films, he became a *chevraman* (one of the boys), the highest Israeli compliment possible.

What was good about Leon, and may have accounted for his success in business, was that once you turned him on there was no stopping him. If something was worth doing, then you gave it everything you had, whether this was singing, dancing, rushing to the Yom Kippur War, saving Russians, or advancing the peace process.

One scene makes me remember this aspect of Leon very vividly. In the mideighties, after the success of the peace process, Leon was given an honorary doctorate by the University of Indianapolis. I had decided to restage this ceremony, and the university president had agreed to enlist the help of the faculty and graduate students and get this all to work properly. In discussing the reenactment with me, the president mentioned that at the preparations for the original ceremony, he had heard Leon hum some Hebrew songs, realized he had a great voice, and had invited Leon to sing something from the podium after officially receiving the doctorate.

This seemed too good an incident not to use in our recreation. Leon was for the idea, and after some discussion we agreed that he would render "Oseh Shalom." This was a song about peace, absolutely appropriate to the occasion. In due course, and after we had filmed Leon getting the doctorate, I explained to the two hundred people in the audience exactly what Leon was going to do. He was going to sing a song of peace in Hebrew, which he did, very well, to be greeted by the politest and most delicate of applause. It was the kind of applause you get from old ladies in a geriatric literary society after a complex discussion on troglodytes and their influence on medieval Christian society. It was certainly not the roar of praise I needed for our film.

Then I had an idea. Leon and I used to sing pop duets in the car, in between journeying from location to location. Since we already had a master version of "Oseh Shalom" in the can, what if he sang a pop song, and we just shot the audience reaction. It couldn't be any worse than what we already had. Leon thought about that a moment and then volunteered to give it a try.

So dressed in his blue doctoral robes and his mortar board and in front of the assembled president, honorary board, and scarlet-gowned faculty and students, Leon prepared to sing. I hushed the audience, gave the cameraman the word *speed* and gestured to Leon to let go.

Maybe I should have mentioned the song was Paul Anka's "I'm Just a Lonely Boy." It is a wonderful song, to which, with arms outstretched to the heavens and with mortarboard akimbo, Leon did full justice. This time he got thunderous applause.

When the film was finished, two or three questions kept coming up again and again. Did I really believe Leon's story? Wasn't this tale of secret help all a bit farfetched? Wasn't this really a film about a puffed-up egotist and ego maniac with delusions of grandeur?

The rough answer is this. I had begun by being an amused doubter but ended up by being convinced of the essential truth of the story and by Leon's sincerity. Yitzhak Rabin had told me of Charney's immense assistance to Israel over the years, most of it unpublicized. I myself saw Leon being greeted at Ben Gurion Airport by a number of Russians he had helped. And Weizman had said to me, very directly, "People sit down opposite each other. The destiny of their country is in their hands. They often need assistance. Back alleys to transmit to each other ideas and possibilities that cannot be said directly. Leon had the attention of the president of the United States. And he certainly had my attention. And that's how he came into cooking the dish of Camp David."

Again there was the letter of Jimmy Carter I used to finish the film. Abbreviated, it reads as follows.

> Dear Leon:
> As a private U.S. citizen you have been very helpful to me in reaching the goal of peace. Thank you for your assistance in these difficult but rewarding months.

And finally, there was the small note that the president had inscribed inside the jacket of Leon's book.

> To Leon Charney . . .
> my fellow Middle East negotiator.
>   Jimmy Carter

When *Special Counsel* was finished we had a big black-tie celebration party in New York. I enjoyed the occasion, but my head was beginning to buzz with an idea for a new film. It was an idea that would need quite a lot of money, and I was wondering whether any of the well-heeled guests at the dinner might be willing to back me. They looked prosperous, but then so did I in a monkey suit, but what lay underneath? To find out, I asked one of the men at my table what he did. Before he could reply, his wife answered for him.

"Don't bother talking to him. I'm the interesting one around here. I've got a house in Australia, one in London, one in the Bahamas, and one in Canada. And we're just looking for an apartment in New York. And I'm very rich."

Ah, I thought, just what the doctor ordered. Unfortunately, she wasn't interested in film. But another lady was. This one was mid-forties, very very pretty, and what Leon would have called "healthily endowed." She was also alone. When the Bahamas lady left us to fill up her plate, my new acquaintance started drumming her fingers on the table.

"I don't know what that other woman's got to boast about. I'm much richer than her, but I don't boast about it. Now tell me. Who are you, and are you married?"

Being a good boy, I told her who I was and that I was married. Leaning over she gestured, in a very conspiratorial fashion, to come closer.

"Ah," she said. "But are you *happily* married?"

I would like to say that I finished up in her bed, and she gave me half a million dollars to make the film. Unfortunately, neither of those things happened. However, after listening to the story of the film, she gave me her thoughts on the matter. "Don't tell these people here you are making a documentary. They'll just get a fright. Tell them you want to make a highly commercial film with loads of sex and a background in Israel and then they'll cough up."

Great advice. I should have listened to her. Then maybe today I'd be rich. But however good the advice it didn't take me much further forward in financing *Waves of Freedom*.

Waves of Freedom, or *The Secret Seas* as it was first titled, was going to be about *aliya beth*, the secret struggle to bring the remnants of European Jewry to Israel between the years 1945 and 1948. Despite the tragedies of the Second World War, in 1945 the British Labor government was still severely limiting Jewish immigration to

Palestine. As a result, a secret war broke out along the shores of the Mediterranean sea between the British and the Jews of Palestine. While the British instituted an air and naval blockade of the Palestinian coast, the Haganah (the main Jewish underground defense force before 1948) was fighting this policy with every weapon at its command. And the most effective weapons were the ships.

Between 1945 and May 1948, over twenty ships sailed for Palestine. Often they were no more than small steamers, river pleasure boats, built to accommodate three to four hundred people at the most. Refurbished and rebuilt they served as transports for almost seventy thousand would-be immigrants. Most of these immigrants were survivors and had suffered incredibly in the war. Their relatives had died. Their families had disappeared. Their homes had been destroyed. For most of them Palestine represented rebirth and the hope of a new life, if only they could get to the shores of this promised land. But few of the ships made it through the blockade. Instead most of the ancient hulks were caught and their passengers, the flotsam and jetsam of Europe, interned in British camps in Cyprus.

Of all these ships, the one that most succeeded in capturing the imagination and the sympathy of the world was the *Exodus*. Caught off the shores of Palestine after a battle with British marines, the stricken *Exodus* was towed into Haifa. Later, the British foreign secretary Ernest Bevin ordered the passengers to be returned to Marseilles. When they refused to disembark at the French port, Bevin ordered the would-be immigrants to be returned to Germany, to Hamburg, to the country of their greatest suffering and pain. The Jews had not succeeded in getting to Palestine, but an immense psychological and moral victory had been won over the British. Here, possibly, was the final straw that broke the will of the British to continue the thankless task of ruling Palestine.

The story of the *Exodus* is very well known, as is the history of the "illegals." In fact, I had already twice told of those sagas in various films I'd done on Israeli history. But in *Waves of Freedom*, I thought I could do something different and provide a different slant on the past. What interested me was the fact that ten out of the twenty or so boats that ran the blockade were both *financed* by Americans and *crewed* by Americans. This seemed to me absolutely fascinating and a winner and yet a story that had never been properly told. So I would go out and do a film about the two hundred

Americans who fought and struggled for Israel's independence by sailing the waves of freedom.

My enthusiasm was dampened a little when Israel television gave me a blank refusal. "Americans—who the hell is interested in them? By the way, the door's over there." Both the BBC and British Independent Television were also supremely uninterested. Just when I was getting ready to blow my brains out, Chris Fennimore, from WQED Pittsburgh, said the idea was fascinating and interesting, and if I would put down the revolver or untie the noose around my neck, we should meet and talk. Chris liked the project and said WQED would show it if I ever raised the money. He also promised me the help of Marcie Setlow, one of the WQED staff, and wished me good luck.

Well, since it still hurts today, let me tell you immediately, I never raised the money. But I grew wise in the process. It worked, or rather didn't work, like this. In searching for development money I talked to about a dozen very rich, very influential New York Jews, introduced to me by my closest New York friend, a wonderfully bright and attractive woman writer, Bobby Cramer. It was no go. If I had been in real estate and wanted to do a film with Goldie Hawn as a young Golda Meir, I would have had them lining up to give money. But films about poor Jews, forget it. Bobby generously offered me her apartment for a fund-raising party, but still chafing over the fact that I wasn't into real estate, I said no thanks.

My second line of approach was the foundations. Having done arm muscle improvement exercises for two weeks, I picked up all the back-breaking foundation books I could find in the O'Donnell Library on West 53rd Street. After two days' work, I listed and wrote to one hundred Jewish foundations that I thought might help me. Three replied. The first told me it wasn't hiring Israelis this season. The second, the Charles Revson Foundation, was much more sympathetic. It liked the idea but had recently given a million dollars or so for the making of the series *Civilization and the Jews* and was temporarily exhausted. This I accepted, particularly as I had worked on the series myself, and it had kept me in toothpaste for a year or so. The last charitable organization, the Memorial Foundation for Jewish Culture, gave me three thousand dollars and regretted that it couldn't give more.

After this experience, I realized I should have paid heed to Jackie Mason. In one of his monologues, Mason chastises Jews for playing around with boats. "What do Jews know about boats? Nothing. Forget them. Jews in boats, impossible. Jews should stay with cooking, and with Chinese meals." Mason was right. Tell a Jewish organization you want to make a film about a hospital, a school, or an abandoned synagogue in Warsaw, and the money comes pouring out. Tell them you want to make an instructional film on baking *chalot*, how to make Sabbath candles, keep kosher or do your own circumcision, and you won't know what to do with the flood of shekels. But a film on Jewish sailors? No way!

I told all this to Marcie Setlow from WQED, who more or less agreed with my grim conclusions. According to her, I should think where the money was and do the film accordingly. "Look, the Levi Strauss company has loads of money. Why don't you do a film about the opening up of California in the nineteenth century. Everyone knows the miners all wore Levi's. We wouldn't have to say that, and the company could give us half our budget. Or we could do a film about the explorers of the Arabian deserts and get Mogul and Standard Oil to back us."

In spite of all our gloomy prognostications, Marcie tried very hard to get money for the film. Often it seemed we were almost there, but usually the promised donor or backer died, had sudden heart surgery, or ran off with someone else's wife at the last moment and needed all his money for the divorce settlement. However, one day she rang me up to say she had succeeded in getting a small grant. The donor's name was Arthur Cantor, a New York film and theater producer who years before had produced a great film about the Yiddish theater titled *The Golden Age of Second Avenue*. Later, Arthur and I became friends. Mostly we meet over great convivial dinners at Bobby Cramer's. All goes well till Arthur asks, "Nu, Alan? What happened with my money?" Blushing, I have to tell him the film was never finished, but that part of his cash paid for a splendid promotion brochure, a hundred copies of which are still in my basement.

My biggest fund-raising disappointment came when I went with Marcie to see a worthy gentleman whom I shall call "Mr X." Mr. X, now in his eighties, had been one of the owners or guarantors of a small shipping line that had bought the *President Warfield* (later renamed the *Exodus*) and had helped refurbish her in Baltimore. I was sure that with such a background Mr. X would give us fifteen thousand dollars. Well, if not fifteen thousand dollars, then at least ten thousand dollars, and with that we could do a lot of research and preliminary filming.

Marcie and I split forces. My task was to give the general background and wind up to the film. Ostensibly, all I wanted from Mr. X was some information about the part he had played in those days. When I was finished, Marcie would come in with the hardest task, making the pitch.

Mr X. had ordered in lunch, and in between mouthfuls of salt beef sandwiches, I did the warm-up, reminding him of the mood of those days, all the time stressing the adventure, the spirit, and the courage and sacrifice of the American sailors. That finished I asked him to tell me of his own participation in those dramatic times and the history of the *Exodus*. Here he started really opening up, with the memories pouring out in a constant stream.

The *Exodus*, then called the *President Warfield*, was built in 1928 as a flagship excursion liner for the Baltimore Steam Packet Company. It had a 171 staterooms, and its task was to sail up and down Chesapeake Bay carrying four hundred passengers. In 1942 she was requisitioned by the War Shipping Administration and lent to the British for use as a troop carrying ship. In June 1944 she took part in the Normandy invasion but after the war was offered for sale as scrap.

On 17 December 1946, the boat was sold to Weston Trading Company. On the surface the company, headed by Captain William Ash—a professional sailor—looked very solid and respectable. In practice, the company was a dummy purchasing front for the Haganah. Mr X's task had been to guarantee funds to the Weston Trading Company to cover the immense repairs that would be necessary before the ship could sail to Europe.

Almost two months later, on 25 February 1947, the *President Warfield* left Baltimore for the Azores. Damaged in a storm, the boat had to dock in Norfolk for repairs. Because of extensive news coverage of the near disaster, stories started leaking out telling of a strange ship with a Jewish and Palestinian crew. To top things off, the *New York Times* printed a story under the title "Palestine Bound Mystery Ship." With British and other pressures mounting to stop the sailing of the ship, Captain Ash sent a message to the *President Warfield*'s captain: "Depart as soon as possible." On Saturday, 29

March, the *President Warfield* sailed for Europe. Weeks later she would pick up seventy trucks of passengers at the small French port of Sete and head for Palestine and her confrontation with history.

After he finished his story, Mr. X turned to Marcie and myself expectantly. "Well, what can I do for you?" Now was the hard part. While Marcie explained what we were doing and how the film would tell the tremendously exciting and moving stories of people like himself and the American sailors, I continued to fantasize. Surely a man with the background of Mr. X would be truly sympathetic to our objectives. Did I say fifteen thousand dollars? Maybe he'd want to give twenty thousand dollars toward such a great project. Maybe he'd suggest we did a series.

"So there you are," finished Marcie. "Anything you can give, however small, would be of tremendous help to us to get the project off the ground."

There was silence. Mr. X tugged at his nose and then smiled.

"No, I don't think so. You see I already give to the UJA."

On my return to Israel, battered, bruised, and more than a little despondent, I was inclined to forget the whole project. Then a small notice caught my eye in the *Jerusalem Post*. It announced that in a month's time a small reunion would take place in Jerusalem of American sailors who had brought the "illegal" boats to Palestine. As part of their visit they would be invited to the president's house as the honored guests of the Chaim Herzog.

This was clearly too good an opportunity to miss. Looking into my bank account, I realized I could just about pay for two days' shooting. So, drawing on my savings, I put together a camera crew and prepared to plunge in.

The important thing to me was to get the stories. Get the stories that had never been told, that were exploding from within, that were bursting to be told. But what kind of stories would these be that would also be of interest to a general public? Well, to start with, who were these men? And what were their backgrounds? I knew that many of them had been sailors in the Second World War, but what had motivated them to leave their homes and embark on such a crazy venture? Clearly they had to tell me what happened on board the boats and what it was like in the camps. And they had to tell me what it was like when they returned to America. Finally, and I knew this would be much harder, I wondered if I could get a few of them to tell me of the effect of those years and that on their later lives.

Yes, I wanted the answers for my film, but I also wanted them for myself and my children. I wanted to know, for my own health and sanity and direction in life, where people looked for inspiration. I wanted to know what got into them and what gave their lives meaning. Maybe, I thought, one or two of the sailors would have worked these things out. It would be nice to know.

In my researches, I had seen a lot of photos from those days. The men look absurdly young and have those good, solid American names such as Larry and Bill and Sid and Sam. And sprinkled here and there is a Manny or a Lou, a Marvin and an Al. In the photos they wear shorts, lean on each other, cross arms, grin, and strike shy, questioning poses. This is how they knew each other over forty years ago. What would they be like today?

Descending from the El Al jumbo jet into the warmth of the afternoon sun, they still looked young. The smiles were still there although most of them had gray hair. Some wore jaunty sailors' caps. A few smoked pipes. Here and there a few of them sported blue and white baseball caps with the words *Exodus 47* emblazoned on the peak. All waved. For a moment I recalled the shot of the wounded and the helpless descending from the decks of the crippled *Exodus* under the guarded eyes of the British tommies. Were these men remembering that as well?

For two days I filmed without stop. These were some of the things the sailors told me.

Harold: I was in law school after the war, and I saw pictures of the people in the camps. I couldn't sit there in my ivory tower and not participate. It was my obligation as much as anyone else. I happened to be in the U.S. and hadn't suffered, but it was my obligation to help.

Dave: There was no escaping the situation. I had relatives in Palestine. I heard about the camps. I was an American sailor. There was no sense of choosing, no sense of obligation. I was chosen.

Paul: As a young man I was living in the Bronx. I'd been a sailor in the war, and now I was living at home with my mother and my sisters. One night I got a call. "Paul, Paul. You wanna help your people?" I didn't know who he was or what he was referring to. I was just a young kid from the Bronx. "If you wanna save your people come down to Lexington Avenue and Seventy-first Street tomorrow morning. You'll see a man with a black leather jacket with the *New York Times* tucked under his arm. If he throws it into the wastepaper basket, go home. We're being followed, and we'll contact you again." I thought, jeez, it must be one of my pals kidding me. So I phoned them. "Hey Al, Joe. You call me?" I wanted to see if it was true.

Anyway, the following morning I stood on that corner. It was one o'clock on a Thursday. A man comes by in a black leather jacket, and I follow him into an office. No preliminaries. "My name's Akiva Skidell, and I understand you can handle small boats. We want you to run craft to Palestine and Cyprus. If you get caught you get hung." I said, "You've got to be kidding." That night I left my sisters and my mother a note and went to Baltimore. I had a choice of the ships, the *Geula*, the *President Warfield*, and the *Trade Winds*. I went on the *Trade Winds*.

Lou: What moved me? We were loading people in the port of Burgas, in Bulgaria. The trains kept rolling out of Europe, rolling out of the night. And the tiny ship was getting heavier and heavier with people, heavier and heavier with Jews. And I had that feeling that I was at the nexus of history.

Joe and Murray sailed on the *Exodus*. Joe is English, tubby, rosy cheeks, almost a dandy. He sports a red rose in his button hole. You would cast him either as a bookie or someone's favorite uncle if you were making a feature. Murray is more serious. I had met him at the house of Eli Bergman in New York, while doing research, and was struck by his gravity and solidity. One feels with him, as with so many of the others, that going on these ships was not a prank, an adventure, but came out of a deep moral necessity. Both Joe and Murray were involved in the battles on the *Exodus*.

Joe: They asked me to climb up the mast and put up the Jewish flag. "But that's dangerous," I said. "The British are shooting." Anyway, I went up the pole. And I got shot. I got shot in the arse. I thought about it for a second and then I said to myself, "Wow. You've been shot." So I came down and told all the guys. I said, "Hey guys, I've been shot in the arse." I expected them to say, "Really? You've been shot? You are quite a hero!" Instead they said, "What? In the arse?" and started rolling around in laughter.

One laughs like Joe's mates. Then you look at one of the old stills. A flag with the Star of David—the Magen David—is flying from the mast while all around steel-helmeted British marines are clambering over the sides. Not quite so funny.

> *Murray:* A British warship had trailed us all the way from France. Close to Palestine it was joined by the cruiser *Ajax*, four destroyers, a frigate, and two mine sweepers. On board our loud speakers played the chorale from Beethoven's ninth. How did we fight? In order to resist the British we rigged wire mesh across the decks, and we sprayed the decks with oil as the Sixth Airborne Division boarded. We had no weapons, so we used cans of corned beef to throw at them. Bill Bernstein, the first mate, got clubbed on the head and died. He had graduated high school in San Francisco and attended Ohio State. One hundred and twenty others were critically wounded.

Many of the Americans, once captured were interned with the refugees in the British prison camps on Cyprus. Some like Harold Katz and Murray Greenfield started digging tunnels in order to escape. Others, like Dave, were eventually taken to Palestine and given their freedom. Because the sailors often wanted to join other rescue ships, it was essential for them to maintain their anonymity and not be repatriated to the U.S.A. This was the case with Dave.

> *Dave:* I was being released from Cyprus under a false name. When the ship got to Haifa I saw on the quay below a young British Palestine policeman whom I knew very well. We used to talk to each other in the camp, and he knew my face. He knew I was an American.
>
> So we are at the top of the gangway. I'm hanging back, but everyone else is pushing forward. I'm being pushed more and more to the front, so in Yiddish I said, "It's the police. I can't go forward. They know me." Well, what with the Jewish talent for conspiracy and improvisation I suddenly find myself with a wife hugging me on one side, and a baby and a blanket on the other. And with us all hugging each other I went down the gangway and walked right past him.

Often one wonders what the British really knew and thought. Al, a radio operator on the *Chaim Arlosoroff* was detained at the Athlit camp, in Palestine.

> *Al:* I didn't want the British to know I was an American, so I made up this garbled version of a Polish-Yugoslav language. Every time they talked to me I answered in this gibberish. Finally the day came

for me to leave the camp. The gate swings behind me, and I turn round for a last look. And it's then that one of the Brits says, "So long, Yank. Take care of yourself." They knew all the time.

After the return to the States there was the question of resuming normal life.

Harold: I had left Harvard Law School intending to return, but when I came back after being on the boats it wasn't so easy. There were two camps. First there were the people who shall remain nameless, who thought I was a renegade and a law breaker and totally undeserving of a place at the prestigious Harvard Law School. And there were others, like Bob Amory, who thought I definitely should be readmitted. "If you exclude this man," he said, "you can exclude all those who fought in the American Revolution."

The dean then asked me to write a letter explaining what I had done and why. I told him I did what I had done out of conviction. I respected laws that aided Jews, not laws that were designed to wound and destroy them. My actions were in accord with the norms of the American people, and I respected that heritage.

I finished my filming by shooting a few last interviews on the lawns of the president's house. Prior to this the Americans had split up for photos: here the survivors of the crew of the *Exodus*; there the aging members of the *Pan York* and the *Ben Hecht*; next to the table the crew of the *Geula*; outside in the gardens the crews of the *Arlosoroff* and the *Haganah*. After the taking of the group photos Israel's President, Chaim Herzog, had made a short but moving speech.

"Forty years ago there were so many challenges to meet. But it was you who were the heroes. It was you few, out of the 6 million Jews in America, who undaunted by official dangers decided to jump into the breach and rescue your people."

One fact stands out that till recently could not be found in any of the history books. Of the sixty-five thousand or so Jews who set sail from post-Nazi Europe to Palestine, more than thirty-two thousand of them, almost 50 percent of the refugees, traveled in vessels largely manned by two hundred or so American sailors. May the men be blessed and may this fact never be forgotten. Few of the men saw themselves as heroes, but most would agree with what craggy, gray-haired Lou Brettschneider said to me with immense feeling on the President's lawn. "The best moment? The greatest moment? Well the moment I felt most exhilarated was when we were in the Black Sea. Everybody was finally on board. We were about to sail. We were singing the 'Hatikva,' and the feeling you had was that you were really doing something worthwhile."

A few years after failing to launch *Waves of Freedom*, I set sail on a very strange new venture. I went hunting for the treasures of God. The question that set off the film was very simple. Are the fabled treasures of the Second Temple still in existence and if they are, then where are they?

The film was brought to me by Boris Maftzir, the head of the Israel Film Service. Boris was trying to put together a history-mystery TV series for Jerusalem's three-thousand-year anniversary, and this concept of a specific treasure hunt had been suggested to him by two talented filmmakers, David Schutz and Amnon Teitelbaum. As both were engaged in other projects, I became the elected film explorer.

Boris suggested the film cover two subjects: a hunt for the Ark of the Covenant; and a search for the golden candelabra that decorated the Second Temple and that disappeared shortly after its destruction. As these two subjects seemed to go off in two totally different directions, I elected to make a film dealing solely with the candelabra, or menorah, as it is called in Hebrew. Boris thought it over, agreed, wished me well, told me not to go over budget, and sent me on my way.

Soon after starting the research, I realized I had stumbled on a growth industry, particularly on the literary scene. History mysteries were all the rage, and if you wanted to make a million you simply dug up some incredible theory, wrote ninety thousand words, and foisted your slender hypothesis onto an avid, thirsty, and naive public.

One British writer whose name I forget actually outlined a formula for these books. You had to be a male, and you wrote them in the form of a quest. Women could appear in the books but only as camp followers. Serious historians had to oppose your theory that aliens built the British Parliament, or that the Egyptians used the Internet, but you would press on nonetheless. Midway through the book you had to have your night of darkness and self-doubt, but that would pass. What was vital was that at least one chapter dealt with pyramids and that your book title involve the Bible and the planets. So you could try *Jesus and the Saturn Code* or *Moses and the Jupiter Visitation*. Finally, to make your book really succeed, you had to smoke a pipe.

I absorbed all this and was impressed. Would I myself come up with some crackpot theories. Probably! Did I want to make a million? Definitely! Could I conjure up a title that used the Bible and the planets? Without a doubt! In fact I only had one problem. I didn't smoke a pipe.

My preliminary research turned up two interesting things. First, a couple of novelists had got there before me in the hunt for the candelabra. In Lionel Davidson's *The Menorah Men*, the candelabra is buried somewhere close to the Dead Sea. Just as it is about to be retrieved it gets covered over by some developer's project. In Stefan Zweig's *The Stolen Candelabrum*, the golden candlestick is brought back to Israel from Constantinople and is hidden and then lost somewhere in the desert. Both make for great reading and are fine as fiction. But the second thing I discovered was that real basic facts about the subject and real research on the disappearance were practically nonexistent. Legends? Yes, there were legends galore. But real facts, forget it.

Tracing the origins and early history of the candelabra was easy. The Bible says Moses came down from Mount Sinai and was instructed to build a giant seven-branched candelabra of pure gold. The Talmud then goes on to explain that the seven branches stood for the seven days of creation and the light itself for the eternity and endurance of law and faith.

Later the candelabra was placed in the Temple of Solomon, which stood for three hundred years before it was destroyed. When King Herod rebuilt the Temple it served both as a place of worship and a treasury. Menachem Broshi, an archaeologist working at the Israel Museum whom I interviewed for the film, told me that "the amount of treasures in the Temple would put to shame the Fort Knox wealth." And clearly among these treasures was the original candelabra or its replacement.

What we know about the subsequent history of the candelabra comes mostly from the historian Josephus. According to Josephus, the candelabra was taken to Rome by Titus after the destruction of the Temple at the end of the Roman-Jewish wars of the first century. Josephus writes about this in *The Jewish Wars*: "At the break of dawn, Titus with the Emperor Vespasian, ascended a tribunal and acknowledged the cheers of the crowd. Before them passed a procession carrying the spoils of war . . . but most prominent were the treasures of the Temple, the golden table, a scroll of law, and the golden seven branched candelabrum."

So far, so good. At least we had the beginning of the film, and I went to Rome to fix that part of the story. This was done by filming in the Forum where the good Romans had put up an arch to Titus and his father, commemorating the son's victories. One side of the arch shows Titus whipping along in his chariot at top speed, while the other side, of course, shows the famous sculpture of the candelabra itself being borne aloft by various Jewish slaves.

Josephus also tells us that the emperor put the treasures in a newly erected Temple of Peace. By the fifth century, Rome had twice been overrun, and the fate of the treasures had become surrounded in mystery. They were no longer to be seen. Where were they? Good question, and your guess is as good as mine.

Well, that's letting the cat out of the bag. I didn't find the candelabra, and I'm not sitting writing this in some sumptuous thousand-dollar-a-day hotel paid for with the money I made by secretly selling the candelabra to some Russian Mafioso or Paul Getty-like collector. I didn't trace the candelabra, but I certainly came across some interesting ideas as to what happened to it, and here are the best of them.

The most well known, and to my mind, the craziest theory is that the candelabra is being held in the cellars of the Vatican. No one quite seems to know how it might have gotten there, but that doesn't stop the speculation. I put this idea to Zizi Naor, a curator at the Italian Jewish museum and synagogue in central Jerusalem.

"Oh, yes. I definitely believe it is there. In 1943 the Germans asked the Jewish community of Rome to deliver fifty kilos of gold to them, which was a very heavy tax. The Vatican then informed the Jewish community that they would help them by loaning part of the gold. No wonder they would do this because they held the candelabra."

As I couldn't get into the Vatican archives to pursue the subject in a serious way, I asked Father Viviano of the Ecole Biblique to give his opinion on the subject. His answer was scathing. "I've never heard such a silly idea in all my life. It's just archaeological titillation, archaeological soft porn."

One of the more serious ideas held by scholars is that the candelabra was seized by the Visigoths when they sacked Rome in the fifth century and taken to Carcassonne in the south of France. This is supported by a line (in *The Vandal Wars*) by the Byzantine historian Procopius: "The Visigoths made off with the candlesticks and treasures of Solomon, a sight most worthy to be seen, for they were adorned in the most part by emeralds, and in the olden times they had been taken from Jerusalem by the Romans."

Well, who was I to question Procopius? To follow up this trail, I headed for Carcassonne, which in any case I'd always wanted to visit because I'd heard the renovated town walls and turrets were pure kitsch. I wasn't disappointed. The old Roman town had been done up in the nineteenth century, and the fortress, its battlements, and twenty-odd red and blue turrets looked like pure Disney. A gaudy carousel at the entrance to the town also reinforced the illusion that you were entering an American theme park.

What surprised me in Carcassonne, however, was that the locals totally believed the story of the treasures being in the vicinity. Their sources for this were legends, folk tales, and the medieval writings of Gregory of Tours. According to Gregory, the treasures were definitely there but had been hidden away from the eyes of the Franks. The hiding place was said to be the town well. A hundred years ago some of the townspeople of Carcassonne formed a society to empty out the well and find the treasures. Much drink was consumed, but no action taken. By contrast the Germans, who occupied Carcassonne in 1940, went to work immediately. Not only did they drain the well, but they also started looking all over the town for the treasures. Like others before them, they found nothing.

Carcassonne gave us good color material. Not only did we film around the well but also captured those gorgeous and slightly ridiculous turrets and town walls. We also filmed in a Templar museum while I pondered whether to shoot one of the wildest but also most intriguing stories I'd heard, which linked Carcassonne, the Templars and a nearby village called Rennes le Chateau.

I'd gotten the story of Rennes from one of those best-selling history mysteries I mentioned earlier titled *The Holy Blood and the Holy Grail*. The book suggests that Jesus was married, left a son, and that son became one of the ancestors of the early Merovingian kings of France—all good Umberto Eco material. In between some historical information on the Cathars and *their* secret treasures, however, the book mentions, almost parenthetically, that the treasures of the Jews might be at Rennes le Chateau, brought there by the Templar Knights. An improbable story? Well, let's see.

In the twelfth century, Baldwin, king of the Crusader Kingdom of Jerusalem, allowed a small group of his followers to live on the Temple Mount, their home, a wing of the El Aksa mosque, the name of the new band of brothers . . . the Knights Templar. According to rumors, the Knights dug inside the El Aksa mosque for seven years. But what were they digging for? Some books maintain they were searching for the Holy Grail. Michael Baigent and Henry Lincoln, the authors of *Holy Blood*, say that may be so, but what they probably found were some of the hidden Temple treasures, which they took back to France with them. And since Carcassonne was one of the home areas for the Templars, why couldn't the treasures have finished up here? So, incredibly, part of the treasures may have arrived in the same area of France at different times and by different routes. If so, what happened to them?

For an answer, I went to film in Rennes le Chateau, about half an hour's drive from Carcassonne. Rennes is set magnificently at the top of a sweep of dark green hills and has fantastic views of the surrounding valleys. It has about a dozen houses, a small church, and a sleepy restaurant. It seems a village that time has passed by, neglected and abandoned. At one time, however, it was one of the centers of the Visigoth kingdom. It is also surrounded by old Templar strongholds and contains one of the great mysteries of France.

In 1885 a new priest came to Rennes, Berenger Sauniere. He was thirty-three years old. His flock consisted of two hundred villagers, his salary ten dollars a year. While repairing the old church and removing an altar stone, Sauniere came across two Visigoth columns. Inside the columns were parchments written in a kind of code. One seemed to be a kind of genealogy going back to 1244. The other contained the lines "To Dagobert III, King, and to Zion, belong this treasure."

Soon afterward, Sauniere visited Paris, a strange visit for a country priest. On his return he started digging around the church and around the countryside. Inside the church he put up a statue to the devil Asmodeus . . . Asmodeus, the guardian of hidden treasures. Suddenly Sauniere started spending vast sums, amounting to three million dollars by the end of his life. He put in modern roads, built a house, and gave immense banquets.

When Sauniere died in 1917, his will revealed nothing. He had transferred most of his wealth to the woman with whom he lived. When she died in 1953, most questions were still unanswered—the source of Sauniere's wealth and what happened in Paris. What seems likely is that Sauniere found a strange treasure and sold it to the church or a private individual, receiving money in return for his silence. But did he find the Temple treasures? Did he find the menorah? Various French journalists think so, and the notes of one book I picked up in Rennes refer to the Israeli secret service being in the village in 1972 to check on the story.

Well, we filmed around Sauniere's house. And we filmed in his dark, gloomy church. And we filmed the devil Asmodeus. It was a good story. Did I believe the candelabra was there, or that some French secret society had grabbed it and would return it to Israel when the time was right? Definitely not. But then I've been wrong before.

I had jumped into the film assuming the lost treasures and the candelabra were in Europe. About half way into my research I started wondering if I was looking in the wrong place. What if, from the start, the key treasures never left the Holy land? There are two lines to this argument, one supported by the extreme orthodox and the other hinted at by recent archaeological discoveries.

What I found out early on in the research was that many Jewish rabbinical sources hint at the existence of duplicates of the lamp and other Jewish treasures. Josephus also writes that he saw *two* lamps being handed over by the priests to the Romans. Was one the genuine candelabra and one a copy? Or were both copies? And if the Romans took a copy, what happened to the true lamp? Could it have been hidden before the Romans sacked the Temple?

Dr. Meir Ben Dov, my archaeological adviser on the film and author of one of the best books about the history of the Temple Mount, certainly believed that thesis was possible. "We dug near the temple area, and we found tunnels and channels and underground structures, so who knows. Maybe the treasure is still there in one of those places."

I also discovered that most Jewish traditionalists agree with this approach. They fervently believe a secret hiding place was built for the treasures. Supported by talmudic commentaries they argue that many of the treasures and the menorah are still hidden on the Temple

Mount. Rabbi Isaac Mutzafi, a noted Jerusalem kabbalistic scholar, went through his books for me and then told me the following. "Rabbi Emek Hamelech, who was a pupil of Rabbi Ari, discusses this point in his writings. He lists all the objects of the temple, including twelve thousand general ornaments, ten thousand harps, smaller vessels, and the robes of the priests and argues that they are all hidden under the sanctuary, at three levels below the Temple Mount."

The ability to explore this theory was impossible in the centuries between Crusader and modern Turkish rule. Jerusalem was neglected and forgotten by the world. All that changed in 1867 when a team of British engineers under Captain Charles Warren made the first scientific survey of the temple area. With the opening up of the area, in swarmed the archaeologists, the seekers of the Ark, and not a few treasure hunters, the first of whom was Captain Montagu Parker. His was a strange story, which I tracked down in the archives of the Palestine Exploration Society in London.

In 1910 Parker, a British explorer, using the theories of a Swedish mystic as a guide, started to look for treasures. Leaving his yacht in Jaffa, Parker came to Jerusalem and paid off or bribed several of the guards at the Dome of the Rock and El Aksa. He then started to dig inside that area, probably the only one who has ever done so. His target was the Ark or some of the other treasures of Solomon's temple. When the diggings were discovered riots ensued, and Parker had to flee for his life, leaving chaos behind him. For a few days, stories of great discoveries graced the front pages of the *New York Times*. When nothing was shown to support the stories, the brouhaha died away, and Parker faded from the headlines.

With all these stories floating around, I turned to Magen Broshi and Dan Bahat, another eminent archaeologist for their opinions. Both were very dismissive. According to Bahat, these stories of buried treasures in Jerusalem were nonsense. Magen was of a similar mind. "Your million-to-one chance of winning the lottery is greater than your chance of finding treasures under the Temple Mount."

While the archaeologists were doubtful about the treasures being under the Temple Mount, they were much more open to the idea that they might have been smuggled out of the Temple before the Romans destroyed it. This might conceivably have been done via the maze of tunnels and drainage canals under the place of worship. But where could they take the treasures? Where could they hide them in safety? Maybe in the Judean desert only a few hours from Jerusalem. This in fact is the idea that drives the opening of Lionel Davidson's novel and was an idea that seemed relatively plausible to me.

When you go down to the Judean desert, through the wadis and past canyons and sand craters that make you think you are on the moon, the Bible suddenly becomes very alive. You sense the area is as old as time. You feel small, insignificant, and diminished as history swirls all around you. It was here that the walls of Jericho fell and here, beside the Dead Sea, that God rained down fire on Sodom and Gemorrah. The area is harsh, barren, forbidding. Here one could hide anything and have the desert preserve it forever. But then how would later generations trace the objects? Reason suggests a map would have been left behind. That's what I was looking for, a map, but where to find it? The answer lay at Qumran.

The Dead Sea Scrolls were found at Qumran in the Judean desert in 1947. Suddenly in 1952 two new manuscripts turned up in the same location. Unlike the other scrolls, they were written on rolled copper. And that was to be their name, the *Copper Scrolls*. Because of fragility, they were sent to England's Manchester College of Technology. There a sensitive electric saw cut through the scrolls, layer by layer, enabling the first scholars to read the scrolls and make an astounding discovery. The scrolls listed sixty-four hiding places of silver and gold. As one of the archaeologists says in the film, "This sounds like something out of Walt Disney or Steven Spielberg Productions, but there it is. The Copper Scrolls are documents that tell you where to find buried treasure. And we're talking the real stuff here: gold, silver, the stuff that would make us all rich."

It was an astonishing find, but the early experts were split as to whether the scrolls were genuine or fake. Magen Broshi, who I'd been talking to throughout the film, was doubtful. "The copper scroll is one of the most enigmatic things I've ever encountered in my life. Whatever angle you take it's an absolute enigma. Are they speaking about real treasures? If you are hiding real treasures you don't proclaim it from a very large-scale notice."

Today the consensus seems to be that the scrolls refer to genuine two-thousand-year-old treasures. Cal McArthur of Johns Hopkins put it this way: "You know this is such an infernally dull document that if it were imaginary you'd think they'd make it a little more exciting. The fact is it's treasure as presented to you by a certified public accountant."

The amounts talked about in the scrolls are enormous. One scholar whose work I was looking at sets the treasures at sixty-five tons of silver and eight tons of gold. Of course, the next question that arises is where was it all from? And that was the question that interested me for the film. The huge list clearly points to a communal treasury. Two thousand years ago there was only one place that fit that description, the Temple. So it seems that we have a document, the Copper Scrolls, talking about Temple treasures or tithes, probably hidden in anticipation of the Roman siege of Jerusalem.

Gradually, the puzzle seemed to be becoming clearer. But who would have hidden the treasures and written the scrolls? Probably the Zealots who defended Jerusalem and guarded the passes to the Dead Sea . . . all areas mentioned in the scrolls as treasure locations.

Now as I dug deeper into this, I wasn't sure if I was getting closer to the menorah, but I was clearly on the path of the other treasures. The story was definitely one to stir the imagination, especially of treasure hunters, but there were also immense problems surrounding the whole business. For example, the first stumbling block to a filmmaker such as myself pursuing a story, or to an archaeologist, is that the scrolls are written in code. Names are vague. Places are named, but their locations are obscure. And the key to unlock the scrolls is evidently held in another scroll.

Even so, the four main locations for the treasures seem clearly to lie between Jerusalem and Qumran, and a number of the sites have already drawn the treasure hunters. The first was an Englishman, John Allegro. Allegro, himself a bit of a maverick and an enigma, was the author of *The Dead Sea Scrolls* and one of the original scholars involved in the mystery of the scrolls. Supported in the late fifties by King Hussein, Allegro started searching close to the eastern wall of the Old City of Jerusalem and by the Golden Gate. His guide was a double passage from the scrolls: "Under the monument of Absalom on the western side, buried at 12 cubits, 80 talents of silver . . . and in the tomb of Zadok, 80 talents of silver. . . . In the cavity of the pillar of the double gate buried at three cubits, a pitcher, a scroll, and 21 talents of silver."

Allegro found nothing, but till the end of his life he believed that the next search would be the one to uncover all the secrets. Like others, he noted that there were ten references to treasures buried beneath the Temple Mount, but because of religious sensibilities the area was left untouched.

Others searchers have followed Allegro but have mostly turned their gaze to the Dead Sea, the region most frequently mentioned in the scrolls. The most famous of them is Dr. Vendyll Jones of Texas, sometimes cited as the model for Indiana Jones of *Raiders of the Lost Ark* fame. Being curious, I finally located Jones in the small town of Arlington near Dallas and went to interview him.

The office is full of books and maps of the Holy Land. On the walls are blown-up extracts from the scrolls. Scattered all over the place are news pamphlets about his work and video cassettes of his various Israel trips.

Jones, a genial former Christian minister, seemed in our conversation to have left orthodox Christianity very far behind. This, he told me, was the result and of his researches. Jones has led various expeditions to hunt for the Copper treasures. In 1969 he claimed to have located the River of the Dome and the Cave of the Columns, two points mentioned in the Scrolls. In the next ten years, he was subject to immense criticism. Ignoring the jibes of what he calls "the swivel-chair academics," he went on searching but came up empty-handed.

Then in 1988 Jones claimed to have made a world-shattering discovery. Jones pauses and then with a smile takes a curious bottle out of his desk. He holds it up to the light, caressing it lovingly. "You know what this is, Alan? The *shemen afarsimon*, the anointing oil for prophets and kings mentioned in the Scrolls. When I found it we really made the world headlines. CBS, CNN—we were on all of them."

The next year brought additional discoveries; the hidden north entrance to the cave, mentioned in the Scrolls and a chamber containing nine hundred pounds of incense thought to be of the same type as that used in the temple. Then Jones's final words. "If we continue to find things in the order they are written, then what we expect to find next will be the ashes of the red heifer."

For years, small groups of religious Jews have been wanting to rebuild the Temple. But for Temple services to continue, the ashes of the red heifer are necessary for purification rites. Thus if Jones does make such a discovery, the production of the genuine ashes could have very profound repercussions on a very delicate political and religious issue. Most of Jones's claims have been treated by Israeli archaeologists and the scientific community with a great deal of skepticism. Nevertheless, Vendyll Jones presses on undeterred, sure that the greatest discovery is just around the corner.

In the end I finished up with loads of theories about the location of the candelabra and the treasures but with no clear indication that any one of them deserved priority. I said previously that I thought that the idea of the menorah being in the Vatican was absurd. Yet a week after my film was shown, I read in the papers that scholars in Italy had come up with new evidence showing that such a theory was indeed feasible. That just shows you.

To conclude my film, I felt it necessary to ask one last question. Is the search for the candelabra necessary or wise? Rabbi Sol Richman, a young, bearded American who runs the Temple Museum in the Old City was very much in favor of the quest. "There can be no greater discovery that can affect mankind than the discovery of the candelabra or the treasures. They would provide a feeling of direct continuum with the past and make the Bible and religion come alive for many people in an entirely new way."

Rabbi Mutzafi, my kabbalistic expert, was much more guarded. "The question is important, and I have to be careful. The people looking for the menorah and the treasures think they will bring redemption and salvation and the messiah more quickly. I strongly disagree. The treasures may help in a general supportive way. But no more. The hunt is an illusion."

Over the centuries the candelabra, the menorah, has shifted from reality to symbol. Selected as the emblem of the modern Jewish state, it touches upon three thousand years of Jewish tradition. For most people, that is enough. Yet it seems to me there will always be people for whom the candelabra represents a dream, a myth, an intangible longing. For some, it symbolizes a reaffirmation of faith and the need to catch something beyond the banalities of our everyday life. And there will always be those other hunters who seek the treasures, those for whom the menorah represents adventure, mystery, an enigma that has to be pursued for itself.

I didn't find the menorah, but the search will go on because the words *the lost menorah* can still quicken the pulse and stir the imagination. And there is always the sense "maybe we are close, and what if tomorrow . . ." So could the words with which Stefan Zweig closes his novel *The Stolen Candelabrum* be a prediction for our times?

Hidden in its secret tomb there still watches and waits the everlasting menorah. Often a hasty foot passes over the ground beneath which it lies. Often a weary traveler sleeps close to where the candelabrum slumbers. No one can tell whether it will remain hidden forever or someone will dig it up when its people come into their own. But only then will the seven branched candelabra diffuse its gentle light in the Temple of Peace.

9 - The Brink of Peace

Flipping idly through a photo album in 1996 and digging into memories, I suddenly realized I had been in Israel twenty-five years. When I'd arrived in the country my boys had been infants. In fact, the first photo in the album was that of a five-year-old Gil playing on the beach in Eilat. Now, incredibly, both boys had been through the army, Gil in the Golani Infantry Division, and Tal as a sergeant instructor in a mobilization unit. Subsequently, Gil had become an architect and had gotten married, while Tal was studying social work. Both Miki and I were working at the university, but filming was still the most important part of my life.

Usually I did about three films a year, but 1996 and 1997 were to be different. During all of that period, I spent most of my time making a one-hour film for Public Television on the Oslo peace process and the turbulent events that followed. For this piece, we shot in Israel, Gaza, the West Bank, Egypt, Jordan, and Norway. In the course of more than a year, I also interviewed almost everyone of importance concerned with the process, plus a few more. But one man was conspicuously missing from the film. This was Yitzhak Rabin, who was assassinated by a young right-wing Israeli in November 1995. He was missing from the film, and he was missing from the heart of Israel.

Rabin was murdered a few months before I was asked to make the film. That event haunted me throughout the film and does till this day. A few days after the killing I wrote the following letter to my sister Phylis and her husband, Alfred, who were still living in London. I put it here because it shows the frame of mind I was in as I approached the film.

Jerusalem. 7.11.95

Dear Phylis and Alfred:
You both phoned yesterday, and I said I would write because what has been happening was too much for a telephone conversation. Well here goes.

At the moment we are in the midst of rain and a sandstorm. One finishes; the other starts. The effect is gray and choking. It would have been appropriate yesterday, the day of Rabin's funeral, but instead we had glorious blue skies. Now the rain beats on the window, and I'm listening to Mozart, trying to pull together what to say.

The news, the events, the speeches . . . I'm sure you've read all about them in the newspapers or have heard about them or seen them on the TV. So what is left to say? Well to begin with images and those small things that are burned into the memory.

I was supposed to give a lecture at the university on Sunday, but all classes were canceled after twelve. Those that took place in the morning turned mostly into open discussions. About noon the students, hundreds of them, started gathering in the forum, the internal center of the university, and lighting candles. Soon this closed-in, ugly, gray concrete plaza was glowing with hundreds of pin pricks of light. Very quickly the forum was packed, and the soft singing began, songs I hadn't heard for years. Not the triumphant old ones like "Nasser mechakeh le Rabin"—"Nasser Waits for Rabin"—but the quiet plaintive new ones, especially "Shir Lashalom"—"A Song for Peace"—which has become almost the anthem of the Left. A few people spoke, mostly to announce an official university memorial meeting in the amphitheater at two. Then everyone, maybe a thousand students by this time, started singing the "Hatikva," the national anthem.

Well, I've heard the "Hatikva" sung many times in my life, mostly rather embarassedly at weddings and bar mitzvahs, but never like this. Not dramatic. Not loud. I would say quietly, humbly, from inside everyone, with a feeling I've never heard before. As you know, *hatikva* means "the hope." Was it, we were all wondering, the hope that Rabin represented? Who knows! But what you heard was a song coming from the center of everyone, with that proudest and most hard of creatures, the Israeli, crying and weeping.

At two o'clock there was a short memorial for Rabin at the university amphitheater. Have you been there, Phyl? Not on a day like this. A crystal clear day, when you see down through the hard brown and yellow desert hills to Jericho and the Dead Sea. Not on a day like this that mocks you with its beauty, and the jagged mountains of Jordan are focused and blue on the distant horizon. It's this strange connection with time and with the past that haunts you the whole time. Twenty-eight years ago, just after the Six-Day War, Rabin stood here in this open amphitheater, under these same skies, and was awarded an honorary doctorate. He spoke then, as I remember, not of the past but of the dream of the future, an Israel that was possible, that could come into being, an Israel of peace that the sacrifices of war had made possible.

Now Sunday, November 5th, and the words are being recalled before maybe twelve thousand students. A gathering of quiet, subdued, shocked young people, holding each other for support. Most left immediately afterwards to go to the Knesset where Rabin's body was now lying in state.

On Saturday evening I had been watching on TV the rally for peace in Kikar Malchei Yisrael, that huge central square in Tel Aviv. What a joyous occasion: banners, songs, young musicians, families with kids. Maybe a hundred thousand people were there, affirming a belief in the peace process, that it was the right road, and—and this is vital—also gathering to affirm "no to violence."

At 10:00 P.M., when I thought everything was finished, I started watching a rerun of *Crocodile Dundee*. Suddenly they started flashing a notice on the screen, "Stay tuned for a special news bulletin." When I switched on the radio they announced there had been an attempt on Rabin's life.

Ten minutes later the TV pictures started coming through, wildly grabbed news from the square in Tel Aviv: pandemonium. Again and again the TV ran the same uncut, sprawling, and wild news flashes: Rabin being assisted into a car and the car hurtling off; horror stricken, screaming faces; rushing panicked figures; and flashes of the young man who had done the shooting being held, protected, by dozens of police.

What is difficult to convey to you is the feeling of those thirty or forty minutes when nothing was known, when one woman kept on repeating from the square, "No, he wasn't hurt, definitely not hurt." Then we got the crowds in front of the hospital but no news. No news. Finally Israel TV says, "BSkyB television has announced that

Rabin is dead." It turns out this was known almost immediately, but we here in Israel had to hear the first announcement through foreign television.

You can't grasp it. Totally unreal. A few minutes ago there he was on the platform, dark suit and shy smile, looking sheepish and awkward as he tries to sing the popular "Shir Lashalom," awkward but immensely happy that so many people had come to affirm that this was the right way, that the path he had chosen to peace was the right way. And then . . . nothing. Obliteration. Silence. End.

Over the past ten years or so, in various films of mine, I've tried to recapture history. One forgets so much. And what is real and important now can't be grasped without a sense of the past. I've shown the great moments: in Jerusalem after the Six-Day War, The return from Entebbe, The peace with Egypt. But there were also the dark moments like the Yom Kippur War and those dead bodies returning from Lebanon. And now this, which must surely be one of the blackest moments, and yet . . . and I'll explain the "and yet" later.

What I think will forever stay in my mind, and is I think the most important part of the last few days, is the tribute of the people to Rabin and what it says about him and ourselves. The visits of the officials, of King Hussein, of President Clinton, yes, they are important . . . but something else has happened that I think swamps all that, which I don't think was captured in the papers or on the foreign news. Let me describe what I think was missing.

It's night. Monday evening, the evening before the funeral. It's 9:00 P.M. Earlier in the day the body has been brought to Jerusalem. Now the coffin, draped in a blue and white Israeli flag, lies in the Knesset. On the television I have seen thousands filing past, paying their last respects, and now it is time to go myself.

It's a warm night, almost a spring night. Most of the roads leading up to the Knesset are closed. So one walks along as if it's Yom Kippur, with no thought for cars. Soon the few people become a mass, a flood, a torrent.

Imagine if you can, Phyl, every twenty or thirty yards another group around an ever-growing circle of candles and flames. This group sits quietly on the ground, arms linked, softly rocking, singing quietly. At their feet flowers, candles, and the small *yarhzeit* (memorial) lights. Over there, stuck into the rocks of the wall, more lights and tributes. One is hastily written by a child, another by an old man. Then more drawings, yellow flowers, scarlet petals, photos. Farther along fifteen young soldiers, again around their candles, stand singing.

It proves impossible to get up to the Knesset. Too many people. Eventually over a million will come. Proportionately that's 40 million Americans or 10 million English. That is the thing that humbles me and gladdens me.

Did I mention the buses? They are laid on free from all over Israel. I ask the small group next to me, some with babies in their arms, where they come from. The answer is Kiryat Shmoneh, in the far north. Another couple with children are from Beersheba. And so it goes. And people lean together for warmth, spiritual warmth, taking and giving.

Yet there are conspicuous absences. Among the hundreds of thousands here in the warm night I've seen maybe one, two at the most, of the ultra orthodox, and of the black-suited Chabadnicks. This may be God's country, but Israel doesn't seem to be their country.

At home we watch the news till midnight. The TV goes on and on: talk and more talk, description, analysis, shock. How did it happen? Eventually I go to bed at two.

At 6:00 A.M. I try again to reach the Knesset and say my own good-bye. But it is even worse (better?) than the night before. The crowds now reach from the Knesset down to the Israeli Museum on one side and stretch up to Shderot Herzl on the other side. And the unbelievable has happened. Everyone is waiting patiently in a winding eight-people-wide queue. A neat quiet queue in Israel? Never did I expect to see that in my lifetime.

And the dawn is different. The sun comes up slowly on tired people, rises over the rose gardens, and then begins to blind with its heat and intensity. And slowly, so slowly, we begin to edge forward to the Knesset gates, a few yards every fifteen minutes. All along the sides of the streets leading past the government buildings and up to the Knesset, there are now thousands of dark green wreaths, candles, scraps of letters, cards. And everywhere are the groups of youngsters who have kept vigil all night.

Every so often I break away from the crowd to read another set of cards or tributes, from the old, from children, from a school in Emek beth Shaan, from Eilat. Many quote a song of the poet Yehudah Amichai."He was a man." Many call him "Abba," Dad, father. The tributes tear you apart. It's hard to pass by without your eyes becoming wet in spite of yourself.

Rabin was not an easy man. I met him about five times under different circumstances. Everyone says he was a man for intimacy, not crowds. In public he was often brutal, cold, seemingly indifferent, determined, firm, respected, but above all distant and removed.

On a person-to-person basis he was very different: warm, engaging, smiling, committed. The last time I interviewed him I remember him shaking hands with every member of the crew. There was the slow, smiling engagement of his eyes with theirs. He looks directly at you, sums you up, and then accepts you. As an army man he gave orders. To listen and consider the opinions of others must have been difficult for him.

As we ascend to the Knesset the packed-in and jammed feeling gets more intense. Here and there in the crowd I see old friends. Bottles of water are passed from hand to hand. A wreath is passed over the heads of the crowd to the Knesset guards. Above us helicopters come and go and circle and hover. Here and there people hold flowers they want to lay by the coffin or the words of a song. By ten I am three yards from the Knesset barrier. Almost there . . . and then they close the gates. The foreign visitors are now coming, and public access is at an end.

So I never got to pass by the coffin, yet it didn't matter. To be there, to be among the hundreds of thousands sharing the same feeling was enough.

In the afternoon, again under the bluest of skies, I went out to line the streets with others and watch the funeral cortege pass by. All the roads were closed. First to come by is the flag-draped coffin on a black gun carriage. You know he's dead, but still there is the shock of actually seeing the coffin. Then comes another carriage totally covered with flowers. I look around. So many youngsters. Again not a single "black" *dati* (religious) guy. And this is not your secular and fashionable Rehavia. This is Shderot Herzl, where many of the ultra-religious live.

One needs to be out, to see the cars, the police, the coffin, the gun carriage because without this element everything slips into an unreal television event. But just five minutes on the streets tells you this is true, this is happening, this has happened.

You've watched the funeral speeches I'm sure. What amazed me, moved me, was watching King Hussein talk. Again memories and emotions interlace. So I'm recalling a piece of archive material that I used in my film about the 1967 war where Hussein, interviewed in London says "Peace with Israel? No, I don't think so. It's impossible, and there is no way." I cried watching him now.

We are all in such a profound state of shock. Stunned. The mourning and coming to grips goes on, but we are all sleepwalking. Last night, after the funeral, I drove through a silent city. Groups were still gathering spontaneously. Along by Terra Santa, scene of so many rallies and protests against the Lebanese war, there were masses of candles and dense crowds of people. It had been a hard day. Most of us had been up at the Knesset, then on the streets, then glued to the TV—and there is a weariness in the bones. On TV I see the crowds still flock into the Tel Aviv square where it all happened. The flowers grow, and the people cry and hold and touch. There is something so personal about it all. Maybe that child's card that I saw that simply says, "We miss you Abba" says it all. Rabin was Abba Father, Dad, showing the way.

On my desk as I write there is a small black ribbon given to me at the university. On the floor there is a pile of newspapers, yesterdays and today's. As I said, outside it is gray, dusty, and raining.

I started off this letter by saying "and yet . . ." And yet I believe something very good may come of all this.

Phylis, you put your finger on it during your visit last month when you said, "There is so much anger here in Israel." It is more. Since the midseventies we have become not just a nation of separate opinions, but a nation full of hate and anger, with a lot of that hate encouraged by the leaders. In fact the name I gave to my film about Israel 1973–93 was *The Dream Divided*. It was a film questioning what happened to the dream and to the nation, and why all the hate. The last two years that hate has grown in fury. It is now raging and out of control. I'm not sure how much you outside Israel see, but a few months ago there were posters going around showing Rabin in Nazi uniform. Plastered over the poster were the words, "Rabin is a traitor." And this slime and garbage was used not so subtly by the opposition, though they professed a hypocritical shock.

I believe Rabin's death has shocked the nation back to fundamental questions. Who are we? What do we believe in? Where are we going? What struck me again and again, and what strikes me now, is the picture of the youngsters reaching out, questioning, determined to go forward, youngsters such as Gil, Tal, and Tzofnat [Gil's wife] who realize that the movement toward peace is the only way. I believe that in a peculiar way the death of Rabin shocked Israel back to first principles, and above all reunified it. It gave all of us a sense of being one people again, a people with a purpose and direction, a people with love not hate.

The extremes on both sides won't alter, but I believe the silent center has woken up. Rabin represented the old Zionist dream and fought for it most of his life. The amazing thing is he turned from hardliner into one who believed that peace could come and could be achieved. And he paid the price for his beliefs. But I think the message is getting through, that there is no other way.

Being a realist I know it takes two to tango, and there may still be more murders and encounters on both sides. Yet I would like to hope that the unity of this country is back in place, as well as its sense of itself, its pride in its history, and its belief in its future. Will the unity last? Will the feelings last? I hope so.

In my diary from the Yom Kippur War I wrote, "Here no one is alone. We share the joys, and we share the pain. There is no future. No tomorrow. No yesterday Only today." The first part is still true. We share the joys and the pain. But as against twenty-two years ago there is a tomorrow, and if Israel is together again it can be a very bright one.

I miss you all and wish you were here. As you are not I send you the warmest hug I have.

Much love,
Alan

Two months after Rabin's death, I got a call from Abba Eban. Did I want to work with him on a film for WNET about the peace process? Do Americans love baseball? Do the English love cricket? What a question. I'd give my right hand to do such a film. But what exactly was happening?

According to Eban, he had been discussing the idea for some months with Bill Baker, head of WNET-New York, and Baker thought it was a great idea. My name had been mentioned as producer. Could I get over to New York where we could pursue the idea further?

This sounded great till I arrived in New York and went to see Tamara Robinson, the effective head of programs at WNET. Tammy had seen my work, approved me as producer director, but as far as getting the project off the ground, there was a long, long way to go. Yes, Bill Baker had liked the concept, but WNET had no money. Period. So, I inquired of Tammy, "How do we get things moving?" Her answer was that I should spend a few months writing a project proposal. With that proposal they could raise money for research and development. How long would that take? Maybe another five months. During research and development, I could write a tentative script; then with the script in hand they could raise money for the actual production. How long in turn would that take? Oh, maybe another six months. When I pointed out to Tammy that at that rate we would be ready to start the film in another five years, she just shrugged. That's the way it was, and good luck.

Eban knew of these difficulties, and on his recommendation I went to see Eli Evans, chairman of the Charles Revson Foundation. Eli knew about the idea, was sympathetic, and believed that if such a film was going to be made it had to snap into action very soon, and not after the millennium. Thus after an hour's conversation, I walked out of his office with the promise of a small grant for writing the proposal. We'd also discussed strategy. WNET had said it would hunt for funds, if Eban would assist and use the proposal to raise money from various people he knew who were concerned with the Middle East. In the event, and this is jumping the gun a bit, almost the entire budget for the film was raised by Eban.

I wrote the proposal in about four weeks, while doing some guest lecturing at Stanford. The opening statement was relatively simple. "No place has been more volatile in the past nor presents such hopes for the future as the Middle East in 1996. In fact few events in our generation have aroused such intense reactions as the Middle Eastern peace process and its dramatic roller coast fluctuations. It is quite clear that the outcome of the struggle will effect the world for decades to come."

Continuing in the same vein, I then sketched out an executive summary.

On September 9th, 1993, Yasir Arafat wrote to Yitzhak Rabin that the PLO recognizes Israel's right to exist in peace and security. On the same day Rabin wrote that the Israeli government had decided to recognize the PLO as the representative of the Palestinian people and would commence negotiations for peace. Together these sensational documents, negotiated at Oslo, set off a peace process which has revolutionized the Middle East. For the first time in fifty years two peoples, involved in a tragic struggle that has witnessed immense suffering on both sides, saw hope for the future.

Thirteen/WNET proposes to develop and produce a one hour television documentary which will trace the evolving peace process. This vitally important program will illuminate the history, dilemmas and immense challenges for change now confronting the Middle East. The outcome of this situation will have major consequences not just for the peoples of the area, but for the West in general.

I then added that Abba Eban would host and narrate the program, that the film marked the resumption of an old partnership between him and WNET, and that the film would expose millions of viewers to one of the key dramas of our time.

After discussing budget and a time plan for the film, the proposal ended with a short discussion of style and approach. "The film will be a combination of essay and story. It will be built as a drama, with incidents, events and happenings illustrating the larger picture. It will show passions and emotions as we depict the turbulent events of the past three years." All this was fine, except for two comments in the last paragraph, which came back to haunt me. "And the film will provoke. It's object is not just to record a process and a series of events in time, but to echo and reflect on the wider issues of war and peace between nations. And finally, the film will be extremely balanced, with both Arab and Israeli views given due airing."

I wrote the proposal in January 1996, delivered it to Abba Eban and WNET, and waited to see what would ensue. Two events transpired. On the positive side Eban very quickly started raising substantial amounts of money. That was great. On the negative side, I watched with horror as the whole peace process started to unravel. First came the shattering terrorist bombings in Jerusalem in February. This was followed by a disastrous mini-excursion by the Israelis into Lebanon which went under the title of "The Grapes of Wrath." Finally the June elections returned Bibi Netanyahu as prime minister by a majority of half of 1 percent. This was a tremendous defeat for Shimon Peres, one of the main architects of the peace process and did not bode well for the future. Netanyahu promised "peace with security," but I had my doubts. What was clear was that though we had started the film with the idea of celebrating the peace process, reality was dragging us somewhere else.

This process was reflected in the working title I chose for the film. In the beginning, I thought of using *Days of Destiny* or *The Road of Hope*. Halfway through the year I changed it to *States of Decision*. By the end of the year, I was ready to call the film *Down the Drain*, as I considered those few words to be the most accurate reflection of the state of the peace process.

By September of 1996, it was clear we had half the production budget, and I begged WNET to let me go ahead. The answer was no. There could be no action till all the money was in the pot. This being the case, I once more traipsed back to my lifesaver, Eli Evans at the Revson Foundation. With cap in hand, I explained the situation and asked him if he could make me a small grant so that I could begin writing a draft script. That way we would have matters well in hand when all the production monies were in. Again showing immense faith in the project and in Eban and myself, Eli decided to back us for another lifesaving sum.

Now we were faced with the really hard problems. What did we want to say in the film? What should be its span? Who should appear? How would we get into the film, and how would we end it? And what was Eban's role?

The last problem was maybe the trickiest. In the past I had made four fairly successful films with Eban. In those films I had written the scripts after a certain amount of consultation with him, and he had generally trusted my judgment and left me alone to get on with the filmmaking. In the peace film, however, he saw his role as chief executive editor and wanted to be consulted on every little detail. Since he was a perfectionist, had virtually raised all the money himself, and had put an immense effort into bringing the project to fruition, I could very much understand his concern. But it wasn't really the money that was the issue. Eban saw the film as possibly his last major comment on Israeli and world affairs and desperately and passionately wanted the film to succeed. The difficulty from my point of view was that Eban wasn't a filmmaker. He was highly astute, a brilliantly intelligent and concerned politician, and maybe one of the world's greatest orators, but he wasn't a filmmaker, and his judgments were not those of a filmmaker. As a result there were a greater number of disagreements than usual between us regarding style, content, and commentary.

Our most violent clash came about over my wish to include in the film the assassination of Yehi Ayash, the Hamas terrorist and bomber mastermind, and the resulting riots in Gaza. I believed that the murder of Ayash, allegedly by the Mossad, had initiated a series of revenge bombings in Israel by Hamas, and it was important that the death and its consequences be shown. Eban kept insisting such a sequence was unnecessary. In the end, it stayed in the film, but I don't think Eban was ever very happy about it.

Clearly, the film was not just a documentary. If it was going to have any value it had clearly to reflect Eban's view. It had to represent the personal observations of one of the world's last great statesmen on one of the most pressing issues of the day. But it also had to be human and down to earth, and moving and emotional, and this wasn't always easy for Eban. This was very acutely reflected in our discussions on the people we should interview. Eban, or "Aubrey" as I was more accustomed to call him, wanted the statesmen. He wanted, and rightly so, to talk to Arafat and Bibi, King Hussein and President Mubarak, Peres and Savir, and Abu Alaa and Seib Arakat. For my part, I wanted to talk to the Arab in Gaza, to the settler in Hebron, and to ordinary people in Jerusalem and on the West Bank.

Another difficulty was that whereas Eban had a very clear perception and brilliant analysis of events leading up to the peace process, he seemed to me less sure of his footing in dealing with events after Oslo. But then who was? Eban was also inclined to be much more optimistic about the outcome of the process than I was, and we would argue considerably as to whether that optimism was justified.

The form of the film was also extremely tricky to deal with because we were telling two different stories, which, unless we were careful, would conflict with each other in terms of style and approach. The first dealt the secret negotiations of Oslo. This was a straight, fascinating narrative story involving wonderful characters such as Norway's Terje Larsen, Professor Yair Hirscheld, and Arafat's banker and adviser Abu Alaa. The second story, and entirely different in its texture and feel was what happened to the peace process after Oslo.

I found this latter story very difficult to formulate till I realized it could be conceptualized in the form of the letter . The two inner arms of the W were the Arabs and Jews who, putting it very simply, were trying to advance the process. The two outer arms of the W were those forces, Jew and Arab, settler and terrorist, who were opposed to the process and in many cases trying to wreck it. In practice, this formulation also fitted neatly into a chronological telling.

Possibly our most serious problem was the ending. How on earth were we going to come out of this unholy mess? What message were we going to leave with the audience? This couldn't wait till the day of judgment, and after consulting with Eban and lifting a few choice quotes from him, I wrote the following in December 1966 as a first draft for the end of the film.

EBAN ON CAMERA
We are at a turning point. I would like to believe that the Middle east has been irreversibly transformed, but it is difficult to predict the future.

EBAN NARRATION
The Arab Israeli dialogue does not exist in a vacuum. It is sited in
an area of fundamentalist passion where revolution and upheaval is
always on the horizon.
   Against this background we can understand what a failure of the
peace process might lead to . . . an inferno of explosive antagonisms
and volcanic hatreds. Generations might have to pass before anybody would attempt such a peace process again.

I had been very wary of Egyptian formalities and bureaucracy, but
at Cairo Airport we were given celebrity treatment. The fact that
we were traveling with Ambassador Abba Eban and were about to
interview President Mubarak was only half the story. The other half
is that I had a superb production manager and co-producer, Elia
Sides. Elia had opened doors and achieved results that seemed impossible. He had paved the way to kings and princes and more
impossible would later get us in to see some key members of Islamic
Jihad and Hamas. I didn't know what to expect of Cairo, but because of Elia it was all going as smooth as a Sunday stroll in Central Park. At least, it was till we tried to leave the airport.
   With Eban there was no problem, because an Egyptian welcoming committee had whisked him off to the hotel in a magnificent
Mercedes. For myself, crew, and equipment, the Egyptians had provided a miniature Russian car that was dangerously overcrowded
with even two people in it. I was very put out, but such a situation
rarely phased Elia. Turning to an Egyptian army officer in the car
park, he told him such things wouldn't do, as we were on a visit of
national importance that included the filming of the president. To
my surprise, the officer immediately commandeered a huge army
van, ignored the protests of the waiting driver, smiled, and wished
us a wonderful stay in Cairo as he waved good-bye.
   After a night at the Hilton Ramses, we got ready for the drive to
the palace. I was worried about time. The interview was for nine
thirty. It was now nine o'clock; the streets were choked with traffic.
In the event, I shouldn't have worried . . . except for my life. We
went in a group of five. Leading the column were two police motor
cyclists, sirens screaming. Following them was a police car, blue
lamps spinning, wheels scarcely touching the ground. Third for
take-off was Eban, sitting sedately in a black chauffeur-driven

Bentley, followed in turn by four security men in a white Honda. Last, but by no means least, was myself, driver, and crew in the equipment van. While the rest of the traffic moved at about ten miles an hour, we hurtled past at about ninety (or so it seemed) probably leaving death and destruction in our wake. I can't be sure because my eyes were closed in fear after we missed an eight-wheeled lorry by two inches.

The interview itself was a bit disappointing. But then I hadn't expected very much. Mubarak was a side player in this particular peace process, and I expected little more than clichés. They were all there, expressed in a very forthright way by a very impressive president, but they were no more than clichés, just about useful for a twenty-second sound bite in the film.

> We are supporting peace with all-out efforts. We would like to reach a fair solution which will lead to a permanent peace and stability in this part of the world. You cannot exclude Syria from the peace process otherwise, and I tell you frankly we will never reach a comprehensive settlement. Egypt suffered for ten years. We sacrificed a lot for peace and are still supporting peace by all means.

If President Mubarak looked the picture of health, Arafat looked anything but. After some difficult negotiations I had crossed into Gaza with Eban, two Israeli journalists, and my crew. When we saw Arafat our first impression was that he was ill. His hands trembled, his face looked ashen, and his whole demeanor spoke of depression. As the negotiations were totally blocked at this time, I could understand the reasons for his mood.

Mubarak we had interviewed alone. By contrast, Arafat was surrounded by six advisers. Eban had decided to do the questioning in this case and started off in Arabic. This startled Arafat who possibly wasn't used to Eban's classical use of the language. Being worried about how this would go over on U.S. TV, I asked them both if they would mind going on in English. Again the answers provided no surprises.

> The Israelis are not implementing accurately and honestly what has been agreed upon and signed at the White House. Mr. Netanyahu has frozen everything: all the negotiations, all the committees. We can't export. Our production is low. I would like to see the complete involvement of the American administration in this issue. It is not an Israeli cause. It is not an Arab cause. It is an international cause.

Eban asked Arafat what message he would like to send to the world about the attitude of the Palestinian nation to the peace process.

> In spite of all the difficulties and the troubles, we are committed to the peace process. This is a strategic choice for the Palestinians, but we are appealing to everybody to protect the peace of the brave.

When Eban had finished, I tried a few more pointed questions. Why had the Palestinian authority published an ordinance threatening death to anybody who sold land to Jews? Why after so many years of armed conflict did he decide to go for a political solution? And how did the reactions of Hamas and Islamic Jihad affect Arafat's plans?

The first question he dismissed with a smile. Those ordinances were not to be taken seriously and just repeated an old Jordanian statute. All this was stated just a week after an Arab businessman was assassinated on the West Bank for such an act of treason. As for the political solution, he had decided on it way back in the seventies.

> We stated our aim and target to achieve peace many, many years ago. You have to remember my speech in the United Nations in 1974, when I said I am coming carrying the olive branch in my hand.

This was interesting, because what I remembered was the handgun that he also carried to the podium. As for Hamas . . .

> Hamas is now different. Some of them, most of them, have accepted to deal with the peace process, and two of them are ministers in my Cabinet.

While Eban returned to Jerusalem, I went on to interview Razi Hamed, a senior member of Hamas, who edited the Gaza Hamas newspaper. His office was over a garage. To enter, you negotiated dark, winding stairs. In one corner of the room was a framed picture of the Dome of the Rock, on the table proofs of the latest edition of the Hamas newspaper. Razi Hamed himself was about thirty, dark. Bearded. Passionate. Angry. Here for once there was frankness, with the usual banalities laid aside.

> Settlement, sovereignty, Jerusalem, refugees, borders, nothing is solved. Because of this I am against Oslo. I am against it because it didn't take into consideration the minimum rights of my people.

When I mentioned to Razi that the Israelis were moving back, that they had left five cities, he was scornful. When I suggested that these events should fill him with hope, he looked disgusted.

> You are giving me two nothings. All the time they say that Israel is ready to withdraw from the West Bank and Gaza and to give the Palestinians more freedom, but it's not here. Nothing. I cannot go to the West Bank. I can't go to the beach without an Israeli check. I don't want to live under the occupation. I want my flag, my identity, my respect, my dignity.

My last questions to Razi were about Arafat and armed resistance.

> There's no democracy here, no political stability. And all the time Israel is pressuring Arafat to fight us. As for the armed struggle, that is not our first option, but Israel doesn't understand any language but the language of force. Therefore we have to go on with the strategy of armed struggle. Israel is expanding the settlements, killing Palestinians, confiscating our lands. So many of the Palestinians say we should go back to military operations. This is a war between two peoples, and nobody can tell me to forget the rest of my homeland, because for me and my parents and my grandparents, we are born in Tel Aviv and Jaffa and Israel.

One of the main difficulties of *Brink of Peace* was crossing borders—crossing into Palestinian territory, Egypt, and Jordan, loaded with film equipment. Nothing was ever simple. When we had started the film under a Labor government, relations had been good between Egypt and Israel. With Netanyahu as prime minister there was a cooling. So to get into Egypt strings had to be pulled at the highest level.

Getting into Gaza for general filming was also complex. Suddenly the Palestinian authority, with no notice, had decreed that massive forms had to be filled in for journalists' visits, and you had to be accompanied by a "minder." More than once I found myself on one side of the border, arguing with Arab police colonels at a security post and talking with Elia on a cellular phone half a mile away on the Israeli side as we tried to figure a way out of the impasse.

Even when border crossing was easy, bureaucracy and unwillingness of minor officials to make decisions could also be barriers. Crossing into Jordan, just north of Eilat couldn't have been simpler, till the Jordanese customs officer started querying us about our TV camera. This problem we had considered in advance and had secured written permission to bring in a video news camera. This wasn't good enough for the customs man. Wasn't a video camera a *small* camera? And could a TV camera be defined as a video camera? In the end we waited for three hours, till long after the post had shut down, while telephone messages went back and forth to Amman, to higher and higher officials, till permission was eventually granted.

Eventually, we crossed into Akaba at nine in the evening. After a quick meal we started the two-and-a-half-hour journey to Petra, where we were supposed to film next morning. Here we had permissions galore—permissions on permissions—enabling us to take our van through the winding hills into the back entrance of the site where we could begin to capture the glorious remains of Petra's Nabatean kingdom. I thought nothing could go wrong. I was mistaken. Four miles into the hills, ready to wind down into Petra, we had stopped at a ramshackle police hut manned by a lone teenage guard. We showed him the passes. No good. The pass said the van could go to Petra but said nothing about its occupiers. I argued logic. Was the van supposed to drive itself into Petra? No use. So back to the tourist office for more passes. The end of the story was inevitable. When we returned to the same police post an hour later, the original guard was gone, and the new one waved us through without any examination at all.

Being preoccupied with the interviews and the filming in Jordan, I had left the archive searches to my associate producer, Larry Price. Larry, supermeticulous, provided me with material on every aspect of the peace process that one could possibly need. Much of it was, in the end, to prove superfluous. There just wasn't time to go into the problems on the Golan, or the miniwar in Lebanon. The key sections that Larry found on terrorism and incitement were, however, vital and terrifying. They were vital because they provided the visual support for the film. And they were terrifying because bunched together they presented a horrific picture of events that time had erased from our minds.

For instance, I had forgotten how obscene were the demonstrations against peace and against Rabin just prior to his death: Rabin adorned with a pig's head, Rabin dressed as a Nazi officer, Zionism being borne a away in a coffin. Most disgusting of all were the scenes in Zion Square. Netanyahu talks from a balcony, while just below the parapet signs call for death to the traitors. Oil torches wave. Fists are shaken in the camera. Boiling tea is thrown at Yael Dayan.

Then there are the pictures of the terrorist incidents: Beit Lid, Afula, Tel Aviv, Bus 13 Jerusalem. Then again Jerusalem. The pictures take on a certain similarity. Always there is the wreckage and the burned, twisted skeleton of a bus or a car. There are the torn, bloodied bodies on the ground, the ambulances, the soldiers assisting, witnesses sobbing as they recount what happened. And always in the background, a small group hunts endlessly for the smallest scraps of human bodies so that they can be prepared for burial.

Over the years one learns to live with terrorism, but it never ceases to shock. And you are never removed from it. You don't live in Florida and read about a bombing in Oklahoma, nor do you live in Oregon and read about the attack on the World Trade Center from a distance. Instead you read about what is happening in your town and to your family and friends. Let me give you my own history.

In 1969 I went shopping early in Jerusalem's Machaneh Yehudah market. Five minutes after I left, a bomb exploded three meters from where my car had been. Thirteen people were killed. A few years later, a young couple I had befriended—British immigrants living just across the staircase from me in Neveh Granot—were killed by a pipe bomb that exploded in Zion Square. Four years ago, a psychologist I know was shot by terrorists in a café in Rivlin Street. Two years ago, an American friend's daughter was killed while traveling by bus to the university. Last year another friend's nephew was caught in a terrorist explosion on Ben Yehudah Street, finishing up with heavy burns and seven nails embedded in his body.

These were the incidents, particularly the bombings of February 1996, that killed Shimon Peres's election dreams. While Peres reiterated the hopes of Oslo, Netanyahu emphasized the security dangers that only Likud could guard against. While Peres smiled and invoked Rabin's legacy, Netanyahu had only one message, Arab violence that he would combat with all his might.

Peres has always seemed to me one of the most tragic, underestimated people in Israeli politics. Unlike the other favorites, he is not a man of the people. His voice is harsh, his body language awkward. He is not an ex-general. He is not a man of open-neck shirts and sandals. And yet his achievements are substantial. He helped build Israel's armament industry. He reduced Israel's hyperinflation. And more than anything it was his vision of a new Middle East that largely inspired the peace movement. He was also the linchpin of the Oslo process, persuading a doubtful Rabin that the Oslo track could bring results.

I interviewed him in his office in Tel Aviv. It was not a good day.

A few months earlier he had been deposed from Labor Party leadership by Ehud Barak. That was clearly still on his mind. Today he was rushed, harassed, and to cap it all we had come late because of immense traffic hold-ups. For the moment he was no longer a major player in the peace process, and we knew we were going to reopen some wounds. In the event his observations were insightful, often funny, and without any sense of regret.

I asked him about negotiations with Syria.

> We wanted to go ahead. Asad said he was ready to meet but couldn't fix a date. So I told the Americans, look, a girl without a date is like a date without a girl. What's the difference? You can't give me a date—how can we meet a date? That's what interrupted the attempts to meet an agreement before the end of the year.

What were his feelings about Arafat?

> When you think somebody is a terrorist, life is very simple. He doesn't laugh. He doesn't cry. He doesn't get excited. But then, all of a sudden when you see him not as a terrorist but as a human being it's a sensation for you. . . . And what we agreed with him was not about a plan but about a method. That instead of fighting each other we shall have a dialogue, to change terror for negotiation.
>
> I also asked him, "Why are we talking all the time about a Palestinian state and Jerusalem as its capital?" He said, "Don't I have the right to dream?" And I said the difference between a dream and an agreement is that for a dream you only need one. For an agreement you need two parties.

Peres's most scathing remarks concerned the delays in the Israeli pull back from West Bank territory.

> By postponing the redeployment and by extending the negotiations in Hebron we lost time and goodwill, and what did we gain? Imagine you would go to a lady, and you would tell her I have some great news for you. Instead of being pregnant nine months, you will be pregnant twenty months. It will be the same baby. Then she will ask, why suffer? Why have pains? What for? And that's really what happened.

To round off the interview, I asked Peres about his vision of peace and what he thought should motivate Israeli behavior. His answer didn't make the final cut of the film but is worth repeating.

> Likud thinks it is enough to get through the skirmishes of yesterday to achieve peace. I disagree. This is not the end of the war. Peace is

the beginning of something new, comprehensive, universal, different. It is a complete new structure.

As to your other question, I think the real identity card of the nation will be its spiritual, moral, and cultural existence. The sources of strength and wealth are no longer territorial or material. Borders and distances are not important. And if there is something which is really characteristic of Jewish existence and history, it is the preference of the moral code over all other attractions in life.

I went to see Bibu Netanyahu, accompanied by Eban. Aubrey had never met Bibi, and I wondered what he would make of a man whose views were so opposed to his own. Eban was a dove. He had spent a life in politics yet never reached that elusive goal of prime minister. And here was this sprightly right-wing youngster, who almost on entering the door of the Knesset had aimed for and immediately grabbed the highest post. Yet there were two things they shared. Both had been Israel's ambassador to the United Nations, and both were superb speakers. Netanyahu's verbal facility always fascinated me. His policies were something else. I always saw him as a gyroscope, someone who spun very fast, always stayed upright, but went nowhere. However, as a film performer he was excellent: blunt, forthright, telling you exactly what he believed in and how he saw things.

The mandate I was given was to bring peace with security, which is, I believe, the only peace we could have. It's not easy because the other side has fashioned a model that says every time they have disagreements . . . they say we are about to descend into a general cataclysmic war in the Middle East. Secondly, they often unleash violence and encourage terror. And of course, that is unacceptable. I don't want a process. I want a resolution. I want an end to the Arab-Israeli, or specifically the Palestinian-Israeli conflict. I happen to believe that is possible if violence is abandoned as a negotiating tool.

Did Netanyahu believe that? The words sounded good, but there always seemed to me to be a gap between Netanyahu's rhetoric and where his policies were leading the country. For half an hour, we went back and forth over everything, but the key questions I left for the end when Bibi's entourage were already banging on the door and demanding that he go onto his next meeting. What did he think of the future of Jerusalem? And an Arab state?

I think Jerusalem is the hardest part. I have yet to see the Palestinian leadership turn to its constituents and say, "Well, we're not going to get it all. It's not all feasible." There has to be a tailoring of expectations on their side both in the territorial dimension and the idea for example, of the right of return of refugees.

As for a Palestinian state, well the term *state* implies a collection of powers that I believe would threaten Israel and would threaten the peace. . . . So rather than deal with semantics, if you ask me point blank on a Palestinian state, then I'll tell you I'm against it because I don't want those powers to accrue to our neighbors in such a way as to threaten the peace.

In the case of Jerusalem, it has been the capital of the Jewish people for the last three millennia. The holiest city for Islam is Mecca, but it's not the capital of Saudi Arabia. We have to ensure the religious importance of Jerusalem by formalizing an arrangement and identifying a settlement that will ensure the unfettered access and worship of three great faiths. But it will not be redivided. And we will not build walls in the center of the city ever again. There are some red lines in the life of a nation, and this is one of them.

What do I see for the future? I would like to see a free country, a free continent, with a liberal ethos, definitely a liberal ethos, producing a good life for ourselves and for our neighbors—for the Palestinians, for the Jordanians, and for the Egyptians.

It was clear to me as the film progressed that I needed a very articulate spokesman on the Arab side, someone who would be as effective in stating the Palestinian case as Bibi was in talking for Israel. Dr. Hanan Ashrawi, Arafat's minister of higher education, seemed the obvious person, yet I approached her warily. I had heard her talk numerous times on television and had always been struck by the bitterness and sharpness of her attacks on Israel. There was nothing that Israel could ever do that was right. But at least she would be provocative, and I doubted that she would talk in platitudes.

What did she think of the actions of Hamas? This was asked a few days after another bombing. Well, no one had the right to transform a political position into means of violence that would claim innocent human lives, but the Israeli fundamentalists were just as dangerous. What were her opinions on Arab democracy? That was a difficult issue within Palestinian society, but the Arabs had a dual legacy of injustice. First, there was the legacy of exile, dispossession, dispersion, and therefore of revolution, secrecy, and armed struggle. Second, there was a legacy of occupation and therefore a mentality of resistance to authority. The two mentalities had to be transformed to fit into a nation-building could.

Gradually, I became aware of a certain pattern. No matter what the question, the answer always ended up with an attack on Israel. Only when I asked Ashrawi about the future of Jerusalem did the answers become a little less vitriolic.

> It is a symbol and expression of our continuity, of our culture, of our history, of our roots. Symbolically it is in the heart of every Palestinian and every Arab. But I don't look at it only as a celestial city. The solution has to be very much terrestrial. I believe sharing Jerusalem is going to be the real solution. If you solve the problem in accordance with legality and with political pragmatism Jerusalem can be the capital of two states.

Thinking of my meeting with Bibi Netanyahu, I asked Ashrawi whether there was going to be a Palestinian state.

> There is definitely going to be a Palestinian state. We have to have historical vindication of our identity, of the identity we were denied all these years. But it is not up to any one else to tell us whether we have the right to a state or not, or to give us permission whether to have a state or not. . . . The moment we are recognized we can divert all our resources, energies and talents into creating a system which is genuinely futuristic and democratic and will allow for real regional and global interaction on the basis of parity.

I'd been in Gaza a number of times since 1967 and had always emerged depressed. This was particularly true during the Intifada. Silent, wary soldiers patrolled the alleys. Children slunk along the walls. The streets were filthy, the garbage piled high. Faces peered through shuttered windows. Smoke rose from burning tires. Everywhere a sullenness hung over the city. The poisonous fumes of hatred penetrated everything. It was a city you fled from and tried not to think about while drinking your safe cappucino on Dizengoff Street.

I knew I had to go back for the film. I wanted to see what had changed. Gaza had been the most bitter and contentious area under Israel occupation. Now, two and a half years after Oslo, I wanted to see what Arafat had done for the city. What I saw was the difference between night and day.

Though the refugee camps still festered, and it was still a place of squalor and poverty, you could almost tangibly feel the new spirit in the air. It was the little things you noticed: the way the children walked upright in the center of the streets rather than by the side of the roads, the smiles, the general cheerfulness of the crowds. Where Israelis had patrolled, order was now being kept by blue-uniformed Palestinian police. Here and there a police woman directed traffic. Where housing had stagnated there was now a building boom. Tractors worked at the end of every road. Concrete blocks were sprouting everywhere. In the center square of the city, just behind the huge billboard poster of a smiling Arafat promising to regain Jerusalem, huge bulldozers were ripping up the gravel prior to building a new roundabout. And everywhere the green Palestinian flags: fluttering from telegraph poles, attached to schools, floating over the marketplace. As I put it later in the film, "a people manipulated for years by Israel and the Arab states was now establishing a national identity."

I came to Gaza to capture the changes and also to interview a number of Arabs. These were "the men in the street" that Eban wasn't so keen on. I'd spoken to quite a number on my research forays but eventually decided to interview just three or four. Were they typical of public opinion? Did they express what the majority were thinking in Gaza and the West Bank? I don't know. They just struck me as articulate, feeling people who I sensed expressed a centrist, balanced point of view. Or maybe I was kidding myself. Maybe I chose them because they were expressing just what I wanted to hear. These are the games we play in making documentaries.

Juma was typical of the Arabs I interviewed. He was about thirty-eight, a part-time policeman, and I talked to him in his house with his kids running round our knees. Juma had served as my guide around Gaza and seemed very honest and forthright. He was the one who pointed out to me the bizarre situation that many people in the city drove "legal" stolen cars. These were cars that were known to be stolen and therefore had to be registered with a red license plate. Once registered they could be driven but not sold. Juma also admitted to the corruption that went on in Gaza and had pointed out one or two of the new businesses that thrived through "connections and blackmail." To my surprise, he also talked freely of the harsh regime in the Gaza jails and the fear of the prisoners who now looked back almost longingly on their time in Israeli prisons.

This he could talk of personally as he and three of his brothers had spent quite a lot of time in Israeli jails during the Intifada. His younger sister had been killed by an Israeli bullet during this time.

Over the course of an hour, I asked him what he thought of Arafat and the general situation.

> When Arafat came into Gaza we went crazy. It was as if the whole world belonged to us. He suffered so much for us in Lebanon and Tunis, and obtained so much. He gave us a land where we Palestinians can eat, move, talk, sit, make love, and breathe freely.

I asked Juma about his thoughts on Hamas.

> They don't want there to be peace. Hamas wants to stir up Gaza and inflame passions. They don't want there to be peace. We are very much disturbed by these crazy people who blow up buses. They didn't dare do this at the time of the Intifada. Why are they trying to kill people now when there is peace?

Finally, I told Juma about Razi Hamed's dismissal of the achievements of Oslo and asked him what he thought.

> We saw that it could be really good for us. We saw that after forty-eight years of war we hadn't gained anything. But after Oslo we obtained many things. We haven't got everything, but we've got a lot. Our children can live without fear of the soldiers coming, without an atmosphere of killing. They can go to school without fear. If a family wants to go out at night and leave the kids, have a stroll, walk, laugh, it's possible.
>
> I want to tell you the truth. We really hope and want that there will be peace here. But Oslo was not enough. The truth is that the Palestinian people and the Israeli people must learn to live together. And that is possible.

Juma's opinion was definitely not shared by Dubek—Dubie Weinstock—an Israeli park ranger I talked to in Gush Etzion. Sitting on a small rock, his jeep parked on the stones below us, Dubek looked me straight in the eyes.

> I say this to anyone who asks me. This land is bitter with blood. Jew. Christian. Arab. Here blood was spilt before 1967, after 1967, and it will be spilt again after Oslo.

Dubek, a solid, balding man in his late fifties, had personal reasons for his pessimism. A few years before, his elder son had been shot and killed by two Arabs. Now he rides around with a rifle in his jeep waiting for the day he will find the murderers.

Elia, my co-producer, had known Dubek a long time and thought he would be able to express for me the feelings of the settlers on the

West Bank. The discussion of settlement was one of the key issues of the film, and I wanted to be sure it was covered well, and fairly. This was essential because although the Israeli Palestinian dispute is about many things, at heart it is a fight about land, about two people's claim to the same territory, the West Bank. In 1977 Israeli Jews had been encouraged by the new right-wing Likud government to settle on the West Bank. Since then their numbers had grown to over 120,000 settlers. Surrounding them, in small towns and hundreds of villages, live over one million Arabs. Dr. Abdel Heide Shafi, whom I had talked to in Gaza, had been very blunt about the whole situation. For him, the Israeli presence in the occupied territories was illegal. The Arabs had a right to all the occupied territories, including Jerusalem, and only their return would make for peace.

Dubek gave me the other side. He had lived in Gush Etzion, a group of kibbutzim and villages south of Jerusalem, till 1947. The Etzion block had been lost in Israel's War of Independence and many of its Jewish inhabitants killed. In 1967, following the Six-Day War, Dubek and others had moved back to the area, resuming, as it were, their birthright. Though I was not myself an advocate of West Bank settlement, I could see that many settlers felt a deep bonding among themselves, the Bible, and Jewish history, and I felt this should be expressed in the film. As far as I could judge, nothing would move Dubek from the rocks and the stones and the trees around Gush Etzion, and I wanted the viewers to understand why.

> They expelled my grandfather from the Old City of Jerusalem in 1936; otherwise we would still be living there. The war didn't begin today; it has lasted many years.
>
> The problem with my people is they have no regard for land. With any other people it would be obvious. How was it possible after two thousand years of exile they couldn't return? I'm trying to maintain the link with the land, with the soil, for myself and for my children.
>
> The link between my people and this land is closer, harder, stronger than any other people has with its land. If a people has been in existence for three thousand years and then decides to return, you can see the proof of its bonding with its land.

This conversation took place in the hills of Gush Etzion. A placid day. High scudding clouds. Dubek found some mint in the grass, and we all drank tea boiled up on the portable stove he kept in the jeep. In the foreground a few sheep. In the distance, the minaret of a mosque. Quiet. Peaceful. Nothing like the bedlam I found in Hebron.

I went to Hebron because an Israeli withdrawal had been delayed for months, and I wanted to gauge the mood after Arafat took over. Hebron is a strange, harsh city—a city where memory rules. Abraham and Isaac are said to be buried there, and a huge memorial, half mosque, half synagogue, has been erected over their graves. Arabs remember the murders committed by Baruch Goldstein who only two years before slew thirty people praying at the mosque. Israelis for their part remember the Jewish residents killed in the Arab riots of 1929.

Today Hebron is a divided city. Here in three tiny enclaves, five hundred Jews cling passionately to their ancient heritage in the town. One of the main buildings in the Avraham Avinu quarter defiantly proclaims that it was stolen from the Jews and then reclaimed. The huge round water towers are adorned with the Israeli blue and white flag. A Magen David is scrawled on the walls. Israeli gun emplacements look down on the casbah. An Israeli soldier with a green beret plays with a child. Behind him people scurry back and forth in the open-air market.

The main street of the Jewish quarter leading to the old Hadassah building is almost empty. Now and then a soldier removes the spiked barrier in the road, allowing a donkey cart to pass. In one of the doorways a young religious Jewish woman, her head covered, is hanging out washing.

When I came to Hebron on research with Elia, many of the settlers refused to speak to us. For them the TV and the media were the enemy. Eventually, we contacted Gershon Bar Cochba, one of the security officers for the Jewish quarter. After a long discussion, he agreed to talk on camera for us when we came back. What I wanted to know was why stay in Hebron? Wasn't the Jewish presence there holding up the peace process? Look at the number of armed guards it took to maintain the safety of their tiny community. Gershon's answer, given in front of Abraham's tomb was even more passionate than that of Dubek.

> Hebron represents the roots of the people of Israel. When Abraham our father came to Israel, the first place he bought land was in Hebron. Abraham, Isaac, and Jacob, the forefathers of our people from thirty-five hundred years ago, they came to this place and lived in this area behind us.
>
> I see myself as part of that thread of Jewish history, living where the link in the chain is weakest. And for me that is in Hebron.

I felt immensely moved by Gershon's words. As a Jew, how could I not be moved by his talk of links to the past? If I denied that, what was being in Israel all about? And yet Hebron is an overwhelmingly Arab city. Its inhabitants see the Jewish presence very differently. As Hanan Ashrawi said to me, "The situation in Hebron is untenable. It's a powder keg ready to explode." Meanwhile, the Jewish settlers remain, their position tenuous, their fears increasing.

The Oslo agreements are clearly one of the most intriguing diplomatic accords of recent years. That they came into being is due to chance and a lucky turn of fate. In 1992 a Labor government had been elected in Israel on a platform of peace. It was clear that direct dialogue was needed between the PLO and Israel. But Israelis were forbidden by law to talk to the PLO representatives. The answer, secret talks away from the eyes of the world, is attributed to various sources. Abu Alaa, a key adviser to the PLO, was the first to suggest Norway as a go-between. Another player was Terje Larsen, a Norwegian working in Gaza, who was trusted by both sides. According to what Larsen told me, he had also suggested to Shimon Peres that a secret back channel was needed to further the peace process. Together Larsen and Abu Alaa concocted the idea of secret meetings in Norway under the guise of an academic seminar. On the Israeli side, the main secret player was a Yair Hirshfeld. A Haifa professor with no government ties but a solid background in the situation, Hirshfeld could meet with the PLO without arousing publicity. In practice, he would be reporting to Yossi Beilin.

In trying to cover the Oslo meetings for my film, I was intrigued by three aspects. First, there was the immense secrecy surrounding the whole operation. This seemed an interesting subject for a film to delve into. Second, I thought it would be good to show where the meetings took place and how atmosphere and isolation, as at Camp David, could affect negotiations. Last, I thought we should examine the human relationships among the Oslo negotiators and how trust was achieved between the participants after so many years of suspicion.

Everyone I interviewed had a tale to tell of the tremendous efforts to maintain anonymity and stop any news of the secret meetings leaking to the press. Because of this, Abu Alaa, a sharp, twinkling ex-banker and Arafat's chief negotiator, was almost prevented from entering Oslo.

The first time I came it was all done so fast I didn't have a visa. So the police stopped me at the airport and said, "Where's your visa?" I told them I didn't have one. "Well who are you visiting?" I said, "I don't know. But I think someone is waiting for me." I didn't want to mention Terri Larsen. Afterwards I said to Terri, "Why do you do it like this?" And he said, "We've got to keep it secret."

Yair Hirshfeld, a very jovial, bonhomie type of guy with a mane of frizzy white hair, had a similar awkward experience. His came when the foreign visitors were asked to use another peculiar stratagem.

The Norwegians asked us to use other names at the hotel. Not our own. One time, I came back to the hotel at about one o'clock in the morning. I had to get the key at the reception, and then the lady on duty asked me, "What is your name?" I looked at her, and I apologized. "I'm sorry but I forgot my name."

Oslo itself was too public a place for the "academic" sessions. As a consequence, Larsen arranged for the private estate of the Beauregard paper company, one hundred kilometers from Oslo, to be put at the disposal of the Arabs and the Israelis. His cover story was that he was arranging an academic retreat for some foreigners to discuss Middle East issues. Here, numerous talks took place between January and May 1993. The object: to build confidence between the two sides and lay down a basis for negotiations.

At Beauregard, I understood what isolation could do. The country house stands in a few acres of lovely wooded grounds. Dark green lawns slope down to the distant roads. Inside the mansion pastel rooms with soft red and green velvet furniture open up into each other. Crystal chandeliers grace the ceilings. An old grandfather clock stands on the stairs. Hunting paintings adorn the yellow walls. For me Beauregard evoked a world of quiet comfort at the turn of the century, a world where all the usual inhibitions could be dropped, a private world where you might risk saying the unthinkable and dare to state the impossible. This at least was how Hirshfeld saw it.

Between us as people the relations were very, very good. We liked each other, and there was a very positive atmosphere. The difficulty was to develop the relationship. To show that while the negotiations go on and one or the other takes a difficult position it shouldn't have a negative effect on our relationship.

In the end, it was Abu Alaa who revealed to me the essence of the meetings that contributed so much to their success.

This I said from the early beginning when we first started to talk together. I said, "Look, if we go back to history, we will speak a hundred years without results. If you are ready to speak about tomorrow, how we are today, and what we want for tomorrow, I think we may reach an agreement."

In May 1993 Abu Alaa insisted on an upgrading of the Israeli delegation. This was possible since Israel had recently legalized meetings with the PLO. As a consequence of the request Uri Savir, director general of the Israeli Foreign Office, was sent to Oslo to take over the discussions. The academic discussions had become official negotiations. Larsen, however, was worried that the fantastic relationship that had been established over the months between Abu Alaa and Hirshfeld would be broken by the arrival of what he described to me as "this spit and polish shoe-shine diplomat." In his small Oslo office, Larsen told me about his first meeting with Savir.

> As Savir came off the plane my heart sank seeing this severe diplomat in his black suit. I thought, this is never going to work, given the informality and the person-to-person trust we had already established. So when we drove to the first meeting, I thought I should give Savir some lines to break the ice. I said, "I'll introduce you to Abu Alaa, point at him, and I'll say to you, "Here is your public enemy number one." Savir looked rather bewildered and didn't comment, which made me very uneasy. But I said those lines. Abu Alaa found it very funny. They took off their jackets and rolled up their sleeves. So it all started well.

The meetings between Savir and Abu Alaa were actually held at a ski cottage near Oslo, used by Norwegian cabinet ministers. When we went to film there I was once more struck, as in Beauregard, by the beauty of the site, the quietness, and the isolation. I asked Uri Savir about his feelings during these first meetings.

> I think I was extremely tense. You cannot in such moments detach yourself from a certain self-awareness about what you are doing. I remember my first walk in the woods around Oslo with Abu Alaa, when we told each other our personal histories. Slowly we developed a common language, which sometimes happens between people, and we were lucky to have that chemistry.
>
> And being alone and creating a Palestinian-Israeli chemistry is really not only the essence of the negotiations—it is also the essence of the agreements which were born out of the negotiations.

In the film, I detailed the ups and downs of the negotiations and the arguments about the contents of the agreement. I also detailed Peres's secret visit to Stockholm to conclude the negotiations and his six-hour telephone conversation with Arafat in Tunis. This was done by using Norway's foreign minister, Jorgen Holst, as an intermediary. What didn't make it into the film were the secret passwords and signs involved in placing that international conversation. These had been established by Larsen.

> To avoid international surveillance, which is cued to names, we made up some very simple codes. We called Yossi Beilin "the son." We called Abu Mazen, the PLO number two man "the holy spirit." Yitzhak Rabin was "the grandfather," and Arafat was "the grandfather on the other side." Mr. Peres was "the father," and Abu Alaa, "the father on the other side." When I talked to Arafat that dramatic night in Stockholm I told him I was with "my father," and I had to repeat it several times before Arafat understood I was there with Shimon Peres.

Abu Alaa, who was then in Tunis with Arafat, was visibly moved when I reminded him about the scene and the phone call. "We were six people in the room. We had tears in our eyes. At that time we thought, well, this is the first step towards achieving Palestine and towards creating and building Palestine and peace." After making tremendous efforts, Elia managed to track down and borrow the videotape that the Norwegian police made of the secret signing between the two sides in Oslo. Each side is welcomed in a luxurious private mansion by Jorgen Holst. Peres and Hirshfeld, Terri Larsen, Larsen's wife, and a few others sit on chairs around the walls. A serious Savir and a smiling Abu Alaa initial the documents; then both make short speeches. What was going through their minds? This is the way Uri Savir put it.

> At the initialing of the agreement I think I had a very strange feeling. It was the contrast between a group of about a dozen people in a small room, the curtains closed, the secret cameras of the Norwegian police taking pictures, and doing something totally clandestine which had enormous historical repercussions.

Although I hadn't finished filming, we started editing in mid-May 1997, giving ourselves till the end of August to finish. Here we were, up against the gun because a broadcast date had already been allocated for mid-October, and the film had to be turned in six weeks before. What worried me most about the editing was that as we were proceeding the whole fabric of the peace process seemed to be crumbling. Israel had started building on Har Homa in south Jerusalem, an action regarded as extremely provocative by the PLO. The negotiations seemed to have entered a deep freeze. Street fighting had resumed in Hebron. A major terrorist attack had occurred in Jerusalem's open-air vegetable market, and a crazy Jordanese soldier had slaughtered six children on a school outing. My fear was that we were saying good-bye to the peace process, and the film would be outdated before it ever hit the screen.

All this seemed hardly to worry WNET. Their big concern was that the film should be balanced and should not be seen as overtly pro-Israel. Because of this they kept picking on little things. Why did the Israelis speak English so fluently, and why did the Arabs in the film speak in such strange, sometimes unintelligible voices. Couldn't I find Arabs with better accents? And why was my language so loaded? Why did I have to call Yitzhak Rabin "general turned statesman?" Wasn't that overdoing it? Couldn't I perhaps just call him "army officer turned politician?"

These matters faded as we struggled to finish the film. This meant numerous sessions with Eban and my script consultant, John Fox, to get the wording of the ending correct. Here we were all in agreement. We wanted a conclusion that would acknowledge all the difficulties and yet would sustain the note of passion and hopefulness that we all felt. This is how it came out, not all that different in the end from what I had scripted nine months before:

EBAN ON CAMERA: The Middle East has been irreversibly
transformed by the Oslo agreements. Things have been said that
were never said before. Things have been done that were never
done before. Written peace commitments have been exchanged.
There are, however, no guarantees for the future. Dedicated oppo-
nents of peace can still dismantle the accords bit by bit, till every
element of friendship, trust, and cooperation has been undone.
That must not be allowed.

NARRATION: The success of the peace process may not lead to
utopia, but it will stop the endless cycle of wars and violence. For
both Palestinians and Israelis a path has been shown in which the

opportunities transcend the dangers. It is a difficult path and daunting. But unless it is vigorously pursued generations might pass before anyone will attempt such a peace process again.

At the beginning of September, absolutely exhausted, I went for a holiday in Denmark and then back to Israel. The film itself, finally titled *On the Brink of Peace*, was screened in October and on the whole got a good press. I thought I was home and dry, but not quite. In November WNET started forwarding to me a few of the protest letters it had received, mostly from right-wing American Jews. There weren't many, but they hurt. *On Camera*, a Jewish magazine devoted to accuracy in Middle East reporting, called the film a "skewed history that blackened Israel's past." Someone called Eban a "biased radical." Others spoke of the film's lack of objectivity and balance. As one person wrote, "The omission and distortion of facts resulted in a portrayal of Israel as the cause of the breakdown of the peace process." The same letter went on as follows.

> In discussing the Palestinian administration Mr. Eban doesn't mention its brutality, denial of civil rights and torture of prisoners. 70% of recently polled Palestinians said they would rather spend a night in an Israeli jail than in a Palestinian jail. Although this documentary is an improvement on your past deliberately inaccurate and inflammatory reports on the Middle East it still falls short of the balanced and objective presentation of information you are obligated to provide the public.

In my written answer to this letter, I said that the program was never meant as *the* final definitive history of the peace process. It represented the personal view of the process as seen by Abba Eban, one of Israel's most distinguished statesmen and one of Israel's greatest defenders in times of stress and difficulty. Having gotten that out of the way I restated what I had been trying to do—not argue the rights and wrongs of each side but present a broad, balanced spectrum of views regarding the peace process. "Given the time at our disposal it was clear that many interesting things would not come up for discussion, from feelings of Arab prisoners towards Arafat to Israel's failure to provide a clear passage between Gaza and the West Bank."

Actually, I was furious at the letters because they expressed such a moral one-sidedness. Yes, I agreed, we should raise hell about what was happening in Arafat's jails. But where were these people when we Jews and Israelis were doing just as bad things to Arabs in our jails in the Intifada. They were silent. Quiet. Hiding. More important was that they had missed the point of the film and the essence of the peace process. The point was that whatever had happened in the past, and wherever blame lay in the past—and it certainly wasn't one-sided—one had to move on. Which brings me back to Yitzhak Rabin.

There is a moment in the film when Arafat and Rabin are seen with Bill Clinton on the lawn of the White House. A momentous decision for peace has been made. Documents have been signed. Arafat reaches across to shake Rabin's hand. Rabin hesitates. This is a murderer's hand, and Rabin's memory is as good as anyone's in Israel. Rabin hesitates and then he grips the outstretched hand. The decision has been made. One must go forward and seize any chance that will end the useless cycle of bloodshed.

Rabin is missing from most of the film, but he dominates it—because he showed the way. I thought, as I wrote earlier, that his death would shock Israel back to first principles. That it would reunify the people. Make us one people, with a purpose and a direction. A people with love, not hate. Three years later, I began to feel that I had never been so wrong in my life. Nothing that I thought would happen had come to pass. In fact, exactly the opposite had happened. By September 1998, Israel was possibly more divided than ever, and hate roamed once more, almost unchecked.

Three or four events characterize what was happening. A small group went to visit Yigal Amir, Rabin's murderer, in prison, to wish him happy birthday and offer him support. Two months later, a television program, the *Cameri Quintet*, ran a skit showing an actor playing Yigal Amir in his cell. Amir looks at the camera and smiles. "I'm fine," he says. "It's nice to know you now realize I was right. Don't worry. I'll be out soon. Then maybe I'll run for prime minister." Then I read in the Haaretz newspaper that Norway was hosting a five-year celebration of the Oslo accords. Bibi Netanyahu declined to attend.

And so it continued. The most significant thing was that, as Israel commemorated its fiftieth anniversary, all references to Rabin were eliminated from the official celebrations. It was as if the man had never existed and had been wiped from the face of Israel.

I finished *On the Brink of Peace* in September 1997. Then nothing seemed to move until Bibi Netanyahu and Chairman Arafat

signed the Wye accord. Despite the agreement, Netanyahu continued to spin. The Israeli government rolled from crisis to crisis, while
Arafat's Palestine Authority wallowed in an advanced state of pa-
ralysis. In Oslo in March 1997, Larsen concluded our discussion
with words that still seem appropriate: "I believe that a long time
ago, the Olso peace process reached a point of no return. It has been
a difficult and a dangerous road. Unfortunately it has also been a
very bloody road. And I regret to say that in future it will be the
same: dangerous, difficult, and bloody. But I believe it is the only
way to go because all the other alternatives are much worse."

10 - *Civilization and the Jews*

In spring of 1998 I was asked to remake and update an old film of mine, *Into the Future*, which dealt with the situation of world Jewry at the end of the century. This one-hour film had first been made for an innovative WNET series, which in its time had garnered a great deal of attention worldwide.

The original program concept had been extremely intriguing. A nine-part series on the history of the Jews and their involvement with Western civilization. But one wondered whether it could it be done. When the idea was first proposed in the late seventies, it looked doubtful. Six or seven years later, under the title *Heritage: Civilization and the Jews*, the series became the PBS hit of the eighties, putting Channel 13/WNET on the map as a serious producer of major documentary work.

Time has blurred who first came up with the idea. Some say it was the brainchild of Bob Kotlowitz, then one of the senior staff at 13/WNET-New York. Others say that it was Abba Eban's. A few say that it originated in the mind of Jay Iselin, then head of WNET. There are even arguments that say the series arose through the initiative of Eli Evans, president of the Charles Revson Foundation. In practice, I think it was a case of circumstances and prevailing moods generating similar ideas in the minds of a number of people at the same time.

In England and throughout the United States, the success of Jacob Bronowski's *Ascent of Man* series and Kenneth Clark's *Civilization* had shown that there was a massive audience for well-crafted TV series dealing with history and culture. The success of Jeremy Isaacs's *The World at War* gave a further impetus to TV stations to investigate new possibilities for long-running series. Then again, in the U.K. Bamber Gascoigne had already dealt with the history of the church and Christianity. So maybe it was now time to examine the Jews who from Moses and the prophets through Einstein, Freud, and Marx could be said to have had a fairly strong part in creating the intellectual and ethical framework of the modern world.

The scene was set almost imperceptibly. At WNET, memos were passed, ideas bandied around, and the name of Abba Eban—who was then teaching at Princeton—put forward as a possible series presenter. But where was the money to get the idea going? Being a noncommercial station 13/WNET would always be dogged by this problem. The answer came in a 1979 development grant of around fifty thousand dollars from the Charles Revson Foundation to Abba Eban to explore the feasibility of a television series on the interaction between Jewish history and Western civilization. Later Revson increased the grant to one million dollars to WNET when Channel 13 assumed responsibility and the series actually took off. To a large extent, the donation was due to the passionate involvement and enthusiasm of Eli Evans, president of the foundation. In the end this meant not just the giving of money but Evans' major work in the enlistment of other donors, support for the series when it seemed to be crumbling, and tremendous backing for the educational and outreach side of the project.

With research and development money in hand, and with Eban and WNET united in a promising marriage, all that was needed was a bright executive producer to get the project up and running. He emerged in the person of Marc Siegel, a very smart and highly experienced New York producer of both Jewish and non-Jewish subjects. Armed with Revson's money Marc's first objectives were to write a detailed proposal for an NEH grant and put together a team. And it was about that time that *Civilization and the Jews* entered my life and dominated it for a few years.

I'd heard about the series over the grapevine and had also read a short note about it in the *Jerusalem Post*. Admittedly, I was a few thousand miles away from the action, but what the hell, I had nothing to lose, and it was worth a try. In that frame of mind, I sat down one morning and wrote a letter to Marc, listing my achievements, and sent it off registered airmail. Two weeks later I got a reply: "Very interested in your letter. Do come and see me when you are in New York. We must certainly talk." *Delighted* is not quite the word for my reaction. *Astonished* and *overwhelmed* convey much more of my feelings when I opened the missile. It was such an unusual letter to receive from a producer: supportive, enthusiastic, welcoming. In the past most of the begging letters I had written had either been ignored or acknowledged with such words as "You've got to be kidding. We have a thousand applicants for this researcher's job. If none of them are any good we'll write to you again. But don't hold your breath."

To my surprise, Marc's warmth and enthusiasm continued in New York when I went there a few months later to finish a Hadassah film. Eventually, after a number of very good lunches and extensive consumption of Marc's whiskey, the position became clear. What had interested him in my note was my experience in filming the Eichmann trial and my overall Israeli background. He had already engaged writers and directors for the first few films, but there was probably a place for me as second-unit director on the various work that had to be done in Tel Aviv and Jerusalem. There was also the possibility, but only a possibility mind you, that I might be able to work as producer on one of the later films.

For a while there was nothing much to be done, and the promises stayed promises. Gradually, however, the work increased, and I found myself doing everything from scenic pickups to recording commentary with Eban. One day, however, Marc phoned me, asking for something different. There was going to be a huge week-long Holocaust-survivors rally in Jerusalem. Could I film it and also interview some of the more interesting of the survivors? If any good or interesting material came out of this, it could be held for the series film on the Holocaust. In other words, could I engage in an open-ended fishing expedition.

Dozens of film crews arrived for the week, all more or less pursuing the same objectives as myself—film the ceremonies and get some good interviews. The first part was easy. My problem working on the series, however, was to consider what would make sense not as news but as film material for programs that would only be made in a year or so. In the event, I went for what touched the emotions the most. Here the most outstanding moment was the massive gathering at Yad Vashem Museum to pay tribute to the partisans of the Warsaw Ghetto uprising, while the saddest was the lighting of the thousands of memorial candles at night at the Western Wall.

Getting good interviews was more difficult. Somehow, in a few days, you had to track down the most interesting people, with the most fascinating stories, and then get them to find time for the filming. All this against the competition of the other crews pursuing the same goals. Even more problematic in regard to the survivors was the impossible and almost insulting question, What was an interesting and fascinating story? For me that was a story that went beyond its own particularity to express some overall truth or special insight into the Holocaust.

One of those moments came when I interviewed Cordelia Edwardson, a Swedish journalist working in Israel. Cordelia, the product of a mixed marriage—Catholic mother, Jewish father—had for various complex reasons been given up by her family to the Gestapo, and after a period in Terezenstadt finished up in Auschwitz. In the death camp she kept asking, "What is a nice Catholic girl from Berlin doing among all these Jews?" Her decisive answer was that she was one of them and identified with them. What also came out of our conversation was not only the retelling of the experiences but Cordelia's passionate belief regarding the division of the world into the forces of darkness and light and the vital need to side with forces of light.

Ernest Michel, then executive director of the UJA, was another one whose history left a vivid impression upon me. Ernie told me three stories, two of which I eventually used in *Out of the Ashes*. The first was a vivid description of *Kristalnacht*, the night when the Brownshirts set fire to most of Germany's synagogues. "My father saw the writing on the wall. He told me to get out. I had a visa for the States, but there were fourteen thousand people before me. With luck I could have gotten out in 1942." Instead Ernie stayed in Germany and was caught by the Nazis. Ernie's second story described the selection process at Auschwitz. "The thumb went up, and the thumb went down. Up you lived. Down you died. But at the time you didn't know what it meant."

The story I didn't use was actually the most interesting of the three.

At the end of the war, Ernie was working as a laborer on a farm in France. "The bells were pealing. The war was over. Suddenly I realized I had a choice, for the first time. The Jews had died, been murdered because they were Jews. No one knew who I was. Now was my chance. If I liked, I could totally abandon my Jewishness. Why should I hold onto it when it only meant death?" This was a question that I was sure thousands must have asked of themselves during those days, but for some reason I never used it.

Likewise, I never used any of the answers I got from Emil Fackenheim. I had looked up Fackenheim because he was known as a philosopher and thinker who had spent years contemplating the Holocaust and its meaning. In one of his books, he had written, "The Jews must not give Hitler a posthumous victory. The eleventh commandment is that the Jews must survive." Fackenheim was fascinating to listen to but difficult to use as his combination of both Scottish and Lithuanian accents made him almost impossible to understand.

The Jerusalem Holocaust survivors' gathering took place in 1981. Two years later, in 1983, Marc Siegel asked me to produce and direct *Out of the Ashes*. This was the film he had been dangling before me since our first encounter. Now, four years later, it was actually happening, or, according to Marc, should happen with a bit of luck. The hesitant framing of the invitation was due to one thing, the series was running out of money. While part of this situation was due to the usual budgeting problems surrounding a big series, part was due to some questionable creative decisions involving the filming of Eban and the creation of a special museum unit.

After his initial investigation of the project, Abba Eban had been invited by WNET to advise on and front the series. While the invitation was mainly due to his outstanding position as a world-famed statesman, historian, and noted orator, it was also hoped that use of his name would work wonders in fund-raising. The only problem was that Eban was then in his late sixties, and some questions must have been raised asking what would happen if Eban fell ill or was called back to politics. While no real answer besides major insurance could be given to these questions, there did seem to be a partial answer—film Eban's opening and closing film lines immediately. Then, if he became unavailable for any reason, there would be something in the can.

While this made sense in theory, it turned out to be nonsensical in practice. What eventually happened was that at tremendous cost Abba Eban, often together with his dynamic and attractive wife Suzy, was dragged all over Europe and through the Israeli deserts to film lengthy speeches for films that had yet to be scripted. Most of the speeches, often lasting two or three minutes, were totally unsuited for the final series and were almost universally omitted by the later directors of the various films. No one knows for sure, but this insurance ploy may well have cost over half a million dollars. In the end, little came out of it except Eban's quote, "They took me up Mount Sinai to talk about the Ten Commandments, but I came down very quickly—before God gave us another ten."

The museum unit was also another tremendous money waster. Here someone had had the bright idea of dispatching a special second unit team to the world's key museums and having them film artifacts that could potentially be used in the different films. Thus one filming session at the Jerusalem museum would contribute footage for six or seven films, and one visit to the British museum would likewise contribute archive for three or four films. In theory this would obviate each different director having to make a special trip to a certain site. It was a wonderful theory but never worked for two reasons. First, the objects were shot without being related to script or context, just on the assumption that they might be used . . . somewhere. Second, most of the producer-directors, including myself, not only disliked having someone else's work shoved upon them, but more seriously could find no place to use the assembled footage. So another few thousands went down the tubes with no positive result.

Besides the above problems, there was another depressing downer to the series. A number of the films in production were themselves showing difficulties, and one had in fact had to be totally abandoned. The eventual situation, then, when Marc asked me to act as producer, was that after almost four years of production, only two films out of nine were near completion. Coupled with all this a rumor was going round the station that because of the money difficulties *Civilization and the Jews* might have to end abruptly in the sixteenth century. Good-bye, the modern age. Good-bye, the French Revolution, Hassidism, Enlightenment, nationalism, America, Marx, Freud, Hitler, and Israel.

Well, the patient didn't die but struggled on with severely reduced budgets. For my own part, this didn't concern me too much, because the allocation for *Out of the Ashes* was still much more generous than any budget I'd worked on before.

Out of the Ashes was to be devoted to the Holocaust and was the eighth and penultimate film in the series. What I'd seen of the early episodes, the Bible-and-after films, seemed to me fairly heavy stuff, but the producers had all my sympathy. They were difficult films to bring to life, being so heavily dependent on scenery, statues, and suggestive reenactments and of necessity totally devoid of interviews and live footage. But occasionally there were brilliant flashes, when it all came together, such as in the film dealing with the Moorish period and the Jews of Spain.

Without realizing it at first, I soon understood that I had in fact been given what could turn out to be the most interesting film of the series. Partially this had to do with subject. The Holocaust was closer to us, more meaningful to us, and more painful and emotionally wrenching for us than any of the earlier films could possibly be. All these elements made for a film which would be much easier for the audience to grasp and relate to than anything dealing with the previous centuries. But the added element that would make the filming so much easier was that I could use photos, recollections, memories, interviews, and archives—basic dynamic and vital film material that had perforce been absent from all those films that dealt with the period before the nineteenth century.

As producer-director of *Out of the Ashes*, I had the total creative responsibility in my hands, and within limits I could shape and formulate the film as I wanted. I could also write it if I wished, but as I had already written two films on Nazi Germany, I wanted a fresh viewpoint. In the end, I asked a highly gifted English writer, Brian Winston, to do the script, while I provided detailed guidelines and outline. Our first task together was to reformulate the boundaries of the film.

In my first discussions with Marc, the film was defined as covering the years 1933 to 1948. In fact, Eban had filmed a piece before I came onto the scene (never used), talking about how much the world had changed between those years. I felt very strongly that these boundary lines were totally wrong. To start in 1933 was to give the whole game to Hitler, and to end in 1948 was to build in the proposition that Israel only came into existence because of Hitler, which I thought was untrue and misleading. I argued instead that the film should start in 1918 and end in 1945. It would start at the end of the First World War—a clear historical watershed—go on to the revolutionary ideas of the twenties, and conclude with victory in 1945, when we would provide a bitter summing up of the Holocaust. Marc agreed with me on the time framework, and the first battle was over.

The second battle had to do with Israel, and it was one I lost. When I had looked at the original outline for the nine-part series, there seemed to me one glaring omission—there was no single film devoted to the rise of modern Israel. By way of contrast the story of America and its Jews took up not only film seven in its entirety, but was also slated to figure very prominently in the last film of the series, *Into the Future*. To make up for the fact that no single film was to be devoted to Israel's emergence, the powers that be had decreed that parts of the story should be threaded through two or three films, one of which was my film on the Holocaust. I thought this was a dreadful decision both politically and creatively, one lacking all tact, sensitivity, and feeling. My objections were to no avail. My instructions were literally to shove in a bit of Israel, and if possible link the story to the flight of the Jews from Germany. These instructions were duly carried out, but the Israeli section always seemed to me to stick out very badly and ruin an otherwise excellent film.

Having fixed the parameters, Brian and I got down to the script. By *script* I mean not just the commentary but the overall shape of the film, the sense of rhythm and the clear layout of ideas. When you get that all well blocked and clearly laid out in a historical essay film, the rest—the filming and the editing—becomes relatively simple. But without a solid script you're dead. Brian and I knew that creating a good script depended (a) on finding the correct focus for the film and (b) on selecting the right topics for the fifty-six minutes.

Usually we thrashed matters out at night over at Brian's apartment in Greenwich Village. With luck, Brian's extremely voluble three-year-old daughter would be in bed, and Brian would be free to march up and down his apartment while gesticulating wildly at some of my madder ideas. For the most part, our disagreements were very rare, and Brian turned out (at least in this film) to be the ideal person with whom to work.

It was clear to both of us that in doing a film on the Holocaust, the historical facts, though horrifying, were accessible and relatively simple to grasp. Both of us had read the major works on the period from Raoul Hilberg and Alan Bullock to Lucy Davidowicz and Gerald Reitlinger, and we were aided by a research assistant who got us other books and articles as and when needed. We also had good access to the Yad Vashem Holocaust archives and were introduced to dozens of potential witnesses. The real problem was where to go with the material. In other words, what should we focus on when the world had already seen hundreds of films on the Holocaust? In practice, we drew up the guidelines relatively quickly. What we wanted to do, and felt had been neglected by other films was

- to show Hitler as the supreme politician rather than just a megalomaniac rabble rouser
- to provide a strong analysis of conditions in Weimar Germany
- to reveal the full extent of Jewish wartime resistance
- to illustrate that not only six million Jews died but also that a culture and a whole way of life disappeared
- to discuss the ambiguous attitude of the allies to Jewish annihilation.

As director I was also guided by three other script considerations. I wanted the piece to be effective emotionally, and I wanted general topics to be illustrated by particular stories. I also wanted to avoid using "experts" for comment. It seemed to me to be enough to have Eban reflecting on the events and showing their importance.

The underlying difficulty, of course, for Brian and myself was deciding which events to highlight in the film. Though we only had fifty-six minutes at our disposal, we had to cover twenty-five years of dense European and Jewish history. In essence we were taking a headline run through history, in which much of importance would have to be dropped through lack of time or merely referred to in passing. That meant we could only provide the outline of events rather than show their full texture and complexity. But in a sense this was helpful in sharpening our focus on the film.

Choosing the main topics was easy enough. They included a quick sketch of the position of Europe's Jews in 1920, the background of the Weimar republic, the election of Hitler, the Nuremberg laws, *Kristalnacht*, the final solution and the death camps, and the Warsaw Ghetto uprising. These were the subjects that had to be in. It was the second-line choice that was difficult but in fact more interesting. Here I opted for certain human stories that would bring the abstract concept of annihilation and the breakdown of civilization down to earth in the most moving way possible. This meant the inclusion of the story of the *St. Louis* refugee ship that was turned back from the United States and Cuba and returned its passengers to almost certain death in Germany. And it meant the inclusion of the story of Oradour, a tiny French village whose six hundred inhabitants were massacred by the SS in spring 1944.

In the end, I was very happy with what was in but was also extremely distressed at the important stories that had to be excluded. The most problematic decision here was the omission of the story of anti-Semitism in Poland prior to 1939 and the description of the pogroms in Lemburg. The whole subject was intensely interesting, but there was just no room for its inclusion in the final film.

Thinking in principle about stories is one thing, but finding the material to support them is something else. After much hunting, we found footage about the *St. Louis* in the archives of the UJA. Knowing the outcome of the story the footage was heartbreaking. One sequence said it all. The ship is in dock, the passengers trapped on board, forbidden to disembark. A woman's face looks out beseechingly from a porthole. Not more than twelve feet away on the quay, a middle-aged woman stretches out her hand in agony and despair.

Researching Oradour was very different. Besides shooting the men in the village square, the Nazis had herded the women and children into the church, machine-gunned them, set the church on fire, and then destroyed the village. Having read all this, I took a train from Paris to see what remained of the village after the tragedy, because Oradour sur Glane was never rebuilt. What I found were whispers and memories. Ribs of houses. Frames of barns. Here a burnt-out car totally overgrown with weeds. There a rusty frying pan swinging on the wall under a gutted roof. The church just a skeleton, with a black charred baby's carriage lying in the corner.

The real story of Oradour was to be found in the village graveyard. Row after row of tombstones all bearing photos and the same hated date. One tombstone of black marble revealed everything. It contained fourteen names and fourteen photos of the members of one family. There were the grandparents, the uncles and aunts, the father and mother, and four children. Some of the photos were serious and full of gravitas. Some showed smiling faces. All had a future. All died on the same day.

This scene at Oradour, that of the *St. Louis*, and one other often reduced me to tears in the midst of editing as the emotions became too overwhelming. All of them said the same thing. How was this possible in the enlightened twentieth century? The last piece of material of this kind was a fragment my film researcher Raye Farr had found buried in some German archives. It showed German troops invading a Russian village. At the point of filming, the troops are separating the men and the women, who are marched off in different directions. The men, mostly middle aged and unshaven, stare blankly at the camera. The women cry and wave hopelessly. What is clear is that they know they will probably never ever see each other again in their lives.

What is rarely realized by nonfilmmakers is that the existence or nonexistence of film materials often dictates the inclusion or exclusion of a story. The Germans, of course, never filmed Jewish resistance, and because of the lack of archives the topic just doesn't exist for many films. For us, the topic was supremely important, and we pushed every which way to bring it alive through interviews and stills. Similarly, the most important event historically may be the most boring filmically and again gets excluded in favor of action. Such an event for us was typified by the Wannsee Conference, which decided on Jewish annihilation. This clearly had to be in the script and was finally covered by filming in situ.

The method of work of Brian and myself was very straightforward. In the beginning, we spent weeks discussing all the issues at hand, formulating our approach, and deciding on the topics we wanted to pursue. Brian then went off for a month before presenting me with a basic forty-page draft outline script. I then took this with me on a ten-day research trip to Europe. On returning I reworked the script with Brian to take in new ideas suggested by the location research. One of the ideas related to Denmark. We had always wanted to say something about the escape of the Danish Jews by sea to Sweden, but archive materials and stills were practically non-existent. After my visit I thought we could stage a simple scene of a small boat leaving the harbor with refugees. It would clearly not be the real thing, but it would say to the audience "Just try for a moment to imagine what it was like."

A second idea related to the death camps. They were a central subject in the film, but no material other than stills existed of the camps prior to their liberation. What I decided to do after visiting Poland was restage the last journey to Auschwitz-Birkenau from the point of view of a Jewish prisoner who sees the woods, the trees, the blossoming flowers, and the blue sky for the last time through the open slat of a jammed railway cattle car. The material would then be cut into the film along with shots of Auschwitz today, barren, broken, deserted. There would be no formal commentary, but I saw how we could use some wonderfully moving personal memoirs to cover the visuals. In the end this became one of the most devastating scenes in the film.

The narration that covered the scene was actually taken from *The Memoirs of Isabella*, by Isabella Leitner, who recites the book's passages in the film. I had met Isabella in New York while investigating death camp survivors. Along with her mother and three sisters, she had been deported from Hungary to Auschwitz in 1944. At first, even though I thought Isabella's story was interesting, I didn't want to use her, finding her brash and slightly aggressive. Then she played a tape for me of a reading of her memoirs that she had given at Yale. It was haunting, devastating. So much so that I couldn't believe it was the voice of the same woman who had just been so off-putting in my office. With very little encouragement, Isabella agreed to recite some of the book's passages in the film. Thus it is her unforgettably moving voice that leads us into the death camp with the refrain:

> The scent of spring wasn't delicious. The earth didn't smile, it shrieked.
> The air was filled with death. Your mother's death.
> We arrived in Auschwitz on May 31st.
> May is damned. May should be abolished. May hurts.
> There should be only eleven months in a year.
> May should be set aside for six million years
> . . . to cleanse the earth.

The research threw up a number of very interesting moments. Some were incredibly saddening, like the visit to Oradour, some of a lighter nature, like our visit to the photographer Roman Vishniac. Like most people having anything to do with modern European Jewish history I was familiar with Vishniac's moving photos of Poland in the thirties. Maybe we could use some of them. Maybe we could actually interview Vishniac for the film. Both ideas seemed possible, so having duly set up an appointment I hurried over one morning to Vishniac's apartment on New York's Upper West Side.

The first thing that hit you about the apartment was its cluttered quality. Tables piled a foot high with books, magazines, and photos. Other photos scattered across the room, on chairs, and even lying on the floor. On the wall, a small plaque dedicated to Dr. Roman Vishniac, photographer, scientist, humanist, engineer, and a dozen other professions. Jokingly, I asked Vishniac why it didn't record that he was a scuba diver as well. As I expected the joke fell flat.

Vishniac, frail and in his late seventies, was eager to talk. And that's where we made the major mistake. My assistant Petra asked him, as introduction, to tell us about his early life in Russia. An hour later, we were still in Russia and hadn't even reached 1920. Only after an hour and a half did we get onto Poland and the thirties. All of what he told us was fascinating but useless for the film, such as the fact that his precious negatives were buried under the floorboards till after the war. But one answer stayed with me long after. This was in response to my question as to how he obtained his best shots, like the one of the frightened little Polish girl cringing up against a wall. "Well," said Vishniac, "occasionally I used to dress up as a German officer, in uniform, and enter the Jewish houses with the German guards. I would then film the reactions of the inhabitants." After that, I never looked at the Vishniac photos in quite the same way again.

The research and filming we did in Poland also threw up some bizarre moments, such as my first meeting with the officials of Film Polski, the Communist government film office, which was providing us with a researcher and a small film crew. After the introductions, I was anxious to get on the road and start research. But this was too easy. First, I had to sit down with my associate producer, Megan, and hear a lecture by the director of Film Polski explaining how and why Poland had never been anti-Semitic. After this, we were treated to an hour film on the history of the Jews of Poland and a half-hour film, also made by the government organization, about Jewish graveyards. Only then, with the morning spent, were we able to move.

I had asked for a driver and an interpreter, but somehow we were joined by three other people whose functions never became clear to me. Or maybe they did. Martin was the production manager, so that made sense. Stefan was always photographing us, while Yosef, who spoke no English, was probably there to keep a political eye on everybody. So we obviously had three workers and two private investigators.

Research and filming went well, till the moment came, on my second visit, when we had to pay the bill. As Megan was carrying all our money, I left her to sort things out with Martin while I had a cup of coffee. Suddenly the coffee was interrupted by a distraught Megan waving a piece of paper in my face. "Take a look at this. Can you believe the cheek?" We had worked with the Poles for three and a half days, and at the most generous estimate the bill could only have amounted to about $4000. Instead it was for $15,000. Examining it carefully I could see why. It was a thing of wonder and beauty and had obviously been composed with the utmost use of creative imagination. Thus under "camera preparation," a task that normally took about ten minutes, I read, "Three days at $250 a day." Lower down there was another enigmatic entry: "Preparation of documents, five days at $300 a day." And so it went on.

Telling Megan to take a drink, a strong one, I pulled Martin aside, showed him the accounts, and started explaining my position. "It's wonderful Martin, and undoubtably every cent is due. But I have a problem. You come from a Communist or socialist country, where this is the way you work and write bills. But I come from an awful, disgusting, capitalist country where, unfortunately, they don't allow more than five minutes to prepare a camera and ten minutes to draw up documents. So maybe these items and a few others ought to go." Being a reasonable fellow, and at least having tried hard, Martin adjusted the bill, dropping $10,000 in ten minutes. But there had to be some face saving. "I'm only doing it, Alan, because I believe this film could be the start of some important co-productions between Film Polski and WNET." I didn't doubt it, and we both drank to that.

Later in the evening, at the wrap party, I experienced the final shock. After Megan's bottle of whiskey had been consumed and toasts drunk to Poland and the United States, Yosef the commissar or KGB man drew me aside and gave me a small package wrapped in black paper. In halting English, which he now suddenly spoke, he wished me luck and swore me to only open the present on the plane. "Of course," I said but naturally opened it ten minutes later in my bedroom. Inside the black paper was a small Polish solidarity badge, the emblem of the fight against communism. Finally I knew what hedging your bets meant.

Toward the end of the film, most of my script decisions were being dictated by budgetary considerations. The ample sums available at the start of the series had vanished, and each week my budget was being cut more and more. One result was that I was told to use location filming rather than archives because, at three thousand dollars a minute for archive rights, location shooting was cheaper. On the whole, this worked well, in Denmark, in Oradour, in Israel, and in Poland. My only hesitation was in the use of this method in Germany.

I considered an understanding of the notorious Nuremberg laws vital for the film and wanted to show that because of them Jews were restricted in professions, work places, and marriage to non-Jews. They were also limited to the extent they could hire rooms, use public places, and travel by public transport. I didn't think much of this could be shown by archive and decided to film illustrative contemporary background shots of parks, buses, stations, shops, workers, and so on in present day Munich. Thus we talk of the past but show a vivid present in full color. I think the concept worked, but at the back of my mind was the knowledge that it could all be misinterpreted as a comment on lack of change in modern Germany, which was not my intention at all.

In *Out of the Ashes*, I worked with a fantastic crew, which included a wonderful editor, Larry Solomon. I also had a few historical advisers of whom the most important was Professor Yehudah Bauer of the Hebrew University. He made few comments, but when they came they illumined everything. I remember asking him once why the Holocaust was so different to any previous slaughter: "Because for the Nazis, the crime of most other peoples was their possession of land, or their military threat. Regarding the Jews, their crime was their sheer existence."

Bauer's words pinpointed for me the main challenge of the film, which was to find a sharp and unforgettable focus. To do this, you had to ask what was the essential message you wanted to leave with the audience? What did you want them to remember when the pictures had faded and the voices were stilled? Bauer's comment was one. Something else I wanted them to remember was the comment made at the beginning of the film about the dawn of a new poisonous age in Europe. Initially I had been worried how to put this over in an interesting way at the start the documentary till Brian came up with a solution. He took the words of Kafka from *The Trial* and suggested we place them over dark, brooding, and oppressive scenes of Nazi night rallies. The effect was chilling as Kafka speaks of the coming of the secret police, the secret arrests, and death in the night, and we see in an instant what the success of the Third Reich meant for Europe. The third essential message is that which Eli Weisel delivers at the end of the film. "There is nothing else my generation can do but bear witness for humanity. They thought they could kill six million Jews and go on as if six million Jews didn't die—but together with the Jews the image of man was destroyed."

Out of the Ashes was a hard film to make, a devastating film to make. I don't mean technically but emotionally. At every point you were confronted with the fact that six million Jews died. Six million of your people. Six million youngsters, elderly, sick, healthy. Six million lives annihilated. And millions of others, civilians, Romany gypsies, homosexuals, all barbarically slaughtered. These facts were always in the background, never to be forgotten. A shrouded cold, dark presence with sightless eyes always hanging over you as you worked, a presence that nudged you when talked about Oradour and gave a sigh when you showed pictures of the Einsatzgruppen shooting naked people at the edge of a trench.

But I wanted to show more than death in the film. What seemed to me essential was also to remind the audience that besides the death of so many, a whole culture had died with them. Therefore, early on in the scripting process I knew it was vital to show the difference between *then* and *now* in reference to Jewish life in Poland. This I thought could be done by contrasting Kazimiercz (the Jewish area of Krakow) in the thirties and today. To start with, Vishniac's photos provided me with some very specific scenes of old Kazimiercz. I then found archive footage of the synagogues and life in Kazimiercz in 1938 and Nazi footage from the forties of Jews crossing the Krakow bridge with all their possessions, to be imprisoned in the ghetto.

While doing location research with Megan, I then hunted out all the scenes depicted in the archives and by Vishniac and realized I had struck gold. The bridge was still there, now crossed by ten-wheel trucks instead of the pitiful horse and carts of the Jews. Vishniac's Izaka Street and Jewish quarter were still there, as was Kazimiercz's magnificent main synagogue, but all was broken, deserted, and lifeless. In the end, the fusion of all the elements worked perfectly, mainly due to my editor's skill in putting it all together. Early on in the picture, we see Kazimiercz vibrating with Jewish life. The synagogue is full of men and boys at prayer and study, and the square in front of the synagogue pulsates with people gossiping and trading. At the end of the film an old man wanders around *exactly* the same locations—the town, the synagogue, the square—which are now stricken and barren. For a moment he visualizes them as they were (a recap of archive footage used earlier) and then hurries away. It is a scene that still affects me very, very much.

While we were making *Out of the Ashes*, all of us on the crew felt that we were creating something special, and with time it all miraculously started coming together. If what I have written so far makes it appear that the planning of the film was very logical and clear, forget it. You start off with logic and then magically intuition and feeling take over and if you are lucky lift the script and film to a different dimension. Often you don't know what you are doing, and only time reveals what you really have done. To me, this is illustrated by two photos I used in the film. The first still shows a little boy of nine in miniature Nazi uniform. His arm is outstretched in the Nazi salute as he greets Hitler at a railway station. The photo is used to introduce a section showing Hitler at the height of his power. The second photo, used at the end of the film, shows a little French boy, of the same age, wearing a beret and an open-necked shirt, carrying a loaf of bread, and looking directly at the camera. It is 1945, and the boy is standing by the shore while the script talks of a new age and change. I had wanted the French boy to symbolize hope but had totally forgotten the previous photo of the German boy in uniform. Only with time did I realize that the former photo acted as a symbol of darkness, and the latter as a symbol of light, and that both were vital to give the film meaning. Such is serendipity.

As I was finishing *Out of the Ashes*, I could feel a general panic pervading the main offices of the series at the WNET building on West Fifty-eighth Street. *Civilization and the Jews* had been in production for six years, which even for Public TV seemed a little excessive. A number of films, including the one on America, were still incomplete. Marc Siegel had resigned as executive producer because of stress. The last film in the series hadn't even been started, and the public and the sponsors were beginning to ask some hard questions, such as when on earth we were going on air. It was against this atmosphere that a decision was made that, come what may, the series would be shown in the fall of 1984, and because *Out of the Ashes* was looking pretty good, I was to be given the last film to produce.

That looked to be a mixed blessing. There was hardly any money left in the kitty to actually finance the film, and it had to be finished in four and a half months, in order to meet the new committed air date. Those were just the initial difficulties involving the kind of horrendous production challenges most producers go through at one time or another. What troubled me more was that the WNET's guidelines for the film, entitled *Into the Future*, seemed to contain major conceptual flaws that almost certainly guaranteed failure. In fifty-six minutes the film was supposed (finally) to tell the story of Israel's birth, relate what had happened in this century to the Jews of Russia, and bring us up to date with the situation of American Jewry. As if that were not enough, the film had also to bring the series to a triumphant conclusion. This all meant that the film would veer off into a dozen competing directions, inhibiting any clear story-telling or thematic development. I took this up with Arnie Labaton, the new executive producer, but to no avail. This is the way things were. This is the way the film had to be. So began a rather hurried and undistinguished piece of filmmaking.

To safeguard myself in the endeavor, I once more brought in Brian to do the script. This was a mistake. In *Out of the Ashes*, he had produced some brilliant writing because he was passionately in-volved with the subject. By way of contrast, *Into the Future* filled him with a number of doubts. The major one was that he believed the film would come out as a simplistic Zionist tractate. This was not good, because he and his socialist friends from England were now having a hard time with Israel's policies in Lebanon and its seemingly repressive actions in regard to the Palestinians. I may be wrong on this matter, but that's how I read his position at the time. In the end, Brian was so torn in his attitude to the film that he de-clined to put his name on it and used his father-in-law's name as a pseudonym.

So, with little money, and dissension surrounding the script, we forged ahead. We told the story of the flowering of Yiddish culture in the early days of the U.S.S.R. We went on to show Stalin's war against the Jews, and ended the Russian section with the demon-strations of the seventies and early eighties calling for the release of the prisoners of Zion. The achievements of American Jewry were praised and intermarriage and the movement to the suburbs dutifully commented upon. Finally, we told the story of Israel, the battle for independence, and said a few words about the mass immigrations of the fifties. We talked of the utopian-inspired kibbutzim, showed a very colorful scene of a Shavuot celebration, and if we didn't make a Zionist propaganda film, it was still one that the UJA would have been happy to show. Where there were problems, we swept them under the carpet so that the film scarcely mentioned the Palestinians, dismissed the difficulties of Israeli Arabs in two paragraphs, and delicately skirted the Israeli imbroglio in Lebanon. Here and there the film had its moments. It finally showed for example the Holocaust survivors' rally I had filmed in 1981, but I had no illusions about it. It was decorative wall paper delivered to order.

Eventually, *Heritage: Civilization and the Jews* went on air, received some good reviews (Neilson ratings measured *Heritage* at fifty-one million viewers, a remarkable figure for public broadcasting), was commented upon favorably, and that was the end of the story for me. Or at least for fourteen years. Then in March of 1998, I got a surprise call from John Fox, whom I had known from the *Heritage* days when he a had acted as a brilliant overall series consultant. John had been asked by 13/WNET to create a DVD (Digital Video Disc) of the *Heritage* series and had been working on the project for two years. To accompany the release of the DVD, the station had suddenly decided to rescreen the whole *Heritage* series sometime late in 1998. In the thinking of WNET, this would also be an appropriate gesture to mark Israel's fiftieth anniversary.

John's phone call related to the new release. In reviewing the series, WNET had realized that while most of the programs had stood the test of time, the last film, *Into the Future* was hopelessly out of date. In fourteen years, the situation in Israel and the U.S.S.R., not to talk of the U.S.A., had changed beyond all recognition. The film could definitely not be shown in the old version, so could I remake and update the film, with John acting as executive producer? And could this all be done in ten weeks with very little money? Well, what did Henry V once say? "Once more into the breach, dear friends." So once more into the breach it was.

Leaving everything, I rushed immediately to New York. Once there I reviewed the film, which I hadn't seen for a number of years, and plotted strategy with John. Only about half of the old film, mainly the section dealing with the birth of Israel, still made sense. The rest would either have to be dropped, modified, or rewritten to accommodate a decade and a half of change. For example, we had previously ended the Russian section with demonstrations calling for the release of Russian Jewry. Since then the U.S.S.R. had collapsed, over-three quarters of a million Russians Jews had emigrated to Israel, and a new party of mainly Russian immigrants had been established called "Israel Bealiya."

Again, in the old film we had concentrated on peace with Egypt. Since then there had been the outbreak of the Intifada, Oslo had come and gone, Gaza had been returned to the Palestinians, and a peace treaty had been concluded with Jordan.

What was devastatingly clear to both John and myself after a number of review screenings was that the film needed a much tougher and more critical approach to its politics and also needed to focus on the problems affecting Israel and world Jewry at the end of the millennium. In other words, let's drop the decorative wall paper, concentrate on some key issues, and generally raise the seriousness of the program. All this we thought could be accomplished with minimum shooting, harder writing, and two or three incisive interviews.

The first section to benefit from this new approach was that appertaining to Israel's relations with its own Arab population and the Palestinians. This was totally revamped, with the dilemmas, the failures, the frustrations, and the successes clearly laid out for all to see. We also expressed a much harder and more incisive view of the changes within Israel. Thus, while the same scenes were shown of the kibbutz, the commentary now let you know that the younger generation was leaving and that the kibbutz movement was in crisis.

The Russian section was in practice the easiest to redo. Here, to gain time, we dropped a lot of the story of Russia in the thirties and instead added the story of the massive Russian immigration of the late eighties and early nineties. This was told via some recent archive footage and featured an interview with Yuli Edelstein. Edelstein had been in prison in Siberia in the eighties, but after coming to Israel had become minister of absorption in Netanyahu's government. Edelstein was a pleasant man who told his story well. In retrospect, I only regretted one thing. That I hadn't asked him why so many Russian Jews who had fought at home for human rights had suddenly become so bitterly anti-Arab and right wing in Israel.

In order to gain time for the new elements we wanted to include, whole sections of the old film had to be totally discarded. This was less painful than it seems since so much of the old film was almost space filler. Out went the scenes of *klezmer* (Jewish gypsy-style music originating in Roumania) players in New York. Gone were the celebrations of Jewish charitable organizations such as the UJA and Hadassah. And into the waste bin went the scenes of a Czech-Jewish exhibition. More controversially and more painfully, we also decided to leave out an interesting discussion of how Judaism and Christianity viewed each other in the twentieth century. So we had space. Some of it we had already allocated, for example to a better discussion of Arab-Israeli relations. But there were still five or six minutes at our disposal. What were the most important things we should be discussing in that window of opportunity?

While getting ready for my trip to New York, I had hastily dropped two books into my suitcase. One was Yaron Ezrahi's *Rubber Bullets: Power and Conscience in Modern Israel*, while the second was Avi Ravitsky's *Messianism, Zionism, and Jewish Religious Radicalism*. Ezrahi I knew as a professor of political science at the Hebrew University. I expected his book to be good, and it was, particularly in regard to his reflections on the death of Rabin and the election of Netanyahu. What was most useful, however, was his analysis of the conflict between "collectivist" national aspirations, upon which the state was founded, and the voices of individualism engendered by Israel's tradition of liberal democracy. For his part Ravitsky, another young professor at the Hebrew University, provided a very fine analysis of the ultraorthodox response to Zionism and the creation of the State. Both books proved invaluable in helping me sort out my thoughts about Israel, current dilemmas, and issues that might be important for the film. But all the philosophic issues had to be brought down to earth, so shortly after arriving in Manhattan I grabbed a notebook and tried making an arbitrary list of the new key talking points. They emerged as follows:

- the cultural divisions in Israel
- religion versus secularism
- state demands versus individual needs
- state Judaism and fundamentalism versus democracy
- the relationship between Israel and American Jewry
- the hopes and challenges for the future.

Many of the points overlapped. A number were raised because of the specific timing of the new film. Thus while John and I worked on the script, the newspapers constantly emphasized the struggle in Israel over a new Parliamentary definition of "Who is a Jew?" It was clear that if the ultraorthodox succeeded in getting their way then, at least as far as Israel was concerned, thousands of American Jews would be virtually disenfranchised.

The result of all this was a growing rift between American Jewry and Israel, probably the most important division between the two centers for generations, with tremendous implications for the future of both communities. In the United States there was a growing anger and disappointment with Israel, which hit me again and again as I traveled round the States giving the occasional lecture. When people heard I was doing a film, they were emphatic. The film must show what was happening and emphasize the dangers of the situation.

The lead-in to all these matters in the film was fairly simple yet emphasized the distance we had come from the old version. I wrote only a few sentences of narration, but they expressed what I saw as the essence of the matter. "For years Israel's preoccupation with security has barred serious discussion of the basic nature of the Jewish state. Now that the success of Israel seems to be assured after years of turmoil, there is finally time to contemplate its central internal problems and challenges."

This was all a little bit provocative because, for one thing, I knew that much of Israel still believed we were under threat. What I did believe was incontrovertible, however, was that after fifty years of statehood Israel was finally being forced to contemplate what kind of a state it was and what kind of a state it wanted to be. Furthermore I saw that development as being extremely healthy.

In the end there was, of course, little time for discussion of all of the matters I had so optimistically jotted down. Also a number of the points were so complex that it would have taken a complete film to begin to do justice to all the arguments. What did go in however was what I hoped was a serious analysis of the growth of Jewish fundamentalism in Israel and a discussion of the widening rift between Israel and American Jewry.

To show how far things had come in Israel I decided to interview Rabbi David Hartman, head of the Shalom Hartman Institute and think-tank in Jerusalem. I chose Hartman because he seemed to me to be incisive, intelligent, impassioned, and fair. I had also read his occasional comments in the *New York Times*, and they seemed to me to be sensible, caring, yet very accurate summaries of growing religious problems. This is what he had to say on Israel's proposed legislation defining "Who is a Jew."

> Judaism is a personal appropriated value, with which people must identify. Given that, I don't see how the State or the legislator can guarantee the future of Jewishness in this society. . . . Therefore I am deeply opposed to an official, establishment rabbinate decree which denies the possibility of a variety of religious orientations. Everything that comes from above religiously is a total failure. Unless it organically reflects the community sentiment in some way, it can't work.

Hartman was also very good in discussing secular nationalism and identity and the inability of the former to provide meaning to identity. "Israelis speak Hebrew. But what they discovered is you can speak Hebrew but not see yourself as a Jew." The problem as he saw it was that the country was looking for its soul, trying to find a way to connect itself to the past without having to give up the possibilities of a new future. When I changed topics and asked Hartman about the relationship between Israel and American Jewry, his answer was very decisive.

> Israel is the public face of the Jewish people. Israel is the public story. The Jews of the world are seen through what happens in Israel. You can't say they're Israelis, and we're from Los Angeles. We are now one people. There's no more two communities any more. There's one Jewish world in a great struggle. And this is extremely important for Israelis to understand. They are the Jewish people, and they carry the burden of Jewish history. And I've often said this in a joking way, but it's a very serious statement, that Israel is too important to be left to the Israelis.

Hartman was very emphatic and definitive in his views, but they were essentially those of an American rabbi who had decided to live in Israel. While meeting with a number of congregations in the States, I had heard slightly different arguments and felt they should be represented in the film. Here, after much research, our choice of an alternative voice fell on Rabbi Irwin Kula, the New York executive director of CLAL (the Jewish Center for Language and Learning). Kula was in his early forties, dynamic, amusing, and seemed at first something of a hippie, coming equipped with blonde beard, dark blue shirt, a wildly blazing tie, and extravagant gestures. His comments, however, were spot on.

I'm raised in America. I'm comfortable as an American Jew. I'm a rabbi in America, so we all speak from our own context. It seems to me at this moment we do not have a model for the Israel-Diaspora relationship. That is the tension. We have never in Jewish history had a strong dynamic, powerful, sovereign state—and at the same time a strong powerful confident Jewish Diaspora. So for the first time we are going to have two powerful and vital places where Jews live and are involved. And it's not we're central or they're central. There are things they can do by virtue of being a majority culture that will be interesting for the history of the Jewish people. And there are things that we can do, as the first time ever having a minority culture that is free, that will be very, very interesting.

Where I thought Kula excelled was in talking about the future challenges and opportunities for Judaism. I had always felt that Jews and Judaism, particularly in Israel, and particularly after the Holocaust tended to look back and measure everything by the past. But the question was "What of the next century?" And it was a question I thought we ought to ask particularly as the film was titled *Into the Future*. Here Kula supplied considerable matter for thought.

In Jewish life something very interesting is happening. We've moved through the period of the physical rehabilitation of the Jewish people. That's the period 1940 to 1970. Now there seem to be enough margins in our physical security. So it seems to me the time has come to say, Okay. Now that I've survived, what's it all about, what's the meaning of my survival? What's the purpose of my survival as a people, as an individual?

The film could not, of course, answer that question, but we did try to show a few of the responses of Judaism to the modern world. Kula had said to us, "The contribution Judaism can make is on the issue of pluralism. Judaism always works best when it has a very wide range of responses to whatever the contemporary moment is." Following Kula's words, we showed the Hasidim trying to build up walls against the outside communities. We showed the Jewish renewal movement. We showed orthodox, conservative, and reform services and in a few brief moments tried to show what invigorated them and gave them life.

All this discussion actually brought us to the end of the film where my editor, Susan Fanshel, had cut together a beautiful and moving sequence linking a Sabbath evening service in New York to a Sukkot (Feast of Tabernacles) service at the Western Wall. In New York, the rabbi raises his glass in front of a warm, happy congregation of a good few hundred. As he sings the blessing over wine, the scene dissolves into the prayers of thousands in front of the ancient wall of the old Jewish Temple.

As the prayers fade away, Eban ends the series with the words Brian had written for him fifteen years before.

> The story of the Jews has an astonishing resonance. Their strange destiny, their achievements, their suffering, and their vision are an enduring part of civilization. For civilization is the binding together of the memory and the experiences of all peoples.
>
> We are all of us the children of history, and for the enrichment of our world we must try each of us to understand our heritage, to judge it in the light of its highest values, and to pass it on as a treasure for all mankind. This is the message of the Jews to the world.

When the film was over and in the can, I took a break, going for a breather to the Italian lakes. There for the first time in months, I could think about the series without being surrounded by all the daily tensions, the hunt for archives, and the pressure to meet a deadline. Suddenly, I realized we had pulled it off, "we" being myself, John, my wonderful editor Susan Fanshel, my production manager Peter Wentzel, and my associate producer Jennifer Berry. It had been pulled off against the odds, against time, and with no budget. Somehow, in spite of all the difficulties and because of a great team, a film had been created that finally said something and that I truly believed was much better than the original.

I also realized something else. In making *Out of the Ashes* and *Into the Future*, I had been uncommonly lucky in being able to comment on some of the most important issues Jews faced in the twentieth century. But one thing was for sure. I'd had enough, and if I wanted to keep my sanity. I would have to say good-bye to filming Jews for at least a good few summers.

11 - Moses, Come Home!

In May 1998, Israel started celebrating its fiftieth anniversary. *Celebrating* is possibly too strong a word. *Reflected on* and *debated* are expressions closer to describing what was happening. Officially, the country was celebrating, but you couldn't always tell that. Twenty-five years before, things had seemed to be simpler, the joy untroubled. Now too many things were happening to allow the party to continue as normal. In the main, the country was agonizing over what to celebrate, who to celebrate, how to celebrate. In Tel Aviv, an exhibition commemorating fifty years of Israel's achievements was held in one of the parks. Hardly anyone came. Maybe they thought Israel's achievements deserved more than booths marking the growth of Israel's arms industry. At one of the official ceremonies the Bathsheba Dance Company refused to perform after being subject to rabbinical censorship. And, as I've mentioned, the name of Rabin was rarely heard at any of the government-supported festivities. So altogether it was a strange time.

During a great deal of this period, I was in the States trying to finish *Into the Future*, so much of my news was gained via the newspapers or through television. Here and there items caught my eye that seemed to reflect the mood in Israel. Often the border between the farcical and the tragic was almost nonexistent. Ariel Sharon, an archenemy of withdrawal from Arab lands, was appointed foreign minister, to supervise the peace process. A certain kabbalistic rabbi, almost a hundred years old, who could hardly hear or speak, was being massively courted by politicians for his necessary blessing. His portrait also adorned gift bottles of olive oil—his blessing presumably passing to all those who received the bottle and who later, as a quid pro quo, voted for the rabbi's SHAS party. In one newspaper, I read that the Chevrah Kedisha, Israel's orthodox burial society, was occasionally performing circumcisions on dead men in order that they should get to heaven as perfect Jews. Turning to the financial pages, I noted that in order to improve turnover, El Al, Israel's national airline, was setting up flights to nowhere. If you were a jaded businessman, you could now evidently rent a Boeing for a day; bring all your colleagues, contractors, and tired workers; drink champagne; fly around aimlessly for four hours; and then land back at Ben Gurion Airport. I don't know if there were any takers, but the flights looked to me as if they might symbolize recent Israeli government policy. Both El Al and the government seemed to be burning energy and going nowhere fast.

One item, however, gave me hope. This was a massive nineteen-part series on the history of Israel since 1948 entitled *Tekumah*, or "Rebirth," produced by Gidon Drori, a friend of mine at Israel TV. What Gidon had done, together with his directors, was not merely celebrate Israel's history but examine it in detail. And this took guts, because Gidon was trying to look behind the masks and the myths, the fables and the fantasies, and ask, "Where have we come from? Who are we? And how did we really get here?" These seemed to me to be the right questions for the time, but for some people they were too much. These were not questions to be asked in 1998, particularly not the questions about Arab feelings over the years that provided material for *Biladi, Biladi,* Arabic for "my country."

As a result of his failure to provide a simple, happy, upbeat television program, Gidon was severely criticized, with various politicians declaring loudly that the series would never be used in Israeli schools. I personally considered the series the best thing that had appeared on Israel TV for years. I also thought it was a tremendously healthy sign for the future because it said if we are to go on, if we are to become a normal state, if we are to become a true democracy, we must have the courage to examine our past and draw conclusions from it. We must consider not just our achievements but also our failures, and then hopefully we can create a better future for all of us.

My own feelings about Israel at fifty were extremely confused. It seemed unbelievable, but I had been in the country for half my life. Years before, in reference to the new Zionist state, my father had said, "Only madmen go there." Many decades later, I still wasn't sure whether my father was right or wrong. I had a very strong love-hate relationship with the place, which had still not resolved itself. Only one thing was clear, Israel charged your adrenalin and filled up the batteries. As opposed to England, things were never still for a moment. But then how did that old Chinese curse go—"May you live in interesting times." I guess by that criterion everyone in Israel was condemned and afflicted. Yet the rabbis considered residence in the Holy Land a blessing. I suppose in the end things just evened out.

While meditating on all these points, I suddenly found myself being asked by the UJA to lecture on Israel at fifty. For my part, I wasn't quite sure if such an effort was necessary as every paper and TV station was covering Israel with a fervor only superseded by their coverage of Diana's funeral and Clinton's dallyings with Monica. The difficulty was that the coverage often seemed to me sour, spiteful, and uninformed. It was as if all the editors had decided to start their pieces with the same words: "Israel has admittedly done great things, but . . ." Gidon's series had been critical but honest. What I was sensing in America was a review of fifty years of Israel that was throwing away the baby with the bath water. If so, then even a few lectures might help people, particularly small Jewish communities, get a better perspective on Israel.

So from May through July, I traipsed across the States, from Florida to Maine and from New York to Oregon, trying to express a few thoughts about the Israel I knew from three decades of filming. The first point was to tell my audience that I believed that the crisis between Israel and American Jewry would pass and that the Israeli government would eventually see sense over the "Who is a Jew" controversy. Allied with that thought, I also stated that as much as American Jews needed Israel, Israel needed America. Although the UJA slogan "We Are One" was looking shaky, I believed it was still essentially true. To illustrate this point, I related a small incident that had happened to me in Jerusalem only a few months before.

I had just boarded a bus and was sitting next to an American girl about twenty-seven years old. This being a Friday, the bus was crowded. Not only that, people were struggling and fighting to get on the bus as if their lives depended on it and they were escaping from a besieged city, which maybe they were. Observing the pushing and the pulling, the elbowing and the jostling, the American girl turned to me in disgust and said, "Animals! That's what they are, animals!" A little taken aback, I asked her how long she had been in Israel. "Five years." After thinking about this for a moment, I asked her why she stayed. "Ah," she said, "because we're all family."

My talks weren't particularly sophisticated and reiterated many points the listeners must have heard before. But my justification for talking was that because of my films I'd probably experienced a much wider section of Israeli life and views and society than most journalists. So, while admitting all of Israel's problems, I argued that the newspapers had lost their sense of proportion in many of their analyses. Occasionally, however, I mentioned journalists who seemed to have got it right. Paul Johnson, writing in *Commentary* had called Israel's creation and survival a "miracle." I tended to agree with him. But then both of us were merely echoing David Ben Gurion who, according to myth, had once said, "You can't be a realist unless you believe in miracles." And what Israel had achieved since 1948 seemed to me to be truly a thing of wonder. The social gap had closed. Israel's economy was thriving and its development over fifty years incredible. The existential threat to Israel's existence had largely gone, and the country was blossoming. All this I presented to my audience for starters. Furthermore, I told them that the story of immigrant absorption, particularly that of the Russians and the Ethiopians, was one of the most amazing success stories I had ever heard. All this of course was not laid out in bare form as above but was clothed with incidents, texture, anecdotes, and details culled from my own experience and memory.

What I often tried to do was simply reverse perspectives. For example, the newspapers, particularly the *New York Times*, had made a great to-do about the changing nature of the kibbutzim. That seemed to me nonsense. Change was to be expected and welcomed. If the kibbutzim had *not* changed after fifty years, then they would really be in trouble.

Going out on a limb, I criticized the Netanyahu government and stated that a viable Palestinian state would come into existence whether we liked it or not and would not threaten Israel. I argued that the West Bank should be given up for practical reasons and also for moral reasons. These remarks were often questioned and sometimes vigorously opposed, but it was my opinion, and that's what people had come to hear.

Occasionally, my anger surfaced. This was usually when I talked about the actions and attitude of the extreme orthodox—the Haredim—and their disdain for the rest of Israeli society. I mentioned their attacks on innocent women whom they believed to be missionaries; their burning of bus stops with offending posters; and their attacks on young people who want an out from orthodoxy. But most of my anger was directed at their contemptuous regard for the army and the scandalous acceptance by politicians of a situation in which part of the country did national service while over thirty thousand orthodox boys were exempt because of their religious studies.

I illustrated all this by telling my audiences about an early morning scene in Jerusalem. It is autumn 1988. My son Tal has just been called up for the army, and has to report at six thirty in the square by the induction center. He is of course not alone. There are another four hundred kids there, together with parents, grandparents, and well-wishers. On the surface, all is excitement. The boys embrace each other. The girlfriends give the last kisses. One wears a sweater with the names of all her classmates embroidered on it. The small brothers and sisters play hopscotch. Fathers and mothers press lunch packets on their kids, hold them, then turn away to hide the tears. One handsome father dressed in heavy black leather riding gear hugs his son and then wheels away his motorbike from which dangles his son's crash helmet. The name on it is *Erez*.

Beyond the crowd, waiting patiently, are seven buses. These are the buses that will take the kids to their units, to paratroop training, to navy training, to the armored corps, to the tank regiments, to the sappers, and to the infantry. Names are being read out from a clipboard by a uniformed sergeant, and as each is called a youngster detaches himself from his parents, gives a last wave, and boards. Finally, it's Tal's turn. Miki and I hug him fiercely, and he is off.

But to where, and to what? No one knows. And as you turn away you know you are sharing those agonizing questions with all the other parents there. How many of these kids will be alive in a year, in two years? Statistically, you know that at least two or three of these wonderful youngsters will be injured, maybe on the border in

Lebanon, maybe just in a training accident. You know this. You hold the knowledge to yourself and just hope your son will be one of the lucky ones to come through the whole experience safely.

All these thoughts are churning up inside you, but then as you turn away you notice two twenty-year-old black-suited Haredi—the extreme orthodox—boys pass by. They look straight ahead. The scene in the square doesn't trouble them. The battles of this country are not their battles. The fate of these youngsters is not their concern. Their rabbi has told them that endlessly, and all that matters is to hurry to the *yeshiva* and learn a few more *pesukim* (verses) from the Torah. You see this, and for a moment your anger blinds you because of the inequity of the system. Then you calm down, go home, and wait for the letter or the telephone call telling you all is well.

In talking, I often kept the image of friends before me. I remembered the Tiger of the Negev who so many years before had told us about the battle for independence. I recalled my friend Giora, who had fought in 1956, 1967, and 1973. And I thought about the constant images of fallen soldiers on television. It seemed now there was a chance for that period of bloodshed to end. So what I stated was that we were facing either peace or a hundred years war, and that whereas the extreme orthodox were prepared to battle on till the last drop of someone's else blood, I wasn't prepared for that to happen.

Finally, I looked at the awful state of dissension in Israel and tried to give it a positive spin. (In *Knives, Tanks, and Missiles: Israel's Security Revolution*, by Eliot A. Cohen, Michael J. Eisenstadt, and Andrew J. Bacevich, the authors maintain that under certain conditions Israel could still face a security nightmare.) As in the film I had just completed, I argued that Israel had reached a new plateau. With major security fears now largely laid to rest, it was time to examine all those questions that had been pushed under the carpet for years, such as the nature of the religious status quo, women's rights, and the deplorable situation of Israel's Arabs. In short, the national passion for self-analysis and questioning was all to the good.

At the end of the lectures, someone would usually stand up and say, "Fine, you've given us a pretty good analysis, but tell us, you've been working as a filmmaker in Israel for almost thirty years. What keeps you there?" As I mentioned earlier, it was a difficult question to answer. My father had been correct when he had said, "You've got to be a bit mad to go there," but I had never really told him why

I had stayed. In the end, the answer closest to my own feelings was that given by the Israeli author David Grossman in an article entitled "Letter from Israel," which appeared in the *New Yorker* on 20 April 1998. Grossman wrote that he considered himself "lucky to be in Israel—"

> not because I think it is Utopia but because Israel is the only place in which a Jewish person can live with the vital ingredients of the history and culture and mental life of all the generations of Jews that have preceded him and can realize them in the creation of a new and modern reality. . . .
>
> Living in Israel is, for me, still a spiritual adventure. It may be exhausting and frustrating, but how could I do without it. This is what it all comes down to: *Not to be foreign.* To belong. To be a partner with equal rights and obligations, a native and organic part of this great body.

On the whole, I think Grossman got it right.

One of the questions I was continually asked during my lectures was what had changed most in Israel during the years I had lived there. It was an impossible question to answer but usually led to a lively discussion. Often I used my telephone response.

During my early visit to Israel when I worked on the Eichmann trial, there was no phone in the hostel where I was staying. Nor was there one in any of the adjacent houses. With luck you might find one battered public telephone booth half a mile away. As far as Israel was concerned, it was as if that symbol of modern society, the telephone, just didn't exist. If you complained that you couldn't work without a phone, the authorities usually referred you to the back of the very slim official telephone book. There, in black and white, were printed the state's priorities for the granting of a telephone. Highest up on the list to receive a phone, if and when available, were the hospitals. Next came the police services and members of parliament. Third came schools. But the most interesting item as far as the ordinary citizen was concerned came way down the list. Here the note merely said: "Priority fifteen: those people who have already been waiting three years for a phone." Today Israel has the highest number of cellular phone users per population in the world. So go talk of change.

When I came to Israel, my choice was quite definitely Jerusalem. Haifa was beautiful but boring, and living in Tel Aviv was like living in a shoddy version of Miami. Jerusalem had history. It had a past. It had mystery. It had atmosphere. It was a place where stones talked and the prophets had walked. And in those quiet, soft years of the early sixties, it also had a shy, quiet beauty. But like the world of the telephones, Jerusalem has also changed over the years, particularly in physical terms.

When you come into Jerusalem from Tel Aviv, you are now greeted not just by the old Jaffa road but by a hideous series of ten-story apartment buildings. Most of them would easily slip into the last three in any competition for the ugliest building in Israel. Such is your glorious entry into the holy city.

Proceeding down a narrow, noisy, dirty, traffic-jammed Jaffa road into central Jerusalem, you see little has changed except for the number of shop signs in Russian. The shops are still dark and poky, with their displays of wigs, corsets, ironing boards, cutlery, nails, hammers, and pails piled one on top of the other. Little of this bothers the customers who go about their shopping with a cheery indifference to standards of presentation that were obsolete in the nineteenth century.

Further on, you pass the open-air market. Even though it has been spruced up, covered over, and cleaned out it is still recognizably the same market that delighted you thirty years ago. The only difference is you have no place to park, the prices have risen, and everywhere young female soldiers patrol in pairs, looking for suspicious objects.

In the old days, I used to go to the cinema at least twice a week. At that time there were about fifteen cinemas in Jerusalem such as the Tel Or, the Eden, the Edison, the Habirah, and the Semadar. Their seats were of wood, the kernels of sunflower seeds were scattered everywhere, and at high emotional points in the film someone would inevitably roll a lemonade bottle down the aisle. Today only the Semadar remains. The rest of the cinemas have been boarded up or taken down to make way for new office buildings. If you want to see a film, you have to forget central Jerusalem and traipse out to one of the two multiplexes in the suburbs. There you get popcorn and comfortable seats, and if a tradition has been lost, nobody seems really to care.

But the loss of the railway station is something else. For years the small railway on Derech Hebron allowed you to embark on one of the loveliest journeys in Israel. The train to Tel Aviv only went twice a day, and even then it meandered along at something slightly less than the speed of George Stephenson's pioneering carriage one hundred fifty years ago, but who cared? The journey was so delightful, especially in spring, cutting through the mountains and offering views of picturesque small villages, green terraces, and white flowering almond trees that were totally hidden from the road. But the trains are gone, the station closed, and the booking office windows thick with dust. However, as if by way of compensation the number of buses on the roads have increased. As the length of most of them has doubled, they tend to swing along the narrow Jerusalem roads like aged sailors returning to ship after a drunken night out.

The old journalist cafés are gone as well and are badly missed, especially Atara. In their place we have had the inevitable American invasion. In spite of a brash competitor that had the cheek to call itself "McDavid," McDonalds thrives. Burger King also blossoms, as does Bonkers Bagels, Ben and Jerry's, Pizza Hut, and KFC. And because Israelis love music, we also have Tower Records.

Like most people who have been in Jerusalem some time, I am aware of the danger of romanticizing the past. But not all the past was good. Nor is everything that has come in its place bad. Walk down Ben Yehudah on a Friday morning in April, and you'll see what I mean. The street has been turned into a mall with a bubbling atmosphere that would not disgrace the Left Bank. Pass by the dozens of cafés that pour out onto the sun-drenched streets of Nachlat Shiva, and you could be on one of the sidewalks of St. Germain-des-Pres. The glasses are raised, the strudel is passed, the iced coffee stirred, and the cheesecake savored. And as you drink and eat, the Russian musicians alternately serenade you with Mozart and Liszt and wild songs from the Balkan forests. Just glance up the treelined street, and you see eighteen-year-old soldiers with shaven heads hugging each other while celebrating a day's freedom and pregnant mothers sailing past with their fifth and sixth babies; and while all this is happening, the darkest and prettiest girls in the world flash their teeth seductively while trying to maintain a precarious balance on five-inch wedged soles. A hundred years have passed, but it seems an eternity since Mark Twain warned his readers to stay away from Jerusalem at all costs.

If he were alive today, I would take Twain on a tour along the new Hass promenade in Talpiot on a sparkling November morning. The sky is blue, the air crystal clear, and with luck the mountains of Jordan stand out brilliantly to the east. And facing you is surely one of the most striking and beautiful panoramic views in the world stretching from the wooded hills of New Jerusalem, past the domes and parapets of the El Aksa mosque and the Old City, to the sharp yellow slopes of the desert. Somewhere off in the distance a dog barks. Suddenly, time stands still, and you can well imagine how the city must have presented its mystic self to the stranger and the pilgrim over the decades and over the centuries.

Of all the changes that have enriched the city since the sixties, none has been more vital than the building of the Cinematheque and the establishment of the Jerusalem Film Festival. And here, close to the Hebron Road on a summer's evening in July, you can experience the city at its best. The film festival is about to open. The night is warm; the moon is full and the heavens clear. Beneath the Cinematheque, in the amphitheater gardens of the sultan's pool, are gathered three thousand people. In front of them, a huge open-air screen is about to show *The Big Lebowski*, the latest offering of the Coen brothers. A jazz band warms up the audience. The stars are coming out. High above the gardens, the magnificent medieval walls of the Old City are superbly illuminated, their spires and their arches, their battlements and their towers starkly silhouetted against the dark blue velvet sky. There is a palpable excitement in the air. Suddenly, fireworks blaze out. The band plays Gershwin, and the festival is on. It is a moment not to be missed.

Yet for all the wonderful changes, there is a sadness in Jerusalem which was never there in the sixties, because it is a city fighting for its soul. As more and more extreme orthodox pour in, the young secular elements of the city are leaving. They see streets closing, education deteriorating, taxes rising to pay for the needs of the religious section of the population that doesn't work, and as a consequence they are abandoning Jerusalem. Soon, they say, Jerusalem will become just a black-coated, black-hatted religious ghetto. If that does happen, then all of us will have lost something precious and irreplaceable.

One Friday, soon after my return from the States, I went up to Kfar Hanassi to see my pal Bert and his wife Tamar. I hadn't seen them for a year or so and was wondering how they were doing. The answer was, fine. They now had five children, two grandchildren, and a son who was on his way to becoming a Conservative rabbi. Quite a jump for a kibbutz-born *sabra*.

In one sense, I came two months too late. I missed the big bash as the kibbutz had just celebrated its fiftieth anniversary. It had been founded on 2 July 1948 and for a long time went under the name of Mansura. Situated some six kilometers from Rosh Pina, and only a few kilometers from the Syrian border, the kibbutz lived for nineteen years under the threat of enemy guns. According to Bert, when he first came, everyone went to work with an old Lee Enfield rifle slung across his back.

I'd visited the kibbutz many times over the years to see my old friends from Habonim days like Bert and Shulamit. It was always a haven of peace and calm, at least it was if you merely came as a visitor. Over the years, I'd seen it grow from a small village, mainly existing on agriculture, to a larger community boasting of a foundry, weekend rest rooms, and an interesting medicinal herbal business. At first everyone had lived in wooden shacks. These have long gone and have given way to comfortable stone houses, each with its own small garden. On my early visits, Bert had driven me down in his tender to the Kinneret for a swim. Today everyone uses the grass-verged swimming pool. There you can lie on your beach towel under the caressing sun, help yourself to the coffee and lemonade from the sheltered pool kiosk, and read your Elmore Leonard in peace. And if it were not for the green Galillean hills in the background, you could well imagine yourself in California if not in paradise.

The kibbutzim have always looked good to the outsider, but I knew that from the inside they could look very different. Bert has been on Kfar Hanassi for over forty years. In his twenties he was very strong physically and was also probably the most popular of all our group. In his early sixties, he is still a handsome man and has retained a lot of his youthful openness and charm. He was, and is, what you could genuinely call a sweet man.

Sitting on the grass with him, drinking Tamar's lemonade, we recalled our first moments in Habonim, and the night after Shulamit's wedding when Bert, myself, and another friend, Paul, all crashed into each other in our fathers' cars. I also reminded him of the fierce battles he had had with his parents, when he had refused to study and rushed off to Israel. After all these years, what did he think about that, his youthful decision, and how did he see the changes on the kibbutz over time?

> Those early years? Bloody awful. I was tired all the time. The heat was immense, the conditions horrible, and the work endlessly boring. Believe me, the romance vanished very quickly. There were times, and I don't think I've told many people this, that I really felt like leaving. A lot of people were quitting the kibbutz at that time. But that would have meant telling my father he was right and I was wrong.
>
> Then you see what it's all about. You get under the surface, and it makes sense: the building of the land, the sense of equality, the way people support each other and try and do something for the community. Of course, my father was correct about studying. I was a bloody fool not to have learned anything. So that all came later.

Today, Bert is a teacher, having done a B.A. and then an M.A. in history. Talking about studies, he grins and confesses to wanting to do a Ph.D. if Tamar will give him the time off. Like many kibbutz-niks, he works outside the kibbutz, with his salary going into the kibbutz pool.

"A lot of the youngsters don't like that. We used to say 'from each according to his ability, to each according to his needs,' but the second and third generations don't accept that. They want to be paid a salary according to the type of work they do, and to hell with anything else. I understand that. It's a different time, a different age."

When I first visited the kibbutz, all meals were taken in the communal dining room, and everything was for free. Today, at least in Kfar Hanassi and a few other kibbutzim, that has changed. Most meals are now taken at home. When the occasional meal is taken in the dining hall, it's paid for by using the smart card that every member possesses.

As Bert puts it, change is the name of the game, and there is even discussion of the kibbutz members owning their own houses, rather than the houses being seen as belonging to the kibbutz. Clearly, there is an existential ideological crisis in the kibbutz, but for Bert, that is good. "The challenges of yesterday aren't the challenges of today. We have to reinvent ourselves. Find a new purpose, a new way. And it can be done. The kibbutz will grow, and it will be different, but if it can keep even a little of its social and ideological purpose, then things will be fine. And was it worthwhile, and would I do it all again? Well, and it may surprise you, the answer is probably yes."

A year earlier, while making *On the Brink of Peace*, I decided to take a crew to Jordan. The object was to film King Hussein, and after a day of waiting around at the palace, we were granted an audience at 4:00 P.M. The interview went well. Hussein was passionate for peace, a changed man from the stumbling, hesitant monarch I'd seen on British TV so many years ago. His sincerity was overwhelming, his feelings genuine, and his concern for the future generations of Jordanians and Israelis intensely moving.

After the interview, we started to pack up very fast, still hoping to catch the six o'clock plane. It was only then that I discovered that a strike at Ben Gurion Airport meant we couldn't get back to Israel. This left us all stranded in Amman with a day on our hands, but with transport and a driver at our disposal, courtesy of His Royal Highness. After some discussion, we all decided to travel to Madeba to see some sixth-century mosaics and then on to Mount Nebo, which was really just around the corner.

Mount Nebo has none of the awe or majesty of Mount Sinai, and in fact calling it a mountain is a bit of an exaggeration. It's more in the nature of a small, bare hill, planted here and there with scrub grasses and cedars. You can walk up or an easy jeep drive takes you to the top, which is now adorned by a small unprepossessing church. While the inside boasts some interesting animal mosaics, the outside—under repair and reconstruction—looks like a hastily put together army barracks, an impression reinforced by the two pleasant but tired Jordanian soldiers who guard the place. But we didn't come for the church. We came to find Moses.

He wasn't there, but his echoes were all around us because Mount Nebo, of course, is where Moses took his first and last look at the Holy Land. And like Moses you stand on top of the mountain, shield your eyes against the sun, and to your surprise you really can see all over Israel. To the left, in the distance, you can see the blue waters of the Dead Sea. In front of you there are a few miles of brown plains and then the mountains rise up around the Judean desert. The wind stops. The images shimmer in the haze, and for a brief moment you connect magically with a lonely man standing here nearly three and a half thousand years ago.

And you wonder, what did he dream? What did he see of the future? What were his hopes? What really went through his mind? What would he have made of Israel today, with its dissensions and its rivalries, and its achievements and its challenges?

One thing seems clear. Moses believed in the future. He had strength. He had vision. He had courage. All the things that seem so lacking in our current politicians. But would he cheerfully have gone into the Israel of the twenty-first century, or as before would he have found an excuse to linger on Mount Nebo?

And therein lies the question that refuses to go away. Did Moses really want to go into the Holy Land? We really don't know. In the Bible it says, "Moses died and was buried, but no man knoweth of his sepulcher until today." Well, that already sounds a bit suspicious. Maybe, as in a good Graham Greene novel, news of his death was just a publicity stunt. The situation becomes even more clouded when the Scriptures tell us, "His eye was not dim, nor his natural force abated." Maybe, even then, Moses was a bit weary of this whole Zionist enterprise and, seeing all the problems, he took the easy way out by just disappearing.

Maybe. I don't know. But standing on Mount Nebo, where the great man had stood many years before, I made a small wish. "OK, Moses. Enough's enough. Like you we had a dream, and now we're halfway there. We are also in a hell of a mess, but things could be looking up. We need your vision. We need your strength. So Moses, come home! We need you desperately."

Postscript: May 1999. I am in western Australia, having been invited to these wild shores to show a few of my films to the Jewish communities of Melbourne, Sydney, and Perth. All is going well, except for one regret. Because of my absence, I am missing the Israeli parliamentary elections and the final tense moments of the prime ministerial race between Bibi and Ehud Barak. "Who will win?" has been the one question dogging me throughout the tour. Mostly I have shrugged and tossed a coin to signify the race could go any way. Inside, however, I am terrified by the prospect of another four years of Netanyahu, dead-end government, and the abandonment of the peace process. At 7:00 A.M. I push back the rumpled bedclothes, switch on the TV, and get the CNN world news. And there it is! With full election results still to come in, Bibi has admitted defeat and conceded victory to Barak. For a moment, my eyes tear over. Maybe Moses needn't come back so fast. Maybe, after all, there is hope.

Selected Filmography
Index

Selected Filmography

Date	Film	Producer or Distributor
1961	*Eichmann Trial*	Capital Cities TV. Tape copies held at the Jewish Museum, New York
1971	*Battle Officer*	Israel TV
1973	*Letter from the Front*	Jewish Agency, Jerusalem
1974	*With These Children*	Hadassah, New York
1975	*Connections*	CBC, Canada
1976	*The Way Ahead*	Technion, Haifa
1977	*Bedouin Musician*	Israel TV
1977	*Frontiers of Archaeology*	Israel TV
1978	*Day of Peace*	ABC TV
1978–83	*Project Renewal*	UJA
1980	*Vision and Assembly*	Keren Hayesod, Jerusalem
1981–84	*Civilization and the Jews*	13/WNET
1983	*Out of the Ashes*	13/WNET
1984	*Into the Future*	13/WNET
1986	*Treasures of the Holy Land*	Israel Film Service
1988	*Jerusalem: The Gates of Time*	Israel Film Service
1989	*A Special Bond*	Hebrew University
1989	*Waves of Freedom*	Araness Communications, New York
1990	*Special Counsel*	Tel Aviv University and LSF
1990	*Intifada*	13/WNET
1991	*A Nation Is Born: Year of Decision*	Channel 4/UK and 13/WNET

1992	*A Nation Is Born: The Dream Divided*	Channel 4/UK and 13/WNET
1994	*We Could Have Danced All Night*	Israel TV
1996	*The Hunt for the Treasures of God*	Israel Film Service and Biblical Productions
1997	*On the Brink of Peace*	13/WNET
1998	*Into the Future* (revised)	13/WNET

Index

Abu Ghosh (Arab village), 23–24
Adams, Michael, 109
Agadati, Baruch, 123, 125
Agranat Commission, 150–51
Ajax (warship), 187
Alaa, Abu, 227–29, 230
Aleck, Lilly (aunt), 26–28
Aleck, Morry (uncle), 27
aliya (emigration), 13, 42, 46–49, 127,
    179
Allegro, John, 197
Alterman, Nathan, 108
Amiad (kibbutz), 52
Amichai, Yehudah, 205
Amir, Yigal, 233
Amory, Bob, 188
Anilewicz, Mordecai, 84
anti-Israeli sentiment, 109–10, 160
anti-Semitism, 163, 244
Antonioni, Michelangelo, 12–13
Arabs, 10–12, 110, 111–12, 163–65,
    225; interviews of, 223–24; nation-
    alism and, 89, 220–21
Arafat, Yasir, 209, 214–15, 219, 224,
    230; Gaza and, 222; Wye accord
    and, 233–34
Argentina, 71
Argov, Shlomo, 157

Arlosoroff (ship), 188
Aron, Wellesley, 49
Asad, Hafez al-, 219
Ash, William, 183
ashes of the red heifer, 198
Ashkelon (Israel), 120, 121
Ashkenazi, Motti, 151
Ashrawi, Hanan, 221–22, 227
Aspis, Helena, 50, 51
Atara (café), 78–79
Athlit camp (Palestine), 187–88
Auschwitz, 77–78, 84, 238, 246
Australia, 159–60
Avrahim Avinu (Hebron), 226
Axelrod, Natan, 123, 125, 132
"Axelrod Was There" (Schorr), 132
Ayash, Yehi, 211

Bachus (nightclub), 80
Bahat, Dan, 195
Baigent, Michael, 193
Baker, Bill, 208
Baldwin (king of the Crusader King-
    dom of Jerusalem), 193
Balfour Declaration (1917), 123
Barak, Aharon, 121
Barak, Ehud, 219, 273
Bar Cochba, Gershon, 226–27

Bar Lev line, 114, 140, 143, 150
Barnet, Bernard (Baruch), 35, 50, 51, 53, 55
Baron, Hetty (aunt), 28
Baron, William (uncle), 28
Bartov, Hanoch, 92
Battle Officer (film), 8–9, 15, 16, 21, 138
Bedouin, 10–12
Begin, Menachem, 117, 129, 151, 153, 154
Beilin, Yossi, 230
Beirut (Lebanon), 161
Belgium, 85
Ben Dov, Meir, 194
Ben Dov, Yaakov, 123, 124
Ben Gurion, David, 2, 9, 72
Ben Hecht (ship), 188
Bernstein, Bill, 187
Bernstein, John, 170
Beth Haan (People's House), 73–74
Beth Haemek (kibbutz), 52, 57
Bethlehem, 79
Bevin, Ernest, 41–42, 180
Biladi, Biladi (film), 261
Blitzer, Wolf, 173
blockades, naval, 88, 179–80
Boris (photographer), 29, 34
Borochov, Ber, 54
Boutros-Ghali, Boutros, 154
Bradman, Don, 35
Brandt, Willy, 83–84
Brettschneider, Lou, 188–89
Brezhnev, Leonid, 150
Brinker, Menachem, 103
British Broadcasting Corporation (BBC), 94, 140, 148
Broshi, Magen, 195, 196
Broshi, Menachem, 190
Bruno, Michael, 121
Built in a Day (film), 124
Burnt Flower Bed, The (Betti), 59
business, family, 31–33

Cameri Quintet (TV program), 233
Camp David, 154, 156, 174, 178

Cantor, Arthur, 182
Cantor, Eddie, 127
Capture of Adolph Eichmann, The (Pearlman), 70
Carcassonne (France), 192
Carter, Jimmy, 151, 154, 155–56, 169, 178
Cast a Giant Shadow (film), 7
censorship, 14–16, 18–22, 148, 260
Chaim Arlosoroff (ship), 187
Chanah (group leader), 52
Charles Revson Foundation, 181, 235, 236
Charney, Leon, 169–78; as entertainer, 171, 175, 177–78; peace process and, 172–74, 178
Chevrah Kedisha (burial society), 261
Chirbat Chiza (film), 22
Christian Phalange, 157, 162
Clinton, Bill, 233
Cohen (member of priestly caste), 1, 20
Cohen, Monty, 92
Commentary (magazine), 13, 77, 263
communal society. *See* kibbutz
Compton, Dennis, 36
Copper Scrolls, 196, 197, 198
Courts, Louis, 91–92, 96
Cramer, Bobby, 181

Daily Worker (newspaper), 39
Damascus (Syria), 145
Danny (friend), 145–47
David (neighbor and POW), 150
Davidson, Lionel, 196
Davis, Sammy, Jr., 172–73
Dayan, Moshe, 91, 107, 152; Yom Kippur War and, 114, 138, 141, 147, 150–51
Dayan, Yael, 217
Days of Rage (film), 165–66
Dead Sea Scrolls, 196
Dead Sea Scrolls, The (Allegro), 197
death camps, 245–46. *See also* Auschwitz
de Gaulle, Charles, 90, 110–11
Degel Hatorah party, 113
democracy, Arab, 221

demonstrations, 217. *See also* protest
    rallies
Denmark, 85
Dinur, Yehiel, 77–78
documentary film, 7–12, 20, 22–24,
    121–22, 124; fund-raising for, 115–
    16, 179, 181–84
Dream Divided, The (film), 147, 207
Drori, Gidon, 261

Eban, Abba (Aubrey), 89–90, 147, 149,
    209, 231; *Heritage: Civilization and
    the Jews* and, 236, 239–40, 259; *On
    the Brink of Peace* and, 208, 211–
    15, 232; *Year of Decision* and, 110–
    11, 112
Edelstein, Yuli, 254
Eden, Anthony, 63
Edrich, Bill, 36
Edwardson, Cordelia, 238
Egypt, 62–63, 88–89, 213–14; and Is-
    rael, 111–12, 151–52, 216; peace
    process and, 15, 154, 172–74, 178;
    Yom Kippur War and, 138, 140
Eichmann, Adolf, 65–78, 83–87; cap-
    ture by Mossad, 70, 71–72; descrip-
    tions of, 74–75, 83–86; trial of, xi,
    65–66, 68–69, 72–74, 76–77, 83–87
Eisenstein, Sergei, 4, 122
Elazar, David, 114, 141, 151
Elkins, Mike, 95
Elyashiv, Rabbi Yosef, 113
emigration, 13, 42, 46–49, 127, 179
Entebbe (Uganda), 160
Eretz Yisrael Awakening (film), 123–24
Estreich, Alec (grandfather), 26–27
Estreich, Moishe (uncle), 28
Ethiopia, 129, 263
ethnicity, 13–14
Evans, Eli, 209, 210, 235, 236
Exodus (film), 80
Exodus 1947 (ship), 41–42, 180–
    89; American sailors and, 184–89;
    Americans and, 80–81; background
    of, 182, 183–84
Ezrahi, Yaron, 255

Fackenheim, Emil, 239
family life, 29–34
Fanshel, Susan, 258, 259
Farr, Raye, 245
Feisal (king of Saudi Arabia), 90, 95
Fennimore, Chris, 181
Fiddler on the Roof (musical), 109
film. *See* documentary film; Zionist
    propaganda film; *specific titles*
film industry, Israeli, 7–8, 11–12
Film Polski, 247–48
Finer, Alfred, 49–50
Finkel, Basil (Arieh), 53, 55, 56
Fink's (bar), 80–81
Ford, Alexander, 125
Fox, John, 253, 259
France, 63, 89, 111, 192–94, 244–
    45
Frankel, Jonathan, 51, 55, 57
Frej, Elias, 152
Friedman, Thomas, 163
Fruchtmann, Milton, 67–69
fund-raising, for film, 115–16, 124,
    179, 181–84, 208–11

Gascoigne, Bamber, 236
Gavron, Danny, 51
Gaza, 163, 164, 222–23
Gaza Hamas (newspaper), 215
Geula (ship), 186, 188
Goeth, Amon, 83
Golan Heights, 97, 143–44
Goldbloom, Judith, 80
Golden Age of Second Avenue, The
    (film), 182
Goldstein, Baruch, 226
Gollancz, Victor, 73
Gordon, A. D., 54
Great Britain, 62, 63, 123
Greenfield, Murray, 187
Gregory of Tours, 192
Grierson, John, 123
Gross, Natan, 131
Grossman, David, 266
Gruninger, Paul, 87
Gush Etzion (Israel), 225

Haaretz (newspaper), 233
Habonim (youth movement), 49–57;
opposition to university of, 56–57;
social aspects of, 49–51, 55; social-
ism and, 52, 53–54; Wolfin and, 50–
51, 53–57
Hadassah (women's organization), 104,
118, 119, 127
Haganah (defense force), 23, 180, 183
Haganah (ship), 188
Hailsham, Lord, 91
Halevi, Binyamin, 74
"Halleluja" (Lewandowski), 171
Hamas, 211, 215, 221, 224
Hamed, Razi, 215, 224
Hamelech, Rabbi Emek, 195
Haogen (kibbutz), 104
Haredim (ultraorthodox), 113, 264–65
Hartke, Vance, 174
Hartman, Rabbi David, 256–57
"Hasela Haadom" (song), 60
Hassidim (orthodox Jews), 9
Hatch, Tony, 4
"Hatikva" (anthem), 108, 189, 202
Hausner, Gideon, 65–66, 68, 69, 84
Hayesod, Karen, 115
Hebrew University, 116, 121, 122, 123,
141
Hebron (Israel), 226–27
Heninger, Otto. *See* Eichmann, Adolf
Heritage: Civilization and the Jews (TV
film series), 81, 235, 236, 239–40,
253, 259
Hernandez, 46–47
Herod (king of Judea), 190
Hertz, Leah, 92
Herzog, Chaim, 188
Highgate synagogue, 35
Hippler, Fritz, 122
Hirshfeld, Yair, 227, 228
Hitchcock, Alfred, 4
Hitler, Adolf, 241–42, 251
Hollywood, 127–28
Holocaust, xi, 237–39, 241, 245–46,
249; Eichmann and, 76, 78, 85
Holocaust, films about. *See Out of the
Ashes*

Holy Blood and the Holy Grail, The
(Baigent and Lincoln), 192
Holy War, The (Sunday Times), 106–7
Hood, Stuart, 4
hora (dance), 130, 131
House of Dolls, The (Katzeknik), 77
human rights, 166–68
Hurd, Douglas, 28
Hurwitz, Leo, 69
Hussein (king of Jordan), 89, 95, 111,
206, 272

I Gave at the Office (film), 118
immigrants, expectations of, 129, 133–
36, 179–80, 254, 263
Intifada (Arab uprising), 15, 163–68
Into the Future (film), 235, 252–59;
key points discussed in, 255–59;
need for update of, 253–55
Iselin, Jay, 235
Israel, 4, 20, 155, 233, 242; American
Jewry and, 256–58, 262; documentary film and, 12–13, 20, 22–24,
121–22; emigration and, 13, 42, 46–
49, 127, 179; ethnic groups of, 13–
14, 15, 120, 216, 254; film fund-
raising and, 115–16, 124, 179, 181–
84; film industry in, 7–8, 11–12; and
Independence Day celebrations, 81–
83; international media and, 160–
63; modernity and, xi, 2–5, 25, 129,
138–39, 266–69; politics and, 19,
166–68, 229, 255, 257, 264–65;
sentiment against, 109–10, 160;
Sinai and, 62–64, 156; Six-Day War
and, 89–90
"Israel Bealiya" party, 254
Israel Emergency Appeal, 93
Israeli (film), 110
Israeli-diaspora relationship, xi, 256–
58, 262
Israel TV, ix, 6–7, 10, 122, 203–4,
261
Italy, 85, 191

Jean Paul (Oxford student), 63–64
Jennings, Peter, 161

Jerusalem, 58–61, 78–81, 105–6, 142, 220–22; Holocaust-survivors rally in, 237–39; modernity and, xi, 138–39, 266–69; terrorism in, 166, 210, 217–18, 226
Jerusalem Film Festival, 269
"Jerusalem of Gold" (song), 107
Jerusalem Post (newspaper), 98, 105, 113, 184
Jew, definition of, 52, 256, 262
Jewish Agency, 104, 115, 116, 134–36
Jewish community partnerships, 119, 120
Jewish National Fund (JNF), 40–41, 125
Jewish Wars, The (Josephus), 190–91
Jews, orthodox, 1–2, 9, 19–20, 113, 205, 264–65
Jihad (holy war), 215
Johnson, Lyndon, 111
Johnson, Paul, 263
Jones, Vendyll, 198–99
Jordan, 217, 272, 273
Jordan River, 102
Josephus, 190–91, 194
Judah at the Crossroads (Koestler), 52
Judaism, future of, 258
Judy (Australian girl), 68–69, 81–82
Juma (Arab interviewee), 223–24
juvenile delinquency, 120–21

Kafka, Franz, 249–50
Kahane, Karl, 175
Kaminsky, André, 6
Karina, Anna, 175
Katusha attacks, 157, 166
Katz, Elihu, 3, 10, 106, 116
Katz, Harold, 187
Kazimiercz (Poland), 250
"Keddusha" (Sulzer), 171
Keren Kayemet, 124, 127. *See also* Jewish National Fund
Ketko, Schlomo, 104
Kfar Hanassi (kibbutz), 52, 57, 101, 269–71
kibbutz, 109, 126, 129; change within, 254, 263, 269–71; films on, 88, 100;

socialism and, 52, 54, 225. *See also specific kibbutzim*
King David Hotel, 80
Kinloss Gardens synagogue, 35–40, 93
Kinneret (kibbutz), 101
Kiryat Shmoneh (Israel), 156, 157
Kishon, Efraim, 98
Kissinger, Henry, 145, 149, 150
Klement, Richard. *See* Eichmann, Adolf
Kneller, Rolf, 132
Knesset (Israeli parliament), 72
Koestler, Arthur, 52
Komorovski, Lilliana, 175
Koppel, Ted, 77
Kotlowitz, Bob, 235
Kovner, Abba, 84
Krakow (Poland), 250
Kristalnacht, 238
Kula, Rabbi Irwin, 257–58
Kulik, Maralyn, 123

Labaton, Arnie, 165, 166, 252
Labor (film), 124
Landau, Moshe, 74
Land of Promise (film), 126
Langford, Barry, 175
Lanzmann, Claude, 133–36
Larsen, Terje, 227, 230, 234
Larsky, Helmar, 124
law, Jewish, 20
Lebanese War, 156–59, 161–63
Lebanon, 210
lecture tour, United States, 262–66
legal profession, ix, 3, 43, 88
Leitner, Isabella, 246
Lentin, Louis, 97, 99, 106
Lesser, Shirley (Shulamit), 53, 54, 55, 57, 270
"Letter from Israel" (Grossman), 266
Letter from the Front (film), 15, 16, 17–18
Levy, Rabbi Harold, 94
Levy, Ram, 22
Life of a Jew in Eretz Israel, The (film), 123
Likud party, 151, 219–20, 225
Lincoln, Henry, 193

Lion of Jerusalem, 62
Lipschutz, Bob, 169, 172, 173–74
Litani raid, 157
London Jewish Chronicle (newspaper), 145
London Sunday Times (newspaper), 91
Luxembourg, 85

Maariv (newspaper), 106
macher (big shot), 115–16, 122
Maftzir, Boris, 189
Maimonides, Rabbi Moses, 36
Malle, Louis, 12–13
Malouf, David, 159
Mankowitz, Wolf, 110
Mansura. *See* Kfar Hanassi
Manual of Jewish Liturgical Song (Levinson), 40
marriage, in Israel, 20–21
Marx, Karl, 39
Mason, Jackie, 172, 182
massacre: Oradour, 244, 245; Sabra and Shatilla, 158, 161–62
Mazen, Abu, 230
McArthur, Cal, 196
McQuarie University, 160
Meir, Golda, 114, 138, 141, 147, 150–51; diplomacy and, 149
Memoirs of Isabella, The (Leitner), 246
Memorial Foundation for Jewish Culture, 181
menorah, 189–200; adventurers and, 195, 197–99; fiction and, 189–90, 192–93, 196, 199–200; history of, 190–91
Menorah Men, The (Davidson), 190
Messianism, Zionism, and Jewish Religious Radicalism (Ravitsky), 255
Metropolitan (magazine), 173
Mevasseret Bridge, 137
Michel, Ernest, 238–39
military exemption, 9, 113
military service, 57–58, 264–65
Miller, Keith, 35
Montgomery, Binks, 63
Moorehead, Agnes, 128

Moses, 190, 272, 273
Mossad, 70, 71–72, 211
Mount Nebo (Jordan), 272, 273
Mubarak, Hosni, 214
Mutzafi, Rabbi Isaac, 195, 199

Naor, Zizi, 191
Narkiss, Uzi, 108
Nasser, Gamal, 62, 63, 87, 88, 89
"Nasser mechakeh le Rabin" (song), 202
nationalism: Arab, 89, 220–21; Israeli, 257
Navon, Yitzhak, 23–24
Nazism, 87, 122, 249–50
Netanyahu, Benjamin, 210, 217, 218, 220–21, 273; Palestinian state and, 263–64; Wye accord and, 233–34
New Woman, Israeli, 125–26
New York Times (newspaper), 263
Nissenson, Hugh, 77
Nixon, Richard, 149, 150
Norway, 227, 233
Notre Dame (hostel), 81
Nuremberg trials, 68, 70

Oblomov (film), 103
Oded the Wanderer (film), 125
Odessa (Nazi escape organization), 48
On Camera (magazine), 232
On the Brink of Peace (film), 208–34; Ashrawi and, 221–22; criticism of, 232–33; Egypt and, 213–14; fundraising for, 208–11; Oslo agreements and, 227–32; Peres and, 218–20; production problems and, 211–12, 216–17; West Bank and, 215–16, 223–24, 226–27
Oradour massacre, 244, 245
orthodoxy, Jewish, 1–2, 9, 19–20, 113, 205, 264–65
Osbourne, John, 52
"Oseh Shalom" (song), 177
Oslo peace process, 210, 212, 224, 227–34; filming of, 201, 208; negotiations of, 227–30; success of, 231–33

Out of the Ashes (film), 238–52; Holocaust and, 241, 245–46; production problems of, 239–40, 249; research for, 243, 244–48, 250–51
Oxford, 58–62

Palestine, 123, 179–80, 222, 263–64
Palestinian authority, 215, 220–21, 232
Palestinian Liberation Organization (PLO), 89, 162, 209, 227, 229; Lebanon and, 156–57
Pan York (ship), 188
Parker, Montagu, 195
Pash, Isabel, 50, 51
peace process, Israeli-Egyptian, 15, 154, 172, 173–74, 178. *See also* Oslo peace process
peace rally, 203
Pearlman, Moshe, 70
Peres, Shimon, 210, 218–19, 230
Peretz, Aaron, 84
Peter (Oxford student), 63–64
Petra (Jordan), 217
Phantom India (film), 12
Pins, Yaakov, 1
Poland, 244, 247, 250–51
Potashnik, Al, 115
Potter, Dennis, 59
Pourquoi Israel (Why Israel?) (film), 133
Preminger, Otto, 80
President Warfield (ship), 182, 183–84, 186. *See also Exodus 1947*
Pressman, Elkan, 60
Price, Larry, 217
prisoners of war, 148, 150
Procopius, 192
Project Renewal, xi, 117, 119–21, 156, 158
Promised Lands (film), 13
propaganda, 2–3, 122–23, 162, 165
propaganda film. *See* Zionist propaganda film
protest rallies, 151, 158
Public Broadcasting Service (PBS), 147, 165, 235
Pudovkin, Vsevolod, 122

Qumran (Israel), 196

Rabin, Yitzhak, 107–8, 151, 164, 205–6, 217; assassination of, 201–4, 207–8; Charney and, 173, 178; Oslo peace process and, 209, 230, 233
Rafi (friend), 145–47
Ramat Rahel (kibbutz), 79
Raveh, Yitzhak, 74
Ravitsky, Avi, 255
Raz, Giora, 103–4, 106–7, 112, 138
Raz, Michal, 158
red heifer, ashes of the, 198
"re-entry" problem, 146
refugees, Arab, 110
Rennes le Chateau (France), 192, 193, 194
revolts, Jewish, 84
Rex House (London), 96
Rhapsody in Green (film), 129–30
Richman, Rabbi Sol, 199
Robinson, Edward G., 128
Robinson, Tamara, 208
Roeh, Yitzhak, 161
Rome (Italy), 191
Ronnen, Mike, 113
Rosenthal, Adele (sister), 29–30
Rosenthal, Gil (son), 96, 139, 159, 201
Rosenthal, Iris (sister), 30, 49, 50
Rosenthal, Irvin (cousin), 30
Rosenthal, Lewis (father), 28–29, 35, 43–45, 58
Rosenthal, Miki (wife), 90, 94, 95, 96, 116, 201, 264
Rosenthal, Monty (brother), 31, 33, 49
Rosenthal, Phylis (sister), 30, 31, 49
Rosenthal, Raymond (brother), 33, 66–67, 99
Rosenthal, Sarah (mother), 28, 29, 32–33, 58
Rosenthal, Sylvia (sister), 30, 108
Rosenthal, Tal (son), 29, 139, 201, 264
Rovina, Hannah, 125

Royal Air Force, 57–58
Rubber Bullets: Power and Conscience in Israel (Ezrahi), 255
Russia, 150, 174, 252, 254, 263

Sabbath, 20
Sabra (film), 125–26
Sabra massacre, 158, 161–62
Sadat, Anwar, 149–50, 151–52, 153, 154
Safed (Israel), 144
Sallah Shabati (film), 133–36
Saltzman, Harry, 110
Samuel, Maurice, 126
San Francisco Chronicle (newspaper), 70
Sauniere, Berenger, 193–94
Savir, Uri, 229, 230
Schlesinger, John, 110
Schutz, David, 189
Scopus, Mount, 105
Sephardim, 120
Servatius, Robert, 68–69, 72
Setlow, Marcie, 181, 182
Shach, Rabbi Eliezer Menachem, 113
Shafi, Abdel Heide, 225
Sharon, Ariel, 142, 157, 158, 260–61
Shatilla massacre, 158, 161–62
Shavelson, Mel, 7
Shavuot (Jewish festival), 113
shemen afarsimon (anointing oil), 198
"Shir Lashalom" (song), 202, 204
Shukeiry, Ahmed, 89
Sides, Elia, 213
Siegel, Marc, 236, 237, 239, 251
Sinai, 62–64, 88–90, 142–43, 156
Six Days to Eternity (film), 107
Six-Day War (1967), 4, 87, 88–108, 112, 225; aftermath of, 101–4; Jerusalem and, 105–6; Jewish diaspora and, 91–94, 96–100, 104–5; news reports on, 94–95; preface to, 88–90; victory celebrations of, 107–8
Skidell, Akiva, 186
socialism, 52, 53–54
Sontag, Susan, 13

Soviet cinema, 122, 123. *See also* Russia
Special Counsel (film), 169, 174–78, 179
Spectorman, Annie (aunt), 27
Spielberg Film Archives, 123
Springtime in Israel (film), 124
Stanford University, 66, 72
Steinman, Rabbi Aharon, 113
Stillets, Jeffrey and Gerald, 34
St. Louis (refugee ship), 244, 245
Stolen Candelabrum, The (Zweig), 190, 199–200
Straschnov, Amnon, 168
Suez Canal, 62–63, 114, 139
Sweden, 85, 245
Switzerland, 86–87
symbolism, Zionist film and, 130–31
Syria, 140, 144, 145, 219

Tanselle, Don, 172
Teitelbaum, Amnon, 189
Tekumah ("Rebirth") (film series), 261
television, 2–5, 15, 16–17, 25, 70, 129; Israel TV, ix, 6–7, 10, 122, 203–4, 261; PBS, 147, 165, 235; 13/WNET, 165–66, 208–9, 235–36, 239–40, 253
Tel Katzir (kibbutz), 100–101
Templar Knights, 192, 193
Temple treasures, 189–91, 194–95, 197. *See also* menorah
terrorism, 166, 210, 211, 217–18, 226
Thant, U, 89
Thirteenth Kilometer, The (film), 131
13/WNET, 165–66, 208–9, 235–36, 239–40, 253
This Is My Land (film), 125
Three-Power declaration of 1950, 89
Tiger of the Negev, 61–62
Titus (emperor of Rome), 190, 191
Topol, 109, 133
Tracey, Andrew, ix
Trade Winds (ship), 186
Trial, The (Kafka), 249–50
trials, disciplinary, 167
Trout, Joann Franklyn, 165

Trumpeldor, Joseph, 50, 53
Tryster, Hillel, 123
Tuhami, Hassan, 152
Twain, Mark, 268
Tzofim (Israeli youth movement), 82

Union of Soviet Socialist Republics (U.S.S.R.), 252. *See also* Russia
United Jewish Appeal (UJA), 119, 127, 128, 159
United Nations (UN), 145
United States, 111, 127–28; lecture tour in, 262–66

Vatican City, 191, 199
Vespasian (emperor of Rome), 190–91
Vishniac, Roman, 246–47
Visigoths, 191–92
Vision and Assembly (film), 118

Waldgrave, William, 28
Wallace, Mike, 163
Wallenberg, Raoul, 85
Wannsee Conference, 70, 245
Warburg, Gaby and Rachel, 95
"War of Attrition," 138
War of Independence (1948), 22, 23, 225
Warren, Charles, 195
Warsaw Ghetto uprising, 238
Waves of Freedom (film), 169, 179, 180, 181–84
We Could Have Danced All Night (film), 122, 131
"We Have Returned to Sharm el Sheikh" (song), 107
Weinstock, Dubek, 224–25
Weisel, Eli, 250
Weizman, Ezer, 111, 154, 173, 176–77, 178
Wentzel, Peter, 259
West Bank, 112, 163, 164, 219; *On the Brink of Peace* and, 215–16, 223–27
Weston Trading Company, 183
What a Wonderful Day (film), 130–31
Where Do You Get Off (film), 128
Wilson, Harold, 90, 111

Wingate, Orde, 53
Winston, Brian, 241, 242, 245, 252
Wisliceny, Dieter, 70
With These Children (film), 118–19
WNET. *See* 13/WNET
Wolfin, Bert, 35, 50–51, 53–57, 101, 269–71
Wolfin, Tamar, 269, 270
Women's International Zionist Organization (WIZO), 119
Woolf, Ronnie, 108
World Zionist Organization (WZO), 115
WQED Pittsburgh, 181
WTN (British television news group), 148
Wye accord, 233–34

Yad Vashem (museum), 238, 243
Yaviv, Chaim, 6
Year Nobody Gave, The (film), 127
Year of Decision (film), 110–14
Yehiam (kibbutz), 67
Yemen War, 89
yeshiva (rabbinical college), 9, 113
Yesterday's Men (film), 22
Yoash (group leader), 51–52
Yom Kippur War (1973), xi, 9, 16, 137–51; aftermath of, 148–51; Egypt and, 139, 142–43; filming of, 142–45; and "re-entry" problem, 145–47; unpreparedness for, 137–41, 150–51
Youth Aliya (voluntary association), 118
youth movements. *See* Habonim; Tzofim

Zionism, 13, 40–41, 48–49, 61–62, 207
Zionist propaganda film, 115–18, 122–32; high romantic era of, 124–25; post-Holocaust era of, 126–27; post-romantic era of, 128–30; study of, 122–24, 130–32
Zuckerman, Arnon, 170
Zuckerman, Yitzhak, 84

Alan Rosenthal was born in England, studied law at Oxford, and has made over sixty films for television. He helped to set up Israel Television and is a senior faculty member of the Department of Communications at Hebrew University in Jerusalem. The recipient of a Peabody Award for journalism and the International Documentary Association's Award for Scholarship, he is the author of *The Documentary Conscience*, *Writing Docudrama*, and *Writing, Directing, and Producing Documentary Films* and the editor of *Why Docudrama? Fact-Fiction on Film and TV*.